the
U.S. Catholic Press
on
Central America

the
U.S. Catholic Press
on
Central America

From Cold War Anticommunism to Social Justice

EDWARD T. BRETT

UNIVERSITY OF NOTRE DAME PRESS

Notre Dame, Indiana

Manufactured in the United States of America

Library of Congress Cataloging-in-Publication Data
Brett, Edward Tracy, 1944–
The U.S. Catholic press on Central America : from Cold War
anticommunism to social justice / Edward T. Brett.
p.   cm.
Includes index.
ISBN 0-268-04341-8 (alk. paper)
ISBN 0-268-04345-0 (pbk. : alk. paper)
1. Press, Catholic—United States.   2. Central America—Press coverage—
United States.   I. Title: US Catholic press on Central America.   II. Title.

PN4888.C5 B74   2003
070.4'49320972'09045—dc21
2002013121

∞ *This book is printed on acid-free paper.*

Contents

Acknowledgments

I would like to thank Andrew Stein, Father Robert Pelton, Father Edward Cleary, and Hubert Miller, who read either all or part of this manuscript and made valuable suggestions that improved it considerably. I also want to express my gratitude to Phillip Berryman, who gave me certain recollections of Nicaragua that I could not find elsewhere. Special thanks go to the library staff at La Roche College—Cole Puvogel, La Verne Collins, Cindy Speer, Darlene Veghts, and Grace Voytosh—who went way beyond the call of duty in tracking down and obtaining documents for me. I also thank the library staffs at St. Charles Borromeo Seminary and the University of Notre Dame and Barbara Lockwood of the Cushwa Center at Notre Dame.

I further thank all my colleagues at La Roche College, but especially Sister Sally Witt, Paul Le Blanc, Michael Brannigan, Sister Rita Yeasted, Michelle Maher, Linda Jordan, Barbara Harrington, Carol Moltz, Susan Todhunter, Josh Belen, Mari Jean Ferguson, Ronald Gilardi, Lynn Archer, and Father Patrick O'Brien, all of whom contributed in one way or another to making this a better study.

Most of all, however, I thank my wife, Donna Whitson Brett. Donna read each chapter of this study several times, lending her expertise on Central American history as well as on grammar and style. Indeed, more than anyone else Donna has contributed to the making of this study. For this reason, and because she has been a wonderful wife sharing the good times as well as the hard times with me for over thirty years, I dedicate this book to her. Finally, I thank my daughters, Erin and Tracy, and my son-in-law Dave Dunlap for patiently putting up with me while I wrote this book.

Introduction

In the last sixty-five years or so, a remarkable transformation has taken place in the U.S. Catholic church's attitude toward Central America and U.S. policy there, an attitude that has been meticulously documented in the U.S. Catholic press. After decades of virtually ignoring the region, by the early 1950s the Catholic press, following the lead of secular journalists, became convinced that a Moscow-directed plot to take over Guatemala had succeeded and was about to spread throughout Central America. Consequently, Catholic popular periodicals for the first time turned their attention to the isthmus, warning their readers of the dangers of the supposed communist regime of Jacobo Arbenz. When Arbenz was overthrown in 1954, the U.S. Catholic press lauded his demise and predicted that Guatemalan authorities, working in cooperation with the church and supported by the U.S. government, would soon create a democracy predicated on the tenets of papal social encyclicals.

Over the next two decades, thousands of North American Catholic missionaries entered not only Guatemala but much of Latin America, committing themselves both to spreading the Catholic faith and to stifling communism by playing a part in a transition to democracy.[1] Their efforts and experiences were followed by Catholic magazines. By the late 1960s, however, it was all too evident that democracy had not become a reality in the isthmus. Elements of the North American Catholic church, including the press, had by now undergone a remarkable change in their attitudes toward Central America and its problems. They abandoned their Cold War mind-set,

1

opting instead for a more complex analysis. Poverty and injustice were now seen as the primary causes of instability and turmoil. But more significantly, the Catholic press now began to view U. S. policy as part of the problem rather than the solution. Basing their analysis in large part on the opinions of U. S. missionaries, journalists for U. S. Catholic periodicals now spoke harshly of their government's conduct, past and present, not only in Guatemala but in El Salvador and Nicaragua as well, labeling it counterproductive and even immoral. The behavior of U. S. corporations in the region received similar negative commentary. Returning missionaries, some professors at Catholic universities, and some bishops[2] joined Catholic journalists in their critical assessment of U. S. actions in Central America. After the 1980 murders of Archbishop Oscar Romero and the four North American Catholic churchwomen in El Salvador, criticism by Catholics grew enormously. Large numbers of priests, nuns, and Catholic laypeople joined like-minded Protestants in forming ecumenical grassroots organizations dedicated to changing the thrust of U. S. policy in the isthmus.[3] Indeed, by the early 1980s, the North American Catholic church, working cooperatively with liberal Protestant churches, had become one of the more effective critics of U. S. conduct in Central America. An incredible about-face had been completed. This is especially remarkable, since never before in its history had the U. S. Catholic church taken a strong negative stand on an issue of American foreign policy.

The purpose of this study is to review and analyze the treatment of Central America and its problems in U. S. Catholic popular periodicals. Chapters 1 through 3 focus on the actual transformation of the U. S. Catholic press from a Cold War–dominated mind-set to one largely steeped in an awareness of the overriding need for social justice in Central America. Chapters 4 through 8 concentrate on how in the 1970s and 1980s the now largely transformed Catholic press responded to a U. S. isthmian policy still premised on the Cold War paradigm that the church had left behind by 1968. In the conclusion an attempt is made to place the church's metamorphosis concerning Central America in the larger context of the history of U. S. Catholicism. It is my hope that this case study will shed some light on the broader dynamics of the U. S. Catholic church's post–Vatican II contribution to the quest for global justice.

CATHOLIC PERIODICALS

Before moving further, a few words are necessary on the Catholic periodicals that are cited in this study. *America, Commonweal, The National Catholic Re-*

porter, and *Our Sunday Visitor* are cited most frequently simply because they contain the most articles on Central America.

America is a Jesuit weekly founded in 1909 to provide commentary from a Catholic perspective on issues and events in politics, religion, and the arts. Although it never reached as large a mass circulation as some other Catholic publications, it has always played an important role in shaping Catholic opinion. It adhered to the standard Catholic line of the hierarchy until the 1950s, when it broke with the norm by opposing Senator Joseph McCarthy. After that the magazine gradually took on a more nonconformist tone and an independent editorial approach. Influenced by the Second Vatican Council, by the late 1960s it had become a major voice for progressive Catholicism. It reached its highest circulation in the early 1980s and today goes out to about 40,000 subscribers. Read by many bishops and other Catholic leaders and highly respected in ecumenical circles, it is probably the most influential U. S. Catholic journal of opinion today.

Commonweal, founded by a lay group called the Calvert Association in 1924, is the nation's oldest English-language independent Catholic periodical devoted to social, political, religious, and literary commentary. Intended by its founders to be the Catholic equivalent to *The Nation* and *The New Republic,* it quickly established a reputation for sophisticated analysis. By the 1930s, it began to express an independence that did not always sit well with the hierarchy. *Commonweal* and the *Catholic Worker* were the only two U. S. Catholic publications that refused to support General Franco in the Spanish Civil War,[4] and the former was one of the earliest to condemn the demagoguery of Father Charles Coughlin, the influential radio priest. In the 1950s it fought against McCarthyism and criticized as too extreme the Catholic anticommunist fervor of the day. But as John Cogley states: "A study of *Commonweal* editorials over the years would show that more often than not the unpopular positions it espoused were later quietly adopted by the wider Catholic community."[5] Not surprisingly, *Commonweal* has always been highly respected by secular journalists and, throughout its history, has had an unusually large number of non-Catholic subscribers. For most of its existence it has been a weekly, but due to increased publishing costs and a declining number of subscribers, today it is a biweekly with a circulation of about 20,000. Nevertheless, it remains highly influential in progressive Catholic and ecumenical circles.

Begun as a diocesan newspaper in Kansas City–St. Joseph, Missouri, in 1964, *The National Catholic Reporter* was too controversial for episcopal tastes and therefore severed its ties to the institutional church. Brash, outspoken, and aggressively liberal, it quickly replaced *Commonweal* in the post–Vatican II era as the Catholic publication that conservative church people most love to hate. Controlled by laypersons, its goal from the beginning has been to cover the church in the same journalistic fashion as one would cover any other organization—that is, with reasonable detachment and independent judgment. As such, it has taken on controversial topics and delved into matters that other Catholic publications have ignored. It was, for instance, the first paper to broach the issue of clerical pedophilia. The *NCR* has developed a reputation for hard-hitting, in-depth reporting and has become a major progressive force within the church. By the end of the 1960s, it had a circulation of nearly 100,000. Today it stands at approximately 50,000.

Our Sunday Visitor was established in 1912 by an Indiana priest in order to defend the church against nativist attacks and demonstrate that Catholics were loyal Americans. The founder's goal was to create a national Catholic weekly newspaper that would be distributed to churchgoers throughout the country through their parishes. His plan was extremely successful, and for over a half century *OSV* dominated the Catholic newspaper field. By 1964 it had reached a circulation of over 892,000. Dioceses withdrew from the chain, however, during the 1970s and 1980s, and only a national edition remained with a circulation of about 200,000. By the mid-1990s, it still had about 85,000 subscribers. Unlike *America, Commonweal,* and the *National Catholic Reporter, Our Sunday Visitor* usually followed the predictable line of the hierarchy and was aimed at attracting a more general, less intellectually oriented Catholic readership. At any rate, it has consistently been considered one of the best Catholic periodicals of its type. On the whole, it has tended to be somewhere between centrist and moderately conservative in its outlook, but in the 1990s it seems to have moved further to the right.

Other Catholic publications that receive substantial coverage in this study are *Ave Maria, The Sign, Catholic Digest, Maryknoll, Extension, World-mission, The Catholic Worker, The National Catholic Register, Crisis, The Wanderer,* and *Social Justice Review.*

Begun in 1865 by the Holy Cross Congregation at the University of Notre Dame as a weekly religious magazine for Catholic families, *Ave Maria* was continuously published until 1970, when it was discontinued due to rising costs and declining circulation. From its inception it contained editorials, news reports, and general interest articles aimed at a popular, rather than a scholarly, audience. For the most part it tended to be centrist to moderately conservative.

The *Sign,* a national monthly, was published by the Passionist Congregation from 1921 to 1982, when it was terminated for the same reasons as *Ave Maria.* Founded to counter the anti-Catholicism of the 1920s, it attempted to interpret significant current events from a Catholic perspective. In the early 1960s, it was the fourth most popular Catholic magazine in the United States, and in 1972 it had a circulation of over 130,000. Like *Ave Maria,* the *Sign* is considered to be one of the better Catholic popular periodicals of the twentieth century. Its viewpoint could be best described as moderately liberal.

Catholic Digest began in the mid-1930s as the "Catholic ghetto's" equivalent to *Reader's Digest.* A monthly family magazine, it is aimed at a wider, less intellectually oriented Catholic audience and has always adhered to the standard Catholic views of the day. Moderately conservative throughout its history, it consistently took a hard-line anticommunist approach during the Cold War.

Maryknoll, begun in 1907 as *The Field Afar,* has long been the most widely read U. S. Catholic mission magazine and as such has had a major impact on the North American concept of missionary work among both Catholics and non-Catholics. Published by the Maryknoll Fathers and Brothers, it is known for its progressive, ecumenical, multicultural approach to mission. It is no exaggeration to say that it has consistently set the standard for other Catholic mission magazines to follow. In the early 1980s it had a circulation of 800,000.

Extension began publication in 1906 under the auspices of Father Francis Kelley's Catholic Church Extension Society. Its goal was to foster support for Catholic missionary endeavors within the United States (the home missions). However, it soon added subjects of a more general religious nature. By the 1950s, it had become one of the most popular Catholic magazines in America, boasting a circulation of over 500,000. *Worldmission,* published from 1951 to 1981 by the National Office of the Society for the Propagation of the Faith, is the only other U. S. mission magazine cited in this study. Its articles were aimed at average Catholics, and it tended to avoid controversy.

The same cannot be said for the *Catholic Worker,* a monthly started in 1933 by Dorothy Day and Peter Maurin as their answer to the communist *Daily Worker.* Throughout its history it has been the most unabashedly leftist Catholic periodical in the United States. Championing the cause of the working class, it has always been highly critical of capitalism. Certainly out of the mainstream of Catholic thought and read primarily by young Catholic leftists, it nevertheless reached a circulation of over 150,000 at its height. It also influenced at least indirectly the U. S. Catholic church's positions on social justice issues after Vatican II.

Born in 1924 and modeled along the lines of *Our Sunday Visitor,* the *National Catholic Register* has consistently stood for political and religious conservatism. In the mid-1990s it had a circulation of approximately 15,000.

In 1995 it was bought by the Legionnaires of Christ, a traditionalist, staunchly conservative Catholic religious congregation.

A journal of lay Catholic opinion on contemporary and church issues, *Crisis* (originally called *Catholicism in Crisis*) was founded in 1982 by the Brownson Institute at the University of Notre Dame because its editors were "dissatisfied with existing Catholic journals."[6] With Michael Novak as its first editor, it was aimed at a conservative Catholic intellectual audience. Nasty in tone, it quickly developed a reputation for its harsh attacks on liberals and liberal Catholics. In the 1980s it had a circulation of about 6,000; by 1999 it had risen to 15,000.

The Wanderer, a national Catholic weekly journal of news, commentary, and analysis, has published continuously since 1867. Owned and operated by laypeople, it is independent of ecclesiastical oversight. Founded in St. Paul, Minnesota, as *Der Wanderer*, it was published in German for German immigrants in Minnesota and the Dakotas. In 1931 an English edition was begun and simultaneously published along with the German edition. In 1957 the German version was terminated. From its inception the paper has been under the editorship of the Matt family. The *Wanderer* has a reputation for staunch conservatism. Indeed, it is considered the most conservative Catholic national weekly in the United States.

Social Justice Review, a bimonthly journal of opinion, began as a German Catholic periodical in 1908 but changed to English during World War II. It is published in St. Louis, Missouri, by the Central Bureau of the Catholic Central Union of America, a German Catholic organization founded in 1855. Its circulation is just under 5,000, and it has a strongly conservative bent.

Other periodicals cited more briefly are *Catholic Mind* (a Jesuit journal dating from 1902), *Origins* (the weekly official publication of the U.S. Conference of Catholic Bishops), and *LADOC* (*Latin American Documentation*, begun in 1968 by the Latin American Division of the USCC but since the 1980s published by Latinamerica Press); all three publish English translations of important church documents. Others are *The Catholic World*, a Paulist monthly begun in 1865 and terminated in 1996; *St. Joseph's Magazine*, a Benedictine publication dating from the 1890s; *St. Anthony Messenger*, a Franciscan family magazine dating back to 1893; *Jubilee*, the "Catholic ghetto's" equivalent of *Life*; and *Priest*, begun by *Our Sunday Visitor* in 1944 exclusively for a clerical readership. Still others are *Continuum* (begun in 1963), *Magnificat*, *Sisters* (a journal for nuns), *Liturgy*, and *U.S. Catholic*.[7]

one

Guatemala to
the Overthrow
of Jacobo Arbenz

P rior to 1945 there was an almost total absence of interest in
Central America on the part of the U.S. Catholic press. Only
eight listings are found in the *Catholic Periodical and Literature
Index*. All are of a generic nature and devoid of any analytical content. A *Catholic Digest* piece, for example, treated the antics of the
pets of U.S. Capuchin missionaries working in Nicaragua.[1] Only a
single point in the Guatemalan articles merits comment, and that
only because it illustrates the attitude of the Catholic church from
the 1930s through the 1950s toward the indigenous population.
Praising the ministry of a priest in Chichicastenango, the author of
a 1934 *Commonweal* article noted with seeming approval:

> The Indian mind . . . is not constituted to comprehend certain
> abstract doctrines of Catholic theology. . . . [Thus,] as a consci-
> entious priest, [he] may not give them Holy Communion.
> Only the Ladinos, who are better educated, may receive all the
> sacraments.[2]

The first noteworthy article was a piece published in 1945 in
the *Sign*. It was a harsh attack on the recently ousted Guatemalan
dictator Jorge Ubico. Although slightly wanting in that it ignored

7

the dictator's comfortable relationship with Guatemala's Archbishop Mariano Rossell Arellano,[3] the piece was on the whole surprisingly perceptive, as the following remark illustrates:

> Guatemala may be taken, in fact, as a case study in the phenomenon of dictatorship in Latin America. . . . Ubico's regime was a monstrosity of ingenuity, efficiency, brutality, and cynicism. For thirteen years Guatemala enjoyed none of the elements of a decent civic life. The usual procedures of dictatorship were followed in the classic manner: liberty of the press curtailed, schools and university rigidly circumscribed, the movement of citizens carefully and often obnoxiously watched, and no criticism, even the mildest, allowed.[4]

But more substantial was the author's negative analysis of the relationship between the dictatorship and the U. S. government:

> [Ubico's] devotion to the interest of the United States . . . was touching. . . . Here we have in a nutshell the essence of dictatorial practice. What Ubico did internally was of little moment. He could assassinate his fellow Guatemalans; he could fill his local jails; he could muzzle the press . . . and yet if he toed the [U. S.] line externally or internationally, his place was safe.[5]

This harsh critique of U.S. policy in Central America stands alone. The North American Catholic press, influenced (as was the secular press) by the Cold War, would not express similar ideas until the 1960s.

The only other article in the Catholic media in the 1940s noteworthy in its perceptive analysis was also in the *Sign*. It was an apologia for the social policies of Costa Rican Archbishop Victor Sanabria Martínez. The piece began by reporting that San José newspapers were labeling Sanabria a communist because he had revolutionary ideas that were shared by the communist party. The author then defended the prelate: "The diminutive archbishop had the centuries-old conviction, too little stressed in our time, that Christianity packs more socio-economic dynamite per square inch than any and every hue of communism."[6] Pointing out that Sanabria's conduct was in accord with papal social encyclicals, the author noted that Sanabria had "entered politics" for pastoral, not political, reasons, since 90 percent of Catholic Costa Ricans were of the laboring class and most of these were economically hard-pressed. Thus, far from being a communist dupe, Sanabria had actually co-opted the communists, defusing their potential influence by having the church take up the just demands of the working class.[7]

From 1945 to 1954 the reports on Central America in U. S. Catholic magazines concentrated almost exclusively on the conduct of the governments of Juan José Arévalo and Jacobo Arbenz in Guatemala.[8] Elected with 85 percent of the vote in what was probably the first honest presidential election in Guatemalan history, Arévalo took office on March 15, 1945, pledging to bring political, economic, and social reforms to a country emerging from thirteen years of repressive rule under Ubico and from centuries of racism, oppression, and extreme economic disparity. The task before him was overwhelming. More than 70 percent of the population was illiterate. The country had very little industry, and labor unions were outlawed. Seventy-two percent of agricultural land was owned by 2.2 percent of landowners. Less than 25 percent of the land was under cultivation, and agricultural production was inefficient and backward.[9]

Modeling his "Spiritual Socialism" on the policies of Franklin Roosevelt, Arévalo produced impressive achievements during his six years in office. Whereas previously only literate men could vote, the franchise was opened to illiterate men and literate women over eighteen years of age. A multiparty political system was created. Labor unions were legalized, and a progressive Labor Code was enacted into law, bringing major benefits to urban workers. Health clinics and schools were also built in rural villages and urban barrios. The success of these reforms is illustrated by the fact that urban wages increased by 80 percent and the mortality rate fell an average of 2.5 percent per year during the reform years from 1945 to 1954.[10] One would think that such progress would bring praise from the U. S. Catholic press, but this was far from the case. Almost from the beginning of his presidency Arévalo was treated harshly, and by the end of his term a few publications were even labeling his administration communist.

Commonweal was the first to comment on the new president. In a 1946 article, Harry Sylvester declared that although Arévalo was "perhaps slightly more friendly to the Church than was . . . Ubico,"[11] he was opportunistic, completely without experience, and "reputedly making tens of thousands of dollars through inflationary conditions he permits to exist."[12] The author concluded, however, on a less negative note, contending that the recent charge of a U. S. congressman that Guatemala was riddled with communist activity was untrue: "Trouble or disaffection of any sort in Guatemala is always attributed to communists."[13]

America first mentioned Arévalo in 1947, criticizing his government for passing a law allowing censorship of religious periodicals and radio stations when they commented on labor or political matters.[14] The editorial was mute, however, on the circumstances leading up to the statute. Ever since Arévalo had taken office, the Catholic lay weekly *Acción Social Cristiana,* the archdiocesan newspaper *Verbum,* and the archdiocesan radio station had been constantly issuing highly questionable charges against the new president and his reforms. They claimed, for instance, that the administration and labor unions were attempting to transform the nation into a communist dictatorship and called for public antigovernment demonstrations.[15] Although it might be argued that the Guatemalan Catholic media did not merit censorship for their actions, they were certainly not innocent victims, as the *America* editorial at least indirectly indicated through its omission.[16]

The first U. S. Catholic magazine to go so far as to label the Arévalo government communist was *Ave Maria.* In a March 1948 issue it printed a short commentary under the headline "Guatemala Goes Red," charging that Guatemala was "being turned into a little soviet state."[17] It further claimed that the Arévalo government's Labor Code was patterned after that of the Soviet Union and that the administration suppressed the right of private property, placed declared communists in public office, permitted foreign communists to enter the country freely while denying entry to missionary priests, and used force to nullify electoral opposition. As its source, it cited "a group of Guatemalan Catholics" who publicly made these accusations while in Cuba "to prove that the government favors communism."[18] No evidence, however, was provided in support of its claims, and today scholars would give them little credence.[19]

America, citing a *New York Times* article as its source, took a similar position, tersely noting that "little Guatemala is the only Central American country that seems to favor Russia more than it favors the United States."[20] Using the rhetoric of McCarthyism, the commentator next attempted to reveal to his readers the Marxist-Leninist modus operandi as it applied to Guatemala: Although Arévalo denied being a communist, he allowed communists to hold key government positions in return for their political support. But once the communists gained a foothold, they maneuvered "to damage U. S. trade by attempting to drive foreign capital out of the country, regardless of harmful local effects."[21] The "Reds" likewise called for labor and social reforms in order to harass American business organizations that refused to kowtow to them. Curiously, the commentator added that Arévalo seemed finally to be realizing that he had been playing a dangerous game and "that U. S. firms in Guatemala greatly benefit his nation and . . . have of latter years treated their employees fairly."[22] Finally, the author issued a dire warning: "Up to now, Soviet infiltration in Central America has maintained a foothold only in Guatemala."[23]

The last-mentioned *Ave Maria* and *America* commentaries are significant in that they show that even before the Catholic media branded as communist the more controversial reform policies of the next Guatemalan government, that of Arbenz, some of its publications had already painted the more moderate programs of Arévalo with a "Red" brush.

When Jacobo Arbenz took office on March 15, 1951, his primary goal was to expand *arevalismo* into the countryside through land redistribution. Arévalo had earlier balked at such a move, fearing the wrath of the powerful landed elite, especially the Boston-based United Fruit Company (UFCO), the largest landowner in Guatemala. But Arbenz, a former army officer with ties to the military high command, felt more secure. Therefore, in June 1952, his administration issued Decree 900, the most comprehensive agrarian reform in Guatemalan history. The law was far from radical. The government could confiscate only those parts of large plantations that were not productive. All cultivated lands were exempt, as were small and medium-sized farms, whether or not they were producing crops. The government was to compensate those whose lands were expropriated, basing the amount on the value of the land declared by the owner for taxation purposes. Expropriated land was to be distributed to landless peasant families in plots not to exceed 42.5 acres each.

In the eighteen months that the program was in operation, 1.5 million acres were redistributed to about 100,000 peasant families, mostly Indians. Since land that had formerly lain fallow was now under cultivation, production of corn, beans, and coffee increased substantially, as did the country's gross national product. Moreover, due to the decreased labor supply, plantation wages rose to over a dollar a day.[24] Nevertheless, Arbenz and his agrarian reform program were anathema to the U. S. government, U. S. corporations, and the Guatemalan Catholic church. Consequently, in June 1954 his regime was overthrown by the U. S. Central Intelligence Agency working in collaboration with elements from the Guatemalan opposition.

In his fifteen months in office prior to the promulgation of Decree 900, only four short articles were written in the U. S. Catholic press about Arbenz and his policies. One appeared in *Commonweal* and three in *America*. The *Commonweal* piece began by placing part of the blame for poor relations between Guatemala and the United States on the United Fruit Company:

One reason for the hesitancy of other people to accept American political ideals as their own has gradually been coming to light in Central America, where for half a century the United Fruit Company has been operating its own tight little empire of plantations, railroads, docks, shipping and friendly governments.[25]

The editorial writer next turned his criticism on the leaders of the Guatemalan government, however, chiding them for rejecting concessions offered by UFCO and warning that they would do well to realize that if the company suddenly decided to pull out of Guatemala, no one would benefit.[26]

The *Commonweal* editorial is noteworthy because it at least placed some of the blame for the turmoil in Guatemala on U.S. business. Few articles in the U.S. Catholic press during the Arévalo-Arbenz era were willing to go that far.

The first *America* article scathingly charged that "the first four months of [the Arbenz] regime have witnessed an amazing growth of communism in Guatemala." Turning to specifics, the piece accused the government of removing three nuns from the staff of an orphanage after inciting the orphans against them. It further claimed that union workers at the institution had formed a "Red cell" and were using the facility's printing plant to print communist literature.[27]

In a second commentary, *America* made more unsubstantiated charges. Citing the *New York Herald Tribune,* the writer stated that "Communists have taken over the [Guatemalan] government and plan to make it the basis of their subversive operations in Central America."[28] He added that the scenario in Guatemala should serve as a wake-up call for what might soon happen in the entire Southern Hemisphere. As far as the church went, he contended that foreign priests were not permitted to live in the country and that native clergy were threatened "for engaging in social works."[29]

America's bias was again demonstrated by what was not stated. Even secret U.S. intelligence documents from the time concluded that Guatemala was not a communist state. A National Intelligence Estimate report from 1953 noted, for instance, that the Guatemalan Labor (Communist) Party had no more than a thousand members and that fewer than half were militants. It stated further that although communists dominated the Agrarian Reform and Labor Code Revision Committees, there were no communists in the Arbenz Cabinet and communists had "made little or no effort . . . to gain control over the Police or Army."[30] A Bureau of Inter-American Affairs policy paper pointed out that "militant Communists in Guatemala are estimated at a few hundred. Of these perhaps two or three dozen are dangerous leaders or agitators," and none seemed to have been "Moscow-trained."[31] It could be added that only four out of fifty-six members of the Guatemalan Congress were communists. Certainly, these statements did not back up *America*'s contention that Guatemala was a communist state.

Concerning the charge of government persecution of the Catholic clergy, the *America* editorial neglected to point out that foreign priests had been forbidden to reside in Guatemala since the country had issued its 1879 Constitution and that the Arévalo-Arbenz regimes were actually the least militant of all Guatemalan presidents up to that time in enforcing this restriction. Indeed, in 1944, just prior to Arévalo's inauguration, there were only 114 priests in Guatemala. In 1950, when Arévalo's term was at an end, there were 149, and in 1954, on the eve of Arbenz's ouster from office, there were 192.[32] Nearly all of the additional 81 priests were foreigners allowed to enter the country by the two reform presidents, even though this was technically against the law.[33]

Once the Arbenz government began to implement Decree 900, the U. S. Catholic press, like its secular counterpart, escalated its negative reporting. But now there was no hesitation to label Arbenz a communist or a "fellow traveler." Almost every U. S. Catholic magazine reporting on Guatemala did so.

In a March 1953 editorial, *America* equated Guatemalan land reform with that of China, claiming that it was a ruse and that its real purpose was a total communist takeover of the country. Nevertheless, the piece noted that true land redistribution in Guatemala was sorely needed.[34]

St. Joseph Magazine soon raised the ante in Cold War excitation in a lengthy article by H. C. McGinnis. Like the above *America* editorial, the piece equated Guatemala's agrarian reform program with China's, contending that it was no more than a false front, aimed at duping peasants into accepting a communist regime.[35] The article went further, however, making wild claims and using the exaggerated rhetoric of McCarthyism:

Guatemala has succeeded Mexico City as the capital of the Reds' fifth column in the Americas.

Shortly after World War II the Kremlin's agents in Mexico found conditions there too unfavorable for the type of operations they planned. Moscow wanted a place from which it could throw tons and tons of propaganda into American countries and from which its agents could come and go without restraint.

The place is Guatemala, where President Arbenz and his government are little more than Russian puppets.[36]

McGinnis next informed his readers that Arbenz was not actually a communist but an opportunist who "finds it so profitable to be so pro-Communist that it is virtually impossible to distinguish him from an official of the Kremlin itself." Lacking a conscience or ideals when there is a fast buck to be made, Arbenz cooperated with Moscow, which perhaps had promised him "a lifelong dictatorship, come the revolution."[37]

But McGinnis went further, warning that the Soviets actually had more in mind for Guatemala than a mere propaganda base:

> Guatemala furnishes the Kremlin with a highly strategic location. . . . The little republic has three airfields . . . [that] can accommodate medium bombers, capable of making the trip to the Panama Canal in just two hours. They can also hit vital military and scientific installations in Texas within three hours. American bases on the Gulf, such as Pensacola, are within equally easy firing distance.[38]

In case the reader had still not gotten the point, the article included a map of North and Central America. Guatemala was depicted in bold color with a large hammer and sickle. Lines emanated from it to seven major U. S. cities; superimposed was the distance in miles between Guatemala and each location.[39]

Finally, after warning that the Soviet Union had already set up additional "undergrounds" in Honduras, El Salvador, and Nicaragua, the author concluded with a call for U. S. intervention: "Resistance to the Arbenz program is mounting steadily, but . . . help from the outside will be needed if Guatemala is not to be smothered by Red tyranny and despotism."[40]

St. Joseph Magazine was not alone in calling for U. S. intervention in the isthmus. *Ave Maria,* charging erroneously that Guatemala was receiving arms and instruction from the Soviet Union, called on the United States to intervene before the communist cancer spread throughout South America. "If we intervene perhaps [the Good Neighbor] policy will be destroyed for decades. On the other hand, is not Moscow now intervening in Guatemala?"[41]

No attack in the U. S. Catholic press, however, reached the extreme of a piece in the *Catholic Digest* by best-selling author Jim Bishop. A classic example of 1950s Cold War overkill, the article displayed its tone in its subtitle: "A nation in our own hemisphere has a communist government worse than Russia's."[42] The piece began with Bishop informing his readers that in the past, Soviet air force generals "did not smile," but "ever since little Guatemala told the world, last spring, that she hates Uncle Sam and loves Uncle Joe, these men have been smiling like Cheshire cats." But their joy, of course, ran deeper: "All Guatemala has to do is to build a 10,000 foot air-strip." Soviet planes could then fly from Siberia, bomb Seattle, San Francisco, and Los Angeles, and land in Guatemala.[43]

Bishop claimed that the Guatemalan agrarian reform program was "much more severe on landowners than anything Moscow would dare put into effect"[44] and that the United Fruit Company had been treated especially unfairly. Since UFCO provided free housing and hospitalization for its workers and paid them twice or three times the wages they could earn elsewhere, the government had passed laws aimed at "preventing the company from taking care of the needs of its workers." It had also "jacked up" UFCO's taxes "indiscriminately" and had begun to put "the same squeeze" on Pan American Airways. Indeed, Guatemalan workers had been "tricked in[to] fighting against their own best interest."[45]

Lest his readers wonder why Guatemalan voters elected Arbenz in the first place, Bishop explained: Guatemalan people were illiterate, so when it came to voting, "they will blandly ask a young communist election official where to make a mark, and will follow his advice."[46] This is why the communists controlled the entire countryside. "Their only opposition comes from Guatemala City, and practically all of this comes from 10,000 women and the Catholic Church."[47]

Bishop further informed his readers that Guatemalan communists were a "much more virulent type" than those in Moscow.[48] Indeed, "Guatemalan Reds boast that they are closer to real communists than the Soviets."[49] As proof Bishop provided the following examples: "In 1952, a man in Guatemala City was arrested for sedition because he sent a wire congratulating President Eisenhower on his election."[50] Also in 1952, "5 men went to jail because they asked the government whether free campaigning would be permitted."[51] Finally, after leaving a meeting, some Guatemalan women had "parts of their faces blown off" by bullets from the guns of Guatemalan soldiers. What was their crime? They had voted against the communists and spoken out publicly against them.[52] Bishop provided no names or supporting evidence to back up his claims.

In June 1954, *America* added a new accusation against "Guatemalan communists," blaming them for the massive general strike in Honduras against the United and Standard Fruit Companies. No concrete proof was presented to sustain the charge, just the rationalization that the strike was too "professionally run" to be the work of any organization other than the communists of Guatemala.[53]

Another *America* article, written by Scripps-Howard journalist Charles Lucey just before the overthrow of Arbenz, merits some attention. It focused on Archbishop Mariano Rossell Arellano of Guatemala City, calling him "the center of anti-Communist resistance in Guatemala" and "the most formidable foe the Reds have in Central America."[54] After effusive praise for the archbishop, Lucey stated that the poor masses looked to Rossell for leadership and deliverance from an oppressive communist government, so much so that in remote areas they had passed around by hand almost half a million copies of the prelate's anticommunist pastoral letter. Lucey further claimed that the government had been forced to back off from deporting Rossell when thousands of angry people, mostly poor market women, came to his defense. His procession from town to town with the venerable Black Christ of Esquipulas, during which he warned the faithful of the dangers of communism in Guatemala, was presented as a spontaneous action without political motivation. A village priest was supposed to lead the procession, said Lucey, but when Rossell learned that government supporters threatened to stone him, the archbishop immediately flew to Esquipulas to take the priest's place. Knowing his popularity with the masses, the authorities did not dare stone him. Lucey further asserted that Rossell's popularity with the poor came from the Catholic-based social program he had established for them, a program that they found far more appealing than that of the procommunist Arbenz government.[55]

Lucey's report was the first article in any U. S. Catholic magazine to focus exclusively on the important role that Rossell was playing in the anti-Arbenz movement. Nevertheless, it was marred by factual errors and a lack of objectivity. Catholics were far from united in opposition to the reform government. Rossell's support came primarily from the clergy and a small right-wing Catholic urban elite. As historian Blake Pattridge pointed out, there were "many Catholics [who] supported the reforms of the [Arévalo-Arbenz] governments and opposed the conservative policies of their church leaders."[56]

There was also friction between Rossell and the Vatican, which saw him as too independent and nationalistic. Rome was especially concerned with his xenophobic attitude toward foreign clergy and felt that his authority had to be curtailed. Consequently, in 1951 the Vatican created four new dioceses. Over Rossell's strong objection, three of the four new episcopal appointments went to foreigners.[57]

Lucey was also silent on the tensions between Rossell and Genaro Verolino, the papal nuncio, who did not view Decree 900 or Arbenz as a serious threat to the church. Rossell ignored Verolino's numerous pleas to tone down his vitriolic rhetoric and refused to inform the nuncio of his plan to issue his anti-Arbenz pastoral letter.[58] The archbishop also received little backing from the rural poor. It was the CIA, not enthusiastic peasants, who spread his anticommunist letter throughout the countryside. E. Howard Hunt, a CIA agent who played a major role in the operation, said that thousands of copies of the letter were dropped from planes piloted by CIA agents.[59] There was also strong evidence indicating that Rossell's antigovernment actions were all part of a CIA plan preparing the way for Arbenz's overthrow. The pastoral letter, which was read at every mass in every church in Guatemala, the procession with the Black Christ, and the rumors which were spread that the government was considering expelling the archbishop all seem to have been part of this brilliantly orchestrated plan.[60] Finally, there was no massive archdiocesan social program for the poor, as Lucey claimed.

Not all reporting on Guatemala in the Catholic press in the months prior to the fall of Arbenz was as biased as that covered above. Commentaries in *Commonweal* were quite perceptive. Like other Catholic periodicals, *Commonweal* did not question the nearly universal North American view that communists had gained control of the Arbenz government. What made its articles unique, however, was that its writers argued that poverty and oppression, rather than communism, were the root causes of the problems in Guatemala and the rest of Latin America and that the growth of communism was inevitable when injustice was ignored.

In a late 1953 piece, a *Commonweal* writer explained that Latins, with good reason, saw capitalism from a different perspective than did North Americans. To them, it was a repressive system characterized by low wages, restricted production, and a growing gulf between rich and poor that led to class warfare.[61] A second commentary chided the Rockefeller commission for ignoring in its report on Latin America the vital issues "of poverty, illiteracy, malnutrition, disease and low productivity." It argued that these were the real causes of dissatisfaction in Guatemala and the reason for the government's struggle with the United Fruit Company.[62]

A third article pointed out that in a society where the democratic opposition and noncommunist union leaders always wound up in jail, it should be no surprise when communists were seen as the only effective opponents of dictatorship.[63]

In another *Commonweal* article, the writer noted that the rise of communism in Guatemala had followed an all too familiar pattern. Military dictators combined with wealthy landowners to create a destitute class of resentful agrarian workers. Communists then entered the picture by posing, not as Soviet agents, but as patriotic nationalists. They increased their prominence by organizing workers and playing a part in education and land reform. The article concluded by remarking that the most potent anticommunist weapon the United States had was its "democratic message."

Unfortunately, however, because of the conduct of our large companies in Latin America, "we have too often been cast in the role of the oppressors." The article also chided the United States for concentrating on helping Western Europe, while ignoring Latin America.[64]

Only one article appeared in the *Catholic Worker* on this topic, but it stood alone for its radically different approach. It was inspired by the accusations of a U.S. priest, Sebastian Buccellato, after he was expelled from Guatemala by the government. Buccellato had claimed in several media interviews that the Arbenz administration was communist and was persecuting the church and that his ouster proved his contention.

The *Catholic Worker* saw the situation differently and expressed its point of view with blistering sarcasm. It began by stating how ironic it was that when the Guatemalan government began a program based on "land for the landless" it was called communist. The author then remarked caustically: "It is strange that a desire for private property should be one of the greatest appeals of Communism, and strange, too, that as soon as a man seeks private property in this day of corporate farming, he is dubbed Communist."[65] Without mentioning Buccellato by name, the writer made his point in no uncertain terms:

> Recently a Franciscan priest was arrested and deported from Guatemala . . . because, as he said, he was teaching religion. Religion in this case meant that he told his parishioners that they should not accept land which had been expropriated from the United Fruit Company by the Government (but with compensation).[66]

Without further comment the article closed by citing the pronouncements of six popes. Their declarations clearly pointed out that the church had traditionally taught that when a few people have land and many are landless, the latter have the right to occupy and cultivate untilled land, even when the legal owners refuse permission.[67]

Of the few articles in the U.S. Catholic press in the early 1950s focusing on Central American countries other than Guatemala, only one merits attention, a June 1954 profile of Thomas Whelan, U.S. ambassador to Nicaragua, in *Extension*. The piece is of interest in that it depicts in a positive light the egocentric assumptions of the ambassador and also his close relationship with Nicaraguan dictator Anastasio Somoza García. The author, John O'Brien, stated with pride that Whelan, a Catholic, was named ambassador even though "he knew little about South America."[68] He further noted that Whelan had an amazing ability to fraternize with Nicaraguans even though he did not speak Spanish. He added with great admiration that after Whelan had been ambassador for six years:

> He called in all the household servants, his chauffeurs and his garden-ers, all Nicaraguans. "Look," he said, "it's no use. I have tried to learn your language, and I am getting nowhere. So you might as well get busy and learn English."[69]

Whelan was characterized as feeling very positive about Nicaragua and its government, calling it "a fine country with a future" and pointing out that it was the only Latin American nation "that has supported the United States on every issue in the United Nations."[70] The article displayed much pride in the ambassador's special relationship with Somoza: "President Somoza addresses him as 'Tommy' and Mrs. Whelan as 'Mibs' and Whelan calls the President 'Tasha.'"[71] The ambassador was depicted as mixing both officially and socially with Nicaraguan officials and occasionally playing poker with Somoza, going to the races with him and sitting in the presidential box, and often accompanying him on his trips through the country.[72] From a review of this article, it is obvious that while the U.S. Catholic press was viciously attacking Guatemalan President Arbenz and his social programs, *Extension* magazine was heaping praise on Somoza's unsavory government and its close relationship with the United States.

To recapitulate, it was not until the late 1940s and early 1950s that the U.S. Catholic press took an interest in Central America. Its focus, however, was almost totally on the administrations of Arévalo and Arbenz in Guatemala. Virtually nothing positive was said concerning Arévalo and his reforms, and toward the end of his tenure in office a few publications even labeled his government communist and claimed that his Labor Code was based on that of the Soviet Union.

Arbenz was treated more harshly. During his presidency not a single favorable comment was made about him or his policies in any Catholic popular periodical. It was accepted without question by all but the *Catholic Worker* that his was a communist government directed from Moscow, and his land reform program was equated with those of China and the Soviet Union. In 1954 the number of attacks on Arbenz escalated and became gradually more irresponsible. Only *Commonweal* made an attempt at objective journalism. *America* played the leading role in the anti-Arbenz onslaught, but the most extreme articles were published in the *Catholic Digest* and *St. Joseph Magazine*. In keeping with the McCarthyism of the time, charges by the U.S. Catholic press were seldom backed up with credible evidence. Moreover, U. S. policy toward Guatemala and the rest of Central America was universally unquestioned by the Catholic media. It was automatically assumed that whatever positions the United States held concerning the isthmus, they were morally defensible. Likewise, U. S. business, although subject to mild criticism, was considered by all but *Commonweal* to be on the whole a positive element in Central America.

Finally, while the Arévalo and Arbenz governments were being castigated, the U. S. Catholic press did not have a negative word for the Nicaraguan dictatorship of Somoza.

two

Carlos Castillo Armas and the Catholic Church

The overthrow of Arbenz marks a most important time in Guatemalan history. A decade of meaningful reform came to an end and was never revived. It was replaced by a return to dictatorial rule. After serving for about three months as the dominant member of a provisional junta created by the U.S. ambassador, John Peurifoy, Castillo Armas was elected president on October 10, 1954, in a plebiscite reminiscent of those formerly held by Ubico. Guatemalans had the option of voting yes or no for Castillo; no other candidate was allowed to run against him. Since fewer than 400 people were bold enough to risk their lives by casting their ballots against him, he received 99.99 percent of the vote.[1]

Although Castillo claimed that providing for the material needs of the poor masses would be a top priority of his administration, his deeds quickly proved that his statement was disingenuous. In one of his first decrees, he disenfranchised the 72 percent of the population that was illiterate. He soon emasculated the labor movement by revoking the legal status of 533 unions and amending the Arévalo Labor Code. The minimum wage was abolished, as was a worker's right to a paid vacation. The work week was extended to forty-eight hours. Many labor leaders were arrested and some were murdered. A Preventive Penal Law Against Communism was promulgated, which was vague enough to be interpreted in such a way as to subject strikers and members of illegal unions to the death penalty. In light of the above, it is no wonder that within a year of the ousting of Arbenz, union membership had been reduced by 72 percent.[2]

Castillo also destroyed Arbenz's land reform program. A law was passed that terminated additional expropriations of unproductive farmlands. A Department of Agrarian Affairs was created to hear appeals from those who had lost land as a result of Decree 900. By the end of the first year of Castillo's administration, over 99 percent of expropriated land had been returned to its former owners. Castillo also abolished the National Agrarian Bank, which had been established by the reform government to extend credit to small farmers. Likewise, he revoked reform legislation prohibiting large landowners from lending small plots of land to their workers in lieu of paying wages. Those peasants who resisted the rollback of Decree 900 suffered the consequences. Within the first two months of Castillo's presidency, about 8,000 had been murdered.[3]

The repressive policies of the new government went further. Political parties were outlawed and rigid press censorship was inaugurated. Not surprisingly, U.S. business fared well. Reform laws restricting foreign investment were annulled, and generous new tax breaks were granted for foreign corporations.[4]

From the perspective of Archbishop Rossell and the Guatemalan clergy, however, the inauguration of Castillo Armas as president meant a new and better day for the Catholic church. Rossell had obviously played an important role in the ouster of Arbenz, with his pastoral letters and high-profile processions. Three days after Castillo entered Guatemala, beginning his "war of liberation," the archbishop celebrated a Mass of Thanksgiving at the national shrine in Esquipulas. With "the liberator" in attendance, Rossell portrayed him as the defender of Christianity and savior of the nation from atheistic communism. In a July 2 pastoral letter, the prelate went further, justifying Castillo's invasion by erroneously claiming that the Arbenz government was responsible for "the jailings, torture, and assassinations of hundreds of workers and peasants," adding that so many were murdered that their bodies could not be found.[5] He elaborated on this theme a month later in a funeral sermon commemorating those who died fighting under Castillo. Comparing their suffering and death to that of Christ, he declared them national heroes who had been cut down for opposing a communist, anti-Christian, anti-Guatemalan regime.[6]

The papal nuncio to Guatemala, Archbishop Genaro Verolino, also played a large role in the rise of Castillo. He was part of the group that chose "the liberator" as a member of the provisional junta. He also flew with Castillo to Guatemala City, thereby giving a church presence to his triumphant entry into power.

This new cooperative relationship between church and state stood in marked contrast to the situation that had existed over the prior three-fourths of a century. To understand its significance one must look back in Guatemalan history. Until 1870 the Guatemalan church was the most powerful national church in Central America. This changed, however, in the 1870s, when the Liberal Party came to power under the combined forces of Miguel García Granados and Justo Rufino Barrios. The Liberals saw the wealth and wide-ranging powers of the Catholic church as an impediment to progress. Thus, they passed a series of anticlerical laws. The University of San Carlos was taken from the church and put under secular control. In fact, the church was taken entirely out of the business of education, being replaced by a public school system. The tithe was abolished, church property was expropriated, and the church was henceforth forbidden to own any property except that expressly needed for religious services. Religious orders were outlawed, and most foreign priests and nuns were exiled. Religious liberty was established, and Protestant missionaries were encouraged to enter the country. The church also lost its control over marriages and cemeteries. Clergy were forbidden to hold governmental office, wear their clerical garb in public, or speak out on political issues. When the church retaliated by excommunicating Barrios and holding processions in protest of the new restrictions, the government outlawed such public displays of religion and expelled the archbishop from the country. In the future, every archbishop through the 1920s would be exiled for at least part of his tenure in office.

All the above measures were codified in the Constitution of 1879, which remained in effect until 1945.[7] Whereas there had been 314 priests in Guatemala before the anticlerical laws, by 1880 only 119 priests remained, and by 1928 only 78,[8] a number that had increased to 114 by 1945, when Arévalo became president.

As a result of the Liberals' devastation of the church, the latter became weak, poor, understaffed, and unable to play more than a minor role in the lives of most Guatemalans. The church worked primarily with the small, conservative upper class. It operated almost totally in the capital city; a few priests worked in provincial cities and nearly none in rural areas.[9] Rural Indians held to their syncretic Catholicism, but without priests. Catholic clergy came from the upper conservative class and had virtually no identification with the poor masses and their needs and problems.

When the energetic Rossell Arellano became archbishop in 1939, he was determined to revitalize the institutional church and make it a major factor in Guatemalan life. An admirer of General Francisco Franco and his Falangist system in Spain,[10] Rossell seems to have envisioned something similar for his nation. He saw Ubico as a potential Guatemalan Franco. He hoped that the strongman might create a Falangist-like authoritarian government in which church and state cooperated, forging an orderly system based on hierarchy, patriotism, and conservative Catholic values. Whereas Rossell's episcopal predecessors had struggled against the Liberal presidents of their day, the new archbishop attempted to work with Ubico. For his part, the Guatemalan *caudillo* welcomed this change of attitude by the Catholic prelate and quietly made minor concessions to the church: Jesuits were allowed to enter the country to run the Catholic seminary, and Belgian nuns were permitted to open a high school for upper-class girls. U. S. Maryknoll missionaries who had been expelled from communist China and Salesian, Marist, Franciscan, and Dominican priests, mostly from Franco's Spain, were able to come to work in Guatemala.[11] For the first time since the 1870s a papal nuncio was accepted for Guatemala and even awarded the prestigious Order of the Quetzal by Ubico.[12] The *caudillo* allowed the church to celebrate a Eucharistic Congress publicly, and it was during his presidency that Catholic Action groups first began to operate in Guatemala.[13] Moreover, unlike other Liberal presidents, Ubico was no friend of the Protestants. He issued a decree which set limits on the number of Protestant missionaries allowed in the country. He required them to register with the government and provide an account of all their projects to the Ministry of the Interior. He was also the first president since the 1870s not to enroll his children in the prestigious American Presbyterian school in the capital.[14]

Although all the above actions of Ubico pleased the archbishop, there was no question but that the status of the institutional Guatemalan Catholic church depended wholly on the whim of the dictator. All church gains were unconstitutional, and by the early 1940s, it had become apparent that Ubico had no intention of amending the Constitution of 1879. Rossell was well aware that if he or his clergy displeased Ubico, all that had been permitted by the government could be nullified immediately.

Rossell remained silent during the overthrow of Ubico and took an apolitical position in the elections that followed.[15] Arévalo and his fellow reformers had made it clear that they intended to break with much of the Liberal past and draw up a new constitution based on democratic freedoms. The archbishop and Catholic clergy had good reason to hope that the anti-democratic religious restrictions of the Constitution of 1879 would finally be repealed. Perhaps with that possibility in mind, the prelate wished the new administration well, issuing a circular just before Arévalo took office assuring the government that it had the support of the church.[16]

When the Constitution of 1945 finally appeared, however, it was a bitter disappointment to the institutional Catholic church, for it retained all of the anticlerical provisions of 1879.[17] From the time of the new constitution's promulgation in March 1945, the Arévalo administration had an enemy in Rossell. The archbishop's wrath only intensified when the reform government, reversing the policy of Ubico, showed favoritism to Protestants. Not only were Protestant missionaries allowed to enter the country in larger numbers than their Catholic counterparts,[18] but they were called upon by Arévalo to play a primary role in his literacy program by opening and staffing rural schools.[19] Indeed, historian Virginia Garrard Burnett goes so far as to claim that the Arévalo regime "marked the beginning of a new era in [Protestant] mission activity in Guatemala."[20]

The archbishop's attacks on the new government began in October, when, in a pastoral letter, he warned Guatemalans of the evils of communism and its threat to their nation. Although Arévalo was not mentioned, Rossell was indirectly insinuating that communist elements existed in the new government.[21] Prior to elections in 1948, the prelate was bolder, issuing a pastoral instruction to the faithful on the duties and conditions of voting. Equating communism with Moscow and the culture of Genghis Khan, he implored the people to vote against any candidates suspected of communist affiliation. Obviously Rossell was telling Catholics not to cast their ballots for pro-Arévalo candidates.[22] When in 1950 Arévalo accused the archbishop of interfering in politics, Rossell responded that the church had no choice but to warn the people of the communist threat.[23] A later pastoral, issued during Arbenz's presidency, gives insight into the archbishop's way of thinking. In it he remarked that the communist persecution of the Catholic church in Eastern Europe was no different than that of the Latin American church at the hands of Liberals and Freemasons.[24] By this time, Rossell seems to have mixed communism, Liberalism, Freemasonry, Protestantism, and the Arévalo-Arbenz reforms into one vague monolithic enemy of the Catholic Guatemalan way of life. Although Protestantism was not mentioned in the above pastoral, there is no doubt that he included it as part of "the enemy." Protestant denominations were trying to "steal" souls from Catholicism; they had also collaborated with the "communist" government in its rural education program. Thus, they were part of the diabolical threat to Guatemala.

When Castillo Armas became president, he saw the advantage of maintaining a close relationship with the Catholic church. For this reason, once in office he called for the establishment of a constituent assembly to draw up a new constitution. Its membership was composed mainly of conservative Catholics friendly with Rossell.[25] The new Constitution of 1956 gave the church nearly all it wanted. It did not grant the archbishop's request that the Catholic church be given a preeminence over other religions, but the church did get the legal right to own and dispose of property. Religious education in public schools was made legal but optional. Religious orders and congregations received juridical status.

Castillo encouraged the entrance of foreign clergy into the country, and whereas there were 192 priests in Guatemala when Arbenz was overthrown, by the end of 1955 there were 242.[26] By mid-1966 the number of priests had grown to 531, and of these, 434 were foreigners. There were also 805 nuns, all but about 100 of whom were foreign, and 96 religious brothers, all non-Guatemalan.[27]

Under Castillo's presidential successor, Miguel Ydígoras Fuentes, civil recognition of religious marriages was allowed, and the Catholic, Jesuit-run University of Rafael Landivar was opened with the help of a large government subsidy. By 1960 there were seventy-seven Catholic schools in Guatemala.[28] When the Constitution of 1966 replaced that of 1956, the church gained even more. Church property became tax exempt, and Catholic religious instruction in public schools was made mandatory.[29] As anthropologist Richard Adams points out, the constitutional changes begun in 1956 and finalized in 1966 amounted to an invitation by the government to the Catholic church to share responsibility for social control within Guatemala.[30]

In the year following the overthrow of the reform government, *America* was the most prolific of the U.S. Catholic periodicals in reporting on Guatemala. Credit for bringing down the Arbenz government was heaped on various sources. Castillo was lauded for engineering a "palace revolution" that had forced the president to resign.[31] He was also singled out on the one hand for lifting censorship and freeing political prisoners and, ironically, on the other for arresting communists and closing down their newspaper.[32] The Guatemalan majority was praised for rising up "to defeat the first specific attempt of Communist imperialism to establish a beachhead in the hemisphere."[33] Highest accolades, however, were reserved for Archbishop Rossell, who was praised for having been the focal point of "anti-Communist resistance" during this turbulent period.[34]

[He] risked exile and perhaps even death in a courageous challenge to the heads of this country's then pro-Communist Government. His profoundly stirring pastoral letter was the spark that wakened this little nation to the danger confronting it.[35]

Rossell was lauded by the *America* staff for his clarion call for a new Guatemala based on the social encyclicals of the popes,[36] and he was given credit for the constituent assembly's resolution to remove the anticlerical laws from the constitution.[37] His July pastoral letter was translated into English and printed in full in *America*'s sister publication, the *Catholic Mind*.[38]

The *America* staff was mute, however, on the part the United States had played in toppling Arbenz. Indeed, its editors chided the French newspaper *Figaro* and the Canadian *Devoir* for claiming that Castillo's forces had been inflated by adventurers from the Dominican Republic who were hired with U.S. money. Such naiveté, according to the editors, showed that the United States still had "a long row to hoe" in awakening the world to the seriousness of the international communist threat.[39]

More significant was the prediction found in several *America* articles that communism would rise again if the new government ignored the cry of the people for social justice. In a surprising admission that never would have been made if the reform government had still been in power, Gordon George stated: "Whether it is convenient to admit it or not, the displaced Arbenz Government and that of Arévalo before it did initiate real reforms."[40] "The Reds," added Charles Lucey, "were able to gain ascendancy because they climbed aboard and claimed for their own the programs on land reform, social security, trade-union development and public education."[41] A comment from a U.S. White Paper on communism was cited in a third article to support the author's contention that the communists were able to rise to prominence only because they supported the just desire of the masses for peace and better working conditions.[42]

In two articles, *Commonweal* made similar comments, but with greater insight. Unlike those at *America*, the *Commonweal* writers refused to rejoice in the downfall of Arbenz or heap accolades on those, including the archbishop, responsible for it.

In the first piece, the author implied that a history of U.S. corporate greed and U.S. government myopia was partly responsible for the sorry state of Guatemalan affairs. After years of authoritarian rule ended with the ouster of Ubico, the U.S. government did little to help the moderate forces within the region. The questionable practices of the United Fruit Company, "not always . . . so innocent as the fluting song of Chiquita Banana,"[43] did not help the situation. Consequently, when some of the moderates obtained power, they gravitated toward the communists, who had the only party with a platform based on land reform and social improvement. The U.S. campaign against Arbenz only made matters worse, for it was widely viewed throughout South America as an unwarranted interference in the affairs of a constitutionally elected government. The editorial concluded with the hope that a moderate, noncommunist democratic government would end up in control, but it predicted pessimistically that this was a long shot at best.[44]

The second article stuck to the same thesis. Labeling Guatemala a "still unheeded story"[45] where so few were willing to make an effort to bridge the wide gap between rich and poor, it cited the harsh realities of its oppressed workers. It then again chided the sorry past conduct of UFCO, noting that it was made to order for communist propaganda. Giving the devil his due, however, it praised the banana company for recently raising its workers' wages from less than fifty cents a day to two dollars, adding that other U.S. companies in the area were beginning to follow its lead. It pointed out further that Arbenz was not himself a communist. He relied on the support of those who were, however, for the simple reason that there were very few noncommunist reformers in the country: "Non-communists either sat idly by or fought needed reform tooth-and-nail,"[46] while communists, for their own reasons, worked zealously for badly needed social change.

Other Catholic publications were more optimistic, if less perceptive, in their analysis of Guatemala and tended to defend the more questionable policies of the new government. *Ave Maria,* for instance, justified Castillo's banning of the Grand Masonic Lodge from the capital city by explaining to its readers that Freemasons in Guatemala were far different from their U.S. counterparts. In Guatemala they had actively supported "the communist regime," said the *Ave Maria* editors, and they opposed "the [Catholic] Church, the clergy, Christianity and all religion."[47]

In another editorial, *Ave Maria* defended Castillo's repression of organized labor and his dismantling of land reform with the following logic:

> The injustice and brutality that was practiced in Guatemala under the Red-dominated government would have caused that regime to fall long before it did if it had not been supported by two strong pillars—the labor unions and the agricultural group. The Reds set the union policies and told the members what they could, and could not do. . . . Illiterate peasants were often goaded by communists to seize land illegally and these seizures were upheld by the government.[48]

The writer next explained that because of the blatant communist connections of labor and agrarian groups, many expected the new administration to destroy them. But instead, Castillo retained and reformed them: "He outlawed a few unions that were completely Red, and suppressed the Red executive board of a few others."[49] He then guaranteed labor the right to organize without interference as long as it stayed out of politics.

Ave Maria further assured its readers that although Castillo had returned back to its former owners most of the land that the Arbenz government had "seized illegally," the displaced peasants nevertheless would be better off in the long run. This was because Castillo had promised them "huge tracts of public lands"; moreover, whereas under the former government the state had profited by renting confiscated private land to peasants, now the land would be given outright.[50] The piece concluded on a reassuring note: "Things are far from perfect in Guatemala but they seem to be headed in the right direction and the country is recovering."[51]

The *Catholic Digest* was less subtle in its justification of Castillo's methods. In an article condensed from the *Chicago Daily News,* author Edwin Lahey stated that the new president had earnestly tried to steer Guatemala "on a middle course between left and far right" but the communists, now underground, were "still as thick as fruit flies." Consequently, "despite his genuine devotion to democratic principles, [Castillo] Armas has found it necessary to operate like a dictator."[52]

Another *Catholic Digest* article merits attention if only because it shows how far some U. S. Catholic commentators were willing to go to put a positive "spin" on Guatemala. After eulogizing two Guatemalan youths who died trying to overthrow Arbenz, author Jim Bishop told his readers why so many Indians had supported Arbenz and his political cohorts:

> When [the Indians] came to the pueblos after a week's work, they found out that they could not buy a drink. . . . The way to get a drink and to stay out of jail was to have a Communist-party card. The Indians did not know what the card was, and couldn't read it, but they wanted it.[53]

In other words, according to Bishop, the Indians' penchant for alcohol, rather than Arbenz's land redistribution program, explained why so many of them supported the reform government.

On July 27, 1957, Castillo was assassinated by one of his bodyguards. Along with the usual accolades, Archbishop Rossell added a new dimension in his eulogy. Even though Castillo had terminated almost every program that the previous two administrations had set up to help the poor, Rossell declared him champion of the downtrodden, asking: "When will the day come that Guatemala may merit another energetic and sincere defender of the interests of the poor, of the weak, of the exploited, of the same calibre as Castillo Armas?"[54]

Although interest in Guatemala had waned in the United States after the first few months of Castillo's presidency, a few Catholic periodicals did comment on him after his assassination. One of the more telling pieces, written by Chicago newspaperman Edwin Lahey, appeared in *Extension*. Like Rossell, Lahey virtually canonized Castillo, effusively claiming that "for the first time since the republic was founded, Guatemala had a true national hero."[55] Describing Guatemala in vivid Cold War terminology, he stated that "this little republic" was "a laboratory experiment in democracy" and that its success was "of prime importance in the grim world-wide struggle between freedom and totalitarianism for the mind and hearts of men." He concluded that there was strong reason to believe that the experiment would prove successful "and produce evidence for the rest of an uncertain world that a 'middle of the road' policy of constitutional democracy and friendship with the United States is the only safe road for a small nation to travel."[56]

Lahey next explained that although there had been many complaints about Castillo's policies, the president had been convinced that his "middle of the road" political and social programs would eventually "launch his nation permanently on a way of life similar to that of the United States, its political god-father."[57] Proof that Castillo was right, according to Lahey, came from the profound shock and sadness expressed by all classes of society upon learning of his assassination. The rich and the poor, the shoeless Indian and the middle-class housewife—"everybody reacted as though a member of the family had met a tragic death."[58] Even the military, which "had tasted constitutional government, and wanted more of it,"[59] announced that it was committed to a continuation of democracy. Indeed:

> Before the slain President was laid to rest, the whole nation was united in sincere pledges to carry out his program, and the danger of a reversion of chaos and military dictatorship seemed averted.
>
> It was in this way that [Castillo] Armas showed his great prestige while dead. Any group that might have tried to take over the government illegally during the emergency would have evoked a spontaneous public outburst of violent reaction.[60]

America paid a similar tribute to the fallen Castillo. Its editorialist noted that although Castillo was being praised in newspapers throughout the United States for having liberated his country, he actually had done much more:

> In his plans for Guatemala, the ousting of Jacobo Arbenz Guzman and his Communist conspirators was to be not the last act of the drama but the first. The last act was to be a democratic society consecrated to the cause of social justice.[61]

The author next painted a picture of Castillo besieged on the right by powerful landowners determined to return to the exploitative past and on the left by impatient students who demanded that "democracy be accomplished overnight."[62] While conceding that Castillo did not grant complete freedom of the press or permit opposition political parties, the editorialist insisted that "he laid carefully the foundations for future democracy" by allowing workers to form unions and refusing to take ownership of expropriated lands away from peasants.[63] These last two claims, of course, were basically incorrect and probably resulted from the "good press" Castillo had received from Archbishop Rossell and the U. S. government and secular media.

Events in Guatemala following the death of Castillo did not measure up to the high expectations of the North American Catholic press. In the 1957 presidential election, the candidate of the National Democratic Movement (MDN), Castillo's party, was losing at the polls to Miguel Ydígoras Fuentes, the candidate of the National Democratic Renovation Party (*Redención*). Thus, the MDN resorted to fraud and declared its candidate the winner. This caused Ydígoras's supporters to take to the streets. This, in turn, enabled the military, which had its differences with the MDN, to intervene and nullify the election. A new election took place in January 1958, and Ydígoras, a former general and public works minister under Ubico, was victorious. His tenure as president is succinctly summed up by historian Jim Handy:

> Ydígoras' five years in office were a farce of incompetence, corruption and patronage. . . . [He was] determined to wring every penny he could from his position. His party, *Redención*, was held together not by any common ideological binding, but solely by the strands of patronage liberally cast about by its leader. One of his first accomplishments in office was to raise the presidential salary to $150,000 annually—making himself the highest-paid head of state in the western hemisphere—and to establish a generous million dollar pension fund. . . . He auctioned off the national *fincas* for the biggest bribes and under his touch all levels of government disintegrated in a morass of corruption.[64]

Ydígoras was finally overthrown in a military coup led by Colonel Enrique Peralta Azurdia on March 30, 1963. There followed three years of military dictatorship under Peralta, and from the time of the coup up until the 1990s, the armed forces were the dominant player in the country's political life.

The rosy reports and predictions by the U.S. Catholic media concerning Guatemala quickly disintegrated after the 1957 election fiasco. Two articles in *Jubilee,* however, continued to be mildly optimistic. One naively credited Ydígoras with attempting to pass an income tax that, if put into effect, would channel money from the rich into projects for the masses. The author claimed, however, that Ydígoras's noble effort was being jeopardized by a small group of communist workers, whose agitation for reforms was giving conservatives "a convenient excuse . . . to label any social change . . . Communist inspired."[65] The second piece predicted that the newly created Maryknoll Catholic schools would produce a generation of anticommunist teachers to replace the procommunist ones currently dominating the Guatemalan school system.[66]

In an *America* commentary written only six months after the assassination and before Ydígoras's election, however, one can already sense the beginning of a feeling of gloom and frustration. Remarking that Guatemala had recently had its share of setbacks—election fraud, military intervention, and economic hardship resulting from a fall in coffee prices—the Jesuit weekly added that extreme rural poverty had kept the country in a condition whereby it remained "an easy prey to Communist agitation." The piece concluded rather stoically: "Castillo Armas gave his people three years of relative stability. We hope that the new regime can give it six more such years."[67] Unlike *America*'s previous editorials, this one said nothing about the tiny nation being on the road to democracy and social justice.

Over the next few years, as Guatemala slipped more deeply into poverty and violence, the North American Catholic press had little to say on the small nation's sad state of affairs. Only two short pieces appeared in *America,* and neither was of much significance. The first lamented the fact that while the Guatemalan Catholic church was suffering from a shortage of priests and money, well-financed U.S. Protestants were aggressively proselytizing.[68] The second praised the work of the rapidly expanding groups of U.S. Catholic missionaries in the region.[69] Even the death of Archbishop Rossell in 1964 went unmentioned in U.S. Catholic magazines.

The only periodical to merit attention for its analysis of Guatemala during this time was *Commonweal.* In a moving piece, Italian economist Nino Marilano informed his readers that everywhere he went in Central America people of all classes told him that if radical change did not soon materialize, a communist revolution was inevitable. Despising and distrusting their wealthy political leaders, these people, who were not inclined toward communism or rebellion, were coming to think that perhaps communism was the only realistic alternative to their present misery. Prices were high and wages low, from thirty cents to fifty cents a day for those lucky enough to have a job. Yet the poor were the only ones who paid high taxes.[70] Everywhere the author was told horror stories of human rights abuses and was told that U.S. aid was counterproductive: "All feel that the American dollars . . . serve in fact only one purpose: to keep in power inefficient governments and to perpetuate the startling contrast of economic misery for the majority and extravagant wealth for the few."[71]

Marilano concluded by warning the United States not to make the mistake of labeling the aspirations of the masses communistic. Their hopes were too human and Christian to be confused with communist brutality, he claimed, "but they are also too urgent to be ignored."[72]

Commonweal was the only U.S. Catholic magazine to comment on the 1963 Peralta-led coup. Labeling the new government "anti-democratic" and "extreme right-wing," the editorialist predicted that, although it called itself anticommunist, in the long run it would further the cause of communism by eliminating the few political moderates who still remained in the country. To bring home its point, *Commonweal* quoted Brazilian Archbishop Dom Helder Camara: "Our rich in Latin America talk about basic reforms, but call Communists those who decide to carry them out."[73]

In summary, when Castillo Armas first came to power, even though he promised democratic reforms, his actions proved that he was not serious. He disenfranchised the poor majority and outlawed political parties. He refused to allow other candidates to run against him and then declared victory with 99.99 percent of the vote in the 1954 plebiscite. He imposed strict press censorship and destroyed labor unions and agrarian reform. Yet the U.S. Catholic press, with the exception of *Commonweal,* convinced itself that he was the democratic savior of his country and the champion of the downtrodden. Catholic periodicals predicted a bright future for Guatemala, one in which church and state would work together, using papal social justice encyclicals and U.S. democratic institutional models as their guide. Indeed, after his assassination, Castillo was even called by one Catholic magazine the first Guatemalan national hero since independence.

The Catholic media's myopia resulted in large part from the fact that Archbishop Rossell championed Castillo's cause, touting him not only as the anticommunist liberator of his country but also as the savior of the Catholic church—the president who nullified the repressive anticlerical laws that had for so long made it impossible for the church to effectively carry out its mission. It should further be noted that the U.S. Catholic press had also been influenced by the U.S. government and by the secular press, which had portrayed Castillo as a moderate, democratic capitalist and an anticommunist Cold War ally of the United States.

Although after the murder of Castillo the Catholic press predicted that Guatemala would hold firm on its path toward full democracy, it quickly became apparent that this was not to be. With their optimistic expectations dashed, North American Catholic periodicals said little in the next few years on the situation in Guatemala. The one exception was again *Commonweal,* which chided Guatemalan military and political leaders for their repressive actions and implored U.S. governmental officials to reevaluate and change their attitudes and policies toward not only Guatemala but all of Central America.

three

The Transformation
of the Latin American
Catholic Church

In 1911 the Catholic Foreign Mission Society of America, popularly known as Maryknoll, was founded. In 1942 it expanded its operations into Latin America, and the following year it opened its first Central American mission in Guatemala. By 1953 twenty-two Maryknoll priests and one brother had been assigned to various areas of this nation. After the fall of Arbenz, the number increased dramatically. By 1960 forty-one missionary priests and nineteen sisters worked in Guatemala, and one Maryknoller had been made bishop of Huehuetenango.

Influenced by the Second Vatican Council (1962–1965), the 1966 General Chapter of the congregation called on its members to place greater emphasis on the needs of the poor. Its missioners in Guatemala initiated numerous self-help projects in an attempt to mitigate the poverty of their mostly Indian parishioners. Eventually many of these projects failed, however, because of an overreliance on outside help and obstruction from local landowners and officials. By 1970 Maryknoll was deemphasizing the U.S.-style parish with its church, rectory, and school as the mainstay of its ministry, while focusing more on new, more radical forms of evangelization.[1] A review of *Maryknoll* magazine from the late 1940s to 1970 should provide the reader with a useful case study of the changes that took place in the U. S. Catholic press's perception of Central America, for *Maryknoll* serves as more or less a microcosm of what was occurring in most Catholic magazines during this time.

Throughout the 1940s and 1950s, articles on Guatemala in *Maryknoll* focused almost exclusively on the U. S. missionary priest or brother and his superhuman efforts. The Indians he ministered to were depicted as superstitious, childlike curiosities, and the rural regions where he labored were pictured as exotic. A 1948 article told of the labors of a Maryknoll priest serving 40,000 grateful Indians in a "fairyland valley."[2] "Tough Work in Fairyland" was the title given to a 1949 photo essay, which noted that "Guatemala's mountain country possesses rare beauty, and its people exotic charm; but for missioners . . . the task is herculean."[3] A second photo article from the previous year referred to the Maya as "good-humored Indians."[4] In a 1947 piece, a missioner remarked that the Indian had an "indifference to the future," as well as an "indifference to sickness and calamity," and believed that "nothing is worth worrying about," since "the wise man lives for the day."[5] Another article described a recently established Indian school in the capital where indigenous youth were trained to be leaders so they could "raise the Indians of Guatemala to the heights of morality, of science, and of culture."[6] One sentence especially betrayed a sense of European superiority and the "white man's burden":

A small group of Catholic women of the city arranged for the [Indian] boys to bathe, dressed them in modern attire, trimmed their hair, and put them on a social level with the white boys, with whom they were to associate and study in the parochial school.[7]

Mayan religious practices were treated with disdain and ridicule. In a 1950 article, future bishop Hugo Gerbermann told of his determination to put an end to the idolatry and superstition of his indigenous parishioners and how they, in turn, "used all sorts of cunning to dissuade me."[8] A second article was more telling. A missionary priest described what was taking place in a remote church while he was baptizing babies:

All the while, an Indian witch doctor was moaning some gibberish up near the altar . . . [and] an Indian was dancing in front of a statue. It was like working in a "Five and Dime" store during Christmas rush.[9]

In these early years, mission success was measured in large part by the number of sacraments dispensed. In a 1950 report, a priest proudly described his journey to a remote village, where he heard six confessions, performed two weddings, and baptized 397 babies, all in only three days.[10] Another Maryknoller told of a rugged horseback ride over mountainous terrain to give a dying man the last rites:

> But the trip was worth while. Instead of just one sick person, I found four. About a hundred villagers went to confession and Communion. Several children made their First Holy Communion, and I witnessed three marriages.[11]

In all the above articles there was no mention of Indian poverty and suffering.[12] Structural injustice and political controversy were also ignored.

By the early 1960s this had changed, albeit only slightly. Poverty was now mentioned, but only in relation to new Maryknoll development programs that were supposed to mitigate it. An article from 1963 pointed out that in Huehuetenango there were 30,000 Indian farmers unable to grow enough food to feed their families and that as a result many suffered from malnutrition. Consequently, Maryknoll had begun a program to teach Indians crop diversification and the use of fertilizer and insecticide. It was hoped that the new methods would increase crop yields, thereby helping Indians retain their land and avoid serfdom.[13] A 1964 report told of a Maryknoller helping lime workers acquire a truck and form a cooperative so that they might break from their economic bondage.[14]

By the late 1960s, Maryknollers were moving in new directions in their mission approach. A 1967 article called "Mission Today" explained that old attitudes concerning the missions were being reevaluated and redefined. In the past, according to the author, mission work had been seen as a frontier apostolate carried out by hardy priests who measured their success in terms of such things as new baptisms, numbers attending mass, and communions dispensed. But this was no longer the case. While the sacramental part of the missionary's work remained important, it was no longer considered enough. Missionaries now saw themselves as bearers of the good news of an international Christian community. Thus, they must be sensitive to the feelings and rights of those among whom they lived. Because of this, most missionaries no longer thought that the U. S.-style parish was a good model for Third World peoples, nor did they still believe that Western European liturgical forms provided the best means for indigenous people to express themselves spiritually. Likewise, today's missioners felt they must develop an understanding of the nonindustrial world's problems and the revolutionary changes that were taking place there. Catholic theology must be integrated with this understanding so that missionaries could support "enlightened government foreign policies."[15]

Another article bore a similar message. Citing several decrees from Vatican II to support his contentions, the author argued that "it is of the essence of missionary work to strip from the Faith its cultural accretions and dubious additions and to present it to the non-Christian in all its pristine vigor and originality."[16] Furthermore, although the missionary church still desired to make converts, it realized this was not enough. It now taught people to be witnesses to the Christian mission. This meant being Good Samaritans in their daily lives. If they were not, then the institutional church had failed.[17]

A third article claimed that a missioner's duty was to carry out Christ's work of liberation. This included "lessening guilt, relieving unnecessary suffering, helping the poor to help themselves and promoting community concerns for social justice."[18] The missionary organized self-help projects because they created hope and caused "men [to] accept one another as brothers growing together in unity and peace."[19] He entered into dialogue premised on mutual respect with those of other faiths.[20] "The new hope of the missionary Church does not come from counting its increase in membership but from counting on its members to be increasingly a living sign—a witness before other men—of God's own saving presence."[21]

In a December 1969 article, a Maryknoll priest described his work in a rural Guatemalan parish. A primary task was the training of Indian catechists. The ministry was crucial since, as members of the indigenous community, they were readily accepted. The author saw his own role as that of a catalyst in the social, economic, medical, and educational fields. Working with Peace Corps experts and other outside specialists, he had helped the community form agricultural cooperatives, savings and loan associations, and a small clinic. The parish had decided not to build a parochial school, reasoning that the overall community would be better served by supporting the local public school. The author concluded by stating that he did not try to make everyone a Christian but that he did attempt to make Christ's presence known to the poor.[22]

A Maryknoll nun in an article published in October 1970 wrote that Latin Americans were striving to shake off not only economic, social, and cultural dependency but also dependency on foreign theology. They had created a theology of liberation, which reflected "upon the need and right of people to exercise their own decisions and determine their own directions according to their culture and history."[23] Maryknoll sisters in Latin America were now rethinking their own ministry in light of liberation theology, the author stated. In so doing, they had come to realize that "salvation and liberation are synonymous."[24] Salvation was "kingdom-centered theology" and "[God's] kingdom is in the here and now."[25] Thus, Maryknoll nuns were working side by side with the Latin American church "to construct a just and fraternal society in which men can live in dignity and be masters of their own destiny."[26]

A Maryknoll priest argued in a 1969 article that "it is no longer enough to build schools, orphanages, clinics, hospitals and other social services."[27] The only effective answer to the communist threat was a Christian revolution in Guatemala, but one that was "peaceful, constructive and educational" and also based on the doctrines of Vatican II and a scientific understanding of the process of social change.[28] Since the upper class would always resist change and since the lower class lacked the leadership needed to initiate it in an orderly fashion, the middle class must take charge of the revolution. What was the church's task in the process? It should train middle-class leaders "through intensive courses, study sessions, workshops and publications."[29] It must also educate the masses, but in such a way that their attitudes and values would be altered to fit the needs of the times.[30] Finally, the author warned that if a peaceful revolution did not take place soon, a violent one would be inevitable.[31]

In an article from 1970, two coauthors attempted to briefly explain the metamorphosis that was taking place among Maryknoll missioners, as well as in the Latin American church in general. When the congregation first came to Latin America, they stated, it brought a more liberal, service-oriented approach to church work. Its methods were admired and imitated. Nevertheless, its missionaries came to realize that they were too paternalistic. They would organize self-help community projects to benefit the poor, but the wealthy would manipulate these projects to their own advantage. "So the rich became richer and the poor, although not exactly poorer than before, have to be as content as Lazarus in the Gospel with the crumbs that fall from the table of the development festival."[32] Many churchpeople concluded that it was futile to continue pressuring the rich to fulfill their obligations to social justice. They became convinced that the poor masses must be active players in their own liberation. Indeed, the Latin American bishops supported this contention at their 1968 Medellín Conference. The church now realized that oppressive economic, political, and social structures, as well as institutional violence, had existed in Latin America for centuries and had kept the poor in misery. The region's suffering was now further compounded from domination by "huge industrial complexes."[33] Because of this, many missioners and other churchpeople "cheer nationalizations, expropriations and profound reforms."[34] One could say that in some respects "Catholic social ideology is now very close to that of the Marxists."[35] Many, however, perhaps the majority, claimed that the church should not mix in social commitment. But abstention was only an excuse. Today's missioner had to decide: "Is he coming to sustain the status quo or to help produce the liberation of a dominated people?"[36]

To summarize, by 1970 the articles in *Maryknoll* magazine on Guatemala and the general mission philosophy of the congregation had undergone a radical change. The Indian, not the missionary, was now the focus of attention. Indigenous culture and religious practices were now respected rather than ridiculed. Maryknollers took pains to remove Eurocentric nuances from their ministry and adjusted their catechetical methods and liturgical rites to fit the indigenous modes of thought. The Indian catechist was now seen as a primary player in presenting Christian teaching to fellow villagers. Aside from the sacramental aspects of his ministry, the missionary priest now considered his role to be that of a catalyst helping to set certain processes in motion.

Although the sacramental part of Catholicism was still considered important, it was by 1970 only one dimension of a larger picture. Missioners saw themselves as deliverers of the liberating Gospel message that all people had a right to dignity and justice, that because of Christ's incarnation, death, and resurrection all were part of a universal brotherhood. Whereas in early *Maryknoll* articles poverty and oppression were almost never mentioned, now they were highlighted. The liberation of the poor had become a major goal of the mission apostolate. Structural economic, political, and social injustice, as well as institutional violence, were explained to *Maryknoll* readers. Whereas in articles published in the early 1960s communal self-help projects were looked at as a solution to Latin American poverty, they were now seen as too often paternalistic and manipulated to benefit the powerful rather than the poor.

Although certainly not advocates of Marxism, by 1970 Maryknollers no longer considered communism the root cause of all Latin American problems. Indeed, they had come to see similarities between their own liberationist analysis and that of the Marxists. Unlike the latter, however, they advocated only peaceful revolution. Likewise, capitalist developmentalism was no longer viewed as a cure-all. Domination by "huge industrial complexes" was now looked upon as part of the problem. It forced the underdeveloped world into dependency on the industrialized countries, claimed writers in *Maryknoll*.

One of the major objectives of a mission magazine is to obtain monetary contributions from its readers. In the 1940s and 1950s *Maryknoll* had reasoned that the best way to do this was by focusing primarily on the missionary and his work. By 1970, however, the magazine had undoubtedly concluded that it was more important to educate its North American readers (and contributors) on the unjust nature of Guatemalan society. Consequently, the Indian and his struggle for justice and a dignified life now became the primary focus of *Maryknoll* articles on Guatemala. A significant change had obviously taken place in the mind-set of Maryknoll.

What happened to cause such a massive radical change in the thinking of *Maryknoll* authors and the congregation's missioners? To understand this, one must review the major developments that took place in the Catholic church in the 1960s. In so doing, one should also come to a better understanding of the metamorphosis that took place at this time in the overall reporting of Catholic publications on Central America.

As has previously been explained, Archbishop Rossell and the Catholic church had played a significant role in bringing down the Arbenz government. Consequently, the church was rewarded by Castillo Armas when the Liberal anticlerical laws were removed from the constitution. Since foreign priests and religious were no longer forbidden to enter the country, the numbers now increased dramatically. Whereas there were only 192 priests in Guatemala in 1954, in 1960 there were 287. This came to one priest for every 11,100 Catholics.[37] Nearly all of the new priests were foreigners. Of these a substantial number were from the United States. Forty-one of the latter were Maryknollers, ten were Franciscans, three were Benedictines, and three were secular priests. There were also nineteen Maryknoll nuns, three Christian Brothers, and two Benedictine brothers working in the country. Thus, by 1960 the U.S. missionary church had made a significant commitment to Guatemala.[38]

Rossell was especially interested in locating his new missionary personnel in rural Indian regions. Because of the acute shortage of priests, the church had been forced to neglect these areas since at least the beginning of the twentieth century. Left to their own devices, the Indians had developed a civil-religious system based on a mixture of Catholicism and ancient Mayan rites. Needless to say, this did not please the church. Neither did the fact that Protestants had begun proselytizing in some Indian villages in 1940 and had had a modest amount of success and that "communism" supposedly had made inroads in these areas due to Arbenz's land reform program. Thus, Rossell encouraged his newly arrived clergy to take assignments in indigenous communities. There they were to teach the Indians theologically correct Catholicism in order to wean them from their syncretic form. They were also to encourage indigenous vocations to the priesthood and counteract the efforts of Protestants and communists.

Let us now take a brief look at the status of the church at this time in the other Central American countries. The pre-1940 Honduran church was even worse off than its counterpart in Guatemala. Traditionally it had been poorer, less influential, and less effective than the other Central American churches. By 1940 it had only a handful of native-born priests and probably the lowest ratio of priests to population in all of Latin America. Yet just as in Guatemala, Protestantism was beginning to make some headway after 1940, and communism was growing in influence among the working class and students by the mid-1950s. If the church was to be relevant, it would have to dramatically increase the number of its clergy and do so quickly. As in Guatemala, the bishops turned to foreign missionaries. Along with priests from Canada and Spain, U. S. Franciscans and Jesuits made a major commitment to the country. By 1947 the number of clergy in Honduras had grown to 122, and by 1960 it had reached 161. This amounted to one priest for every 9,950 Catholics. By this time U. S. Franciscan and Notre Dame nuns had also sent personnel to the country.[39] Over 80 percent of the clergy and religious in Honduras were foreigners.

Thanks to the long and competent episcopacy of Archbishop Luis Chávez y González (1939–1977), the clergy shortage in El Salvador, although severe, was not as bad as that of Guatemala and Honduras. By 1950 several Spanish Jesuits had committed to work in the archdiocese of San Salvador, and the seminary in the capital had produced more than a few diocesan priests. Although there was less need in this tiny nation for U. S. missionaries, by 1958 three U. S. Franciscan priests and one Salesian were working there. In 1960 the Maryknoll fathers had committed to expand their Central American operations into this country. By 1960 there were 282 priests in El Salvador, that is, one priest for every 7,600 Catholics.[40]

Since the anticlerical Liberal attacks on the church in Nicaragua and Costa Rica were of shorter duration and less severe than in the other three Central American countries, the shortage of priests was less acute. In 1960 there were 228 priests in Nicaragua, one priest per 4,550 Catholics. U. S. Capuchins had made a substantial commitment to the area, as had the Christian Brothers. U. S. Carmelite, Maryknoll, and St. Agnes nuns also worked there. In Costa Rica there were 249 priests in 1960, one per 4,220 Catholics. Of these there was a large contingent of U. S. Franciscan friars and sisters.[41]

Thus, by 1960 all five Central American countries, but especially Guatemala and Honduras, suffered from a shortage of priests and religious. Foreign missionaries from North America and Europe had lessened the severity of the problem but only to a small degree. If the Central American church was to play an effective role, many more priests, nuns, and brothers would be needed. The Central American bishops felt the problem was especially acute because Protestants had become more aggressive in their proselytizing in the isthmus. But more worrisome than Protestant competition was the fear of the spread of communism, especially in light of the successful revolution in Cuba under Fidel Castro.

Problems resulting from a shortage of clergy were not limited to the Central American church. They were shared by the Catholic church throughout Latin America, and the Vatican was well aware of the situation. Therefore, Pope John XXIII decided that dramatic action was needed. In August 1961 he sent Monsignor Agostino Casaroli to a conference of U. S. male religious superiors being held at the University of Notre Dame. There Casaroli delivered a papal request. All U. S. religious orders and congregations were asked to send 10 percent of their personnel to Latin America over the next decade to help revive the church. Although the 10 percent figure was never reached, thousands of U. S. Catholics—priests, sisters, brothers, and laypeople—would answer the call. The importance of this papal request cannot be overestimated. As author Gerald M. Costello points out:

> The speech he [Casaroli] delivered that day would rank as one of the most significant in the history of the church. It served as a blueprint for the United States' full scale mission involvement in Latin America; its words set in motion a series of events that were to alter thousands of lives and change the face of the church on two continents.[42]

The U. S. Catholic missionaries who responded to the papal challenge were largely the descendants of European immigrants who a generation or two earlier had come to the United States in search of a better life. They were proud, patriotic citizens whose families had achieved the success and prosperity of the middle class. Their civic pride was further enhanced by the fact that John F. Kennedy had recently been elected the first Catholic president of the United States. Consequently, these new missionaries entered Latin America with a Cold War mentality. Although they knew little about Latin America, they saw themselves as a crusading force dedicated not only to spreading the Gospel message but also to raising "backward"

Latins from underdevelopment to democratic capitalist prosperity, thereby stifling the threat of communism. Generously financed by U. S. money, they built parish churches and schools modeled after those they had left behind in their hometowns. They saw the U. S. government as their ally and praised Kennedy's announcement of the creation of the Alliance for Progress and Peace Corps.[43] They plugged into these programs when possible, establishing development projects in an attempt to ameliorate the desperate economic condition of their needy parishioners.

It should further be noted that these U. S. missionaries differed considerably from their Central American counterparts. The native clergy, especially in countries with the lowest ratios of priests to Catholics, tended to work with urban middle- and upper-class parishioners. They had been raised in an environment where disparity between rich and poor and widespread poverty had long been the norm and therefore was considered somewhat acceptable. The Central American clergy was fully cognizant of how the institutional church had been devastated by Liberal anticlerical laws. By 1960 this had changed, and in all five Central American countries relatively friendly governments were now in power. Understandably, the native clergy was reluctant to challenge the status quo and chance a return to an unhappy past.

U. S. Catholic missionaries, on the other hand, were shocked by the misery they saw, a misery that exceeded their experience in the United States. It was not long before they felt the need to involve themselves in reformist programs, unaware that their labors might not always be appreciated by an elite class that saw a change in the status quo as threatening to its interests. Needless to say, to many Central American priests, the North American idealistic attitude seemed naive at best and potentially dangerous. Native clergy, who had always had to operate on a shoestring budget, likewise resented that these upstart U. S. newcomers always acquired the financial resources needed to put their plans into effect, regardless of how ill conceived some of these plans might be.

By the early 1960s, then, the Central American church was already beginning a process of revitalization made possible in no small part by an influx of energetic, if perhaps somewhat naive, North American missionaries. This process would be profoundly affected over the next decade by the Second Vatican Council (1962–1965). Pope John XXIII's encyclicals *Mater et Magister* (1961) and *Pacem in Terris* (1963) set the tone by calling on the well nourished to feed the hungry of the world, while warning against colonialism and new forms of imperialism. From a Third World perspective, however, the final document of the council, *Gaudium et Spes,* was especially significant. It condemned the hoarding of wealth and power for the benefit of a small segment of society, while stating that the right to private property must be weighed against the benefits to society accrued from public ownership. But more importantly, it stipulated that all persons are entitled to the basic necessities of life and in extreme cases are morally justified in taking from the excessive wealth of others.

Gaudium et Spes also introduced a radically new methodology to Catholic theological study:

> Instead of proceeding in the time-honored fashion, discussing theological or biblical principles and then applying them to a present-day situation, Gaudium et Spes reverses the process: it begins with a careful analysis of the de facto situation, then turns to sacred scripture and theology for reflection on that situation, and finally, as a third step, makes pastoral applications. Theological reflection thus becomes the second, not the first, step.[44]

Gaudium et Spes likewise went beyond the traditional philosophical and theological approach, employing the social and behavioral sciences.

The Latin American bishops did not play a leading role in the early proceedings of Vatican II. Soon, however, they were enthusiastically immersed in the council, holding regular meetings with conciliar theologians and serving on conciliar commissions. Indeed, several decades later, in his recollections of Vatican II, Archbishop Marcos McGrath of Panama would go so far as to credit the Latin American bishops with creating the social conscience of the council.[45] Returning to their dioceses with a new awareness of the Christian commitment to social justice, most Latin prelates were determined to apply what they had learned to the home front. Plans were soon made to hold a general Latin American episcopal conference at Medellín, Colombia, in order to apply the principles of Vatican II to the Latin American situation. After two years of preparation, the conference was held in 1968. The importance of the Medellín Conference cannot be overestimated. Using the methodology of Gaudium et Spes, it changed the direction of the Latin American church from one aligned, at least indirectly, with the power structure to one that sided with the poor and oppressed. As Edward Cleary writes:

> The final document would say, in brief, that the church is a sinful church in a sinful (unjust) society, one marked by structured inequalities. Latin America, it went on, is a region suffering from two massive evils: external dominance and internal colonialism. Change was obviously

called for and the church wished to take part in the change. The church chose the side of the poor. It must reach out to them, and to the whole continent.[46]

Comunidades eclesiales de base (Christian base communities, or CEBs) were the key element in the church's commitment to the poor and oppressed. Adopting and expanding on the consciousness-raising techniques used by the Brazilian educator Paulo Freire in teaching literacy to the poor, the church began training catechists who formed small, grassroots groups of campesinos (peasants) and urban poor for Bible study and prayer. Biblical passages were read and the group would reflect on them, rooting them in the actualities of their everyday lives. The catechist was to serve as coordinator rather than leader. It was hoped that group members would come to view their lives from a Gospel-based perspective. In the more radical CEBs,[47] members eventually concluded that it was not God's will that they suffer; as God's people they were created not to serve the rich but to have human dignity. They realized that they had a right to basic physical necessities for themselves and their families. In reflecting on the Gospel of Luke, for instance, they learned that Jesus called the rich landowner who hoarded his grain a fool (12:16–21) and that he said, "It is easier for a camel to pass through the eye of a needle than for a rich man to enter the kingdom of God" (18:25); they also reflected on the parable of the rich man and Lazarus (16:19–31). In the other books of both the Old and New Testaments, they learned more about God's commitment to the poor and oppressed. Edward Cleary explains the reflective process of the radical model of the CEB more fully:

> They interpret the exodus as applying to them. They read Amos about helping the widow and the orphaned. And they reflect on Jesus as the one who came to liberate them. They are quick to catch on that liberation is more than spiritual. Often their discussion centers on not having to live in the unfavorable conditions that they once thought unchangeable. Health, education and landownership become topics of reflection, replacing resignation and suffering, as in the past.[48]

Inspired by Gaudium et Spes, some Latin American theologians developed a new theology in the late 1960s, just prior to the Medellín Conference. It came to be known as liberation theology. Briefly stated, this theology attempted to interpret Christian faith from the perspective of the poor and oppressed. This meant critiquing society and the ideologies sustaining it, as well as the church and the activities of its members, but always from the perspective of how well the needs of the suffering poor were being met.[49] Liberation theology relied heavily on biblical prophetic tradition and sometimes resorted to Marxist analysis in posing questions. Consequently, some of its critics accused its theologians of being more communist than Christian and of advocating violent revolution. But as Phillip Berryman notes, a study of the writings of the major liberation theologians shows that they devoted surprisingly little attention to Marxism and had virtually nothing to say about violence.[50] Nevertheless, the theology of liberation would remain a highly controversial subject both in and outside the church up through the 1980s.

In the year prior to the Medellín Conference, the debate over what direction the U. S. missionary church in Latin America should take was greatly intensified by two developments. The first was the publication of an article in *America*, "The Seamy Side of Charity," written by Monsignor Ivan Illich. In 1961 he had been asked by Father John Considine, the director of the National Catholic Welfare Conference's Latin American Bureau, to set up and direct a training center for new missionary personnel assigned to Latin countries. Considine realized that if large numbers of U. S. priests, religious, and lay missioners were to be sent south in response to Pope John's appeal, more than on-the-job training was needed. Thus, Illich was charged with creating a structured program. He chose Cuernavaca, Mexico, as the location for his school.

Illich was well aware that most North Americans had prejudiced attitudes toward Hispanics. He likewise realized that many missioners entered their Latin American assignments with superiority complexes, seeing themselves as teachers bringing to a backward people answers to their problems. To eradicate this type of attitude, he chose to employ "shock" techniques that would brutally challenge chauvinistic tendencies and preconceived notions. His methods proved quite controversial and resulted in a high student dropout rate. Some critics accused him of harboring anti-American attitudes and using ill-conceived, unorthodox techniques. But he weathered the storm and became highly respected in both North and Latin American church circles.[51]

Illich's "Seamy Side of Charity" was published to coincide with the opening of the fourth annual meeting of the Catholic Inter-American Cooperative Project (CICOP). Created by Considine's Latin American Bureau, CICOP provided a platform for Latin church leaders and scholars to express their views to a U. S. audience. Highly successful, its 1967 meeting in Boston attracted a large audience, including many U. S. bishops. Copies of Illich's article were handed out to attendees. As Costello so aptly puts it: "No single document since Monsignor Casaroli's appeal at Notre Dame ... had as much impact on the future course of U.S. mission work in Latin America."[52] Terming it "a blistering indictment of every imaginable aspect of the Latin American mission program," he adds that it "stood the U.S. church on its ear."[53] But in truth, as mission scholar Mary McGlone points out, in spite of all the attention it received, Illich's article was merely repeating what many missionaries and some bishops from both the United States and Latin America had already been saying, albeit in a less publicized, belligerent way.[54]

In summary, Illich charged that the U.S. missionary program south of the border amounted to no more than an attempt to keep Latin America in the Western ideological camp. His words were sharp and sarcastic:

> Men and money sent with missionary motivation carry ... a foreign policy message. They also bear the mark of North American capitalism of the 1950's. ...
>
> This kind of foreign generosity has enticed the Latin American Church into becoming a satellite to North Atlantic cultural phenomena and policy. ... The Latin American Church flowers anew by returning to what the Conquest stamped her: a colonial plant that blooms because of foreign cultivation.[55]

But North American money and missioners did more. They seemed, at first glance, to give new life to an outmoded church, long considered an irrelevancy. The church was now reputed to be a trusted agent running programs aimed at social change. Some good was actually produced. But when there was potential for genuine, radical change, the church, fearful of the ramifications, withdrew its support. In the hands of priests, the true nature of these programs was disguised: in reality, they were nothing more than "publicity for private enterprise and indoctrination to a way of life that the rich have chosen as suitable for the poor."[56] Eventually the recipient of these programs did get the message: the priest stood on the side of big business, the Alliance for Progress, democratic government, the AFL-CIO, "and whatever is holy in the Western pantheon."[57]

After drawing parallels between U.S. church intervention in Latin America and U.S. military intervention in Vietnam, Illich contended that the North American mission program actually could make a bad situation worse: Latin bishops became dependent on U.S. funds and were therefore turned into abject beggars. Countless churches and schools were built and staffed with imported priests and religious. The end result was that "a patently irrelevant pastoral system is artificially and expensively sustained," while any notion of attempting to create a meaningful replacement was dismissed. Finally, with the coming of enough foreign priests to fill the many vacant parishes, the need to consider laymen for evangelical tasks was removed, as was the need to reexamine the structure of the parish and the function of the priest. The church would also feel secure enough to back away from exploring the use of the married diaconate and new forms of celebration of the Word and Eucharist. In other words, the infusion of clergy would make it possible to avoid much-needed reform.[58] Illich concluded by sarcastically commenting that the heart of the discussion should not be *how* to send even more men and money but rather *why* they should be sent at all.[59]

"The Seamy Side of Charity" was certainly intemperate. But whatever the case, Costello is correct in his assessment:

> A few would agree totally with Illich, others would see some elements of truth in what he had to say, and still others, perhaps most, rejected his arguments, sometimes bitterly. But after the article appeared, few people involved in the Latin American mission enterprise, if any, could carry out their assignments without re-examining what they were doing, without asking themselves if, perhaps, there *was* something after all to what Illich was saying.[60]

Nine months after the appearance of "The Seamy Side of Charity," another development occurred, this time in Guatemala, that rocked the U. S. mission program to its very core. Six U. S. Maryknoll missionaries, three priests and three nuns, were expelled from the country after it was discovered that they were involved in forming a "Christian guerrilla front." To comprehend what took place, a brief review of the radicalization process experienced by the major participants should prove helpful.[61] Sister Marion Peter (Marjorie) Bradford was the first of the group to be assigned to Guatemala. She was sent in 1954 to teach at the Colegio Monte María, a school for affluent girls that Maryknoll had opened in Guatemala City at the bequest of Cardinal Mario Casariego, the conservative successor of Archbishop Rossell. It was hoped that the sisters would instill a social conscience in their students, many of whom, it was reasoned, would later marry future leaders of the country and pass a concern for the poor on to them. In the early 1960s, Bradford became involved in the *cursillo de capacitación social* (course of social empowerment) movement, which was cropping up in some parts of Latin America in response to Vatican II. Soon she received permission to leave her assignment at Monte María so that she could devote her energies to teaching the urban poor. In 1964 she became part of a radical

Christian student group, which held meetings at a downtown building nick-named the Crater. The group, which was committed to peaceful revolutionary change, used the *cursillo*-CEB methods of analysis in their discussions. In mid-1966 Father Blase Bonpane joined the student group when he was assigned to Guatemala as national director of the *cursillo de capacitación social*.

Father Thomas Melville was assigned to the country in 1957 and sent to work with Indians in Huehuetenango, where he helped form cooperatives. Later he organized an Indian resettlement program in the Petén. Arthur Melville came to Guatemala in 1961, where he was pastor of a parish in Huehuetenango. Like his brother, he became involved in the cooperative movement. Sisters Mary Leo (Catherine) Sagan and Marian Pahl worked with him in his parish.

Eventually Sister Marian Peter, Thomas Melville, and others organized a student vacation project in which affluent university students committed to work in poverty-stricken rural areas in Huehuetenango and Quiche for six weeks during the November–December university recess period. The plan was a success, with over ninety students, many of them from the Crater group, participating.

Frustrated by the death squad murders of a former student and several cooperative leaders and by what they felt was a lack of commitment to the poor by Guatemalan church leaders, the Maryknollers decided to form a Christian guerrilla movement with some of the students who were involved in their social project. Arthur Melville and the two nuns in his parish joined them. Their actions were influenced, says Thomas Melville, by Vatican II, *Pacem in Terris*, Ivan Illich's article, and the writings of Camilo Torres, a revolutionary priest who was killed in battle in Colombia in 1966.[62] A Spanish priest who had joined the circle of revolutionaries developed second thoughts and revealed their plans to his religious superior. Soon the Maryknoll regional superior, John Breen, was informed, as were the U.S. ambassador to Guatemala and Cardinal Casariego. All six Maryknollers were expelled from the country, but the Melvilles and Bradford flew to Mexico, where they went into hiding and attempted in vain to re-form the group.

On January 16, 1968, guerrillas from the Fuerzas Armadas Rebeldes (FAR) killed two U.S. military attachés in Guatemala City. Although the six Maryknoll revolutionaries were not involved in the assassination plot, the next day the story of the "Maryknoll guerrilla priests" was headlined in newspapers throughout the country. It remained front-page news for more than three weeks and also received top coverage throughout the world. The reputation of Maryknoll in Guatemala, and by extension that of all U. S. missionaries working in the country, was tainted almost beyond repair.

As the following author shows, the importance of the Melville affair is hard to overestimate:

> It made headlines worldwide, created an uproar within Maryknoll, invested both the Society [male branch] and the Congregation [female branch] with a politicized image it proved difficult to shake, and jeopardized the work of the church in Guatemala for years to come.
>
> Revolutionaries in Latin America hailed this example of militant commitment by Christians to the cause of the oppressed. For most Maryknollers, however, it would appear as a naive, dangerous, and unwise action that neither benefited the poor nor served the overall mission of Maryknoll. But it did raise the question: Was the institutional path to social progress adequate? If not the way of the Melvilles, then how in a world of injustice to make Christ's gospel concrete?[63]

This last point is especially relevant. If nothing else, the Melville incident would force the U. S. Catholic church and especially its missionaries, just as Illich's *America* article did, to rethink their blueprint for Latin America.

Indeed, Father David Kelly, in his regional report on Maryknoll in Central America, states that in the aftermath of the Melville episode, when the Guatemalan press and many politicians were calling the congregation a communist front and demanding that all its members be expelled from the country, the Guatemalan hierarchy said not one word in its defense. Even more shattering, not "even one portion of the local Christian community" came forth to make a single public statement on Maryknoll's behalf.[64] Surely such lack of support must have caused many Maryknollers to conclude that their work actually meant little to the people.

Thus, because of culture shock and frustration at the massive poverty and suffering that they experienced all around them, and influenced by the Illich article and the Melville affair, large numbers of U. S. missionaries in both Central and South America readily took to the message of *Gaudium et Spes,* the Medellín Conference, and liberation theology. They argued that their congregations should abandon their traditional ministries and concentrate exclusively on working with the poor through such methods as the formation of CEBs. Furthermore, they felt that missionaries should abandon their U. S.-style parishes and schools and share the lifestyle and culture of the poor. Other missioners, however, disagreed, and polarization took place within their communities. Indeed, 1968—the year of Medellín—marked the high point in numbers of U.S. Catholic missionaries serving in Latin America. Over the next several years the number would steadily and rapidly decline. Although this was partly due to the crunch in religious vocations that was beginning in the U.S. church, it was also because most missioners who were uneasy with the direction of their fellow missionaries opted out of Latin American ministry.[65]

By the later 1960s, North American Catholic periodicals no longer relied on the U.S. government, the U.S. secular press, and the Latin American Catholic media as their primary sources for information on developments south of our border. Although these sources remained important, they had been eclipsed by the analysis of Catholic missionaries, most of whom worked with the rural poor and were therefore often eyewitnesses to what was taking place. Consequently, as these missionaries became more critical of U.S. conduct in Latin America, so did the North American Catholic press. The earliest documentation of the Catholic press's new direction, however, is found not in articles treating Central America but rather in those written in response to President Lyndon Johnson's intervention in the Dominican Republic. Not surprisingly, *Commonweal* was first to strike. A short piece from May 1965 not only condemned the intervention but bluntly claimed that, although we refused to admit it, U.S. actions throughout Latin America "are governed by considerations . . . naked in their self-interest."[66] A second piece stated that whatever good Kennedy's well-meaning but conservative Latin American efforts had achieved was destroyed by Johnson's Dominican meddling. The author called for a redirection of U.S. policy south of the border so that it would benefit the dispossessed majority rather than the middle and upper classes.[67] Another *Commonweal* article contended that U.S. heavy-handedness in Latin countries only gave right-wing generals an excuse to use violence. It lamented that a decade which had begun with promising programs like the Alliance for Progress and Peace Corps had "taken a nasty turn," negatively affecting moderate leftist political groups.[68] In the next year, *Commonweal* accused Johnson of favoring rightist Latin American dictatorships over the reformist governments that Kennedy had supported.[69] A second article chided the United States for selling weapons to dictators for counterinsurgency purposes.[70]

But it was an *America* article from May 1966 that was especially surprising in its critical tone. It began by citing Senator Robert Kennedy's warning against alliances with governments whose cry of "communism" was only an excuse for the perpetuation of privilege. In a major shift from its former conservative Cold War logic, *America* next postulated that the problems of the underdeveloped world could be solved only by governments willing to take radical measures. Yet these were precisely the governments that antagonized the United States by nationalizing U.S.-owned property, while spouting anticapitalist rhetoric. The U.S. must learn to tolerate such governments, it warned, because they were the only viable alternative to communism. If we opposed them, we would only be helping, not hindering, the real communists.[71]

It was a new publication, the *National Catholic Reporter*, however, that would soon take the lead among Catholic periodicals in its outspoken criticism of U.S. conduct in Latin America. This weekly, run by laypersons, quickly developed a reputation for its willingness to take to task either church or state authorities for what it perceived to be their failings, and it would soon displace *Commonweal*, said John Cogley, "as *the* daring Catholic publication."[72]

The *NCR* first commented on Guatemala in June 1967, when it described a military counterinsurgency operation. In hard-hitting fashion, the author stated:

> The army is being aided by right-wing terrorists, and the terrorists are being assisted by U.S. military aid received through the Army. The result has been a bloodbath.[73]

The piece claimed that the Mano Blanca death squad, which assisted the army by kidnapping and executing peasants, was equipped with machine guns and rifles donated through a U.S. military aid program. It added that of the 2,000 or so people killed in the military sweep, only forty to fifty were actually guerrillas.[74] Yet in his presentation of background information, the author held to the rhetoric typical of the past, referring to "the pro-Communist regime of Col. Jacobo Arbenz" and asserting that under Arbenz "communists organized massive peasant land invasions."[75]

The *NCR* was the first national Catholic periodical to report on the Melville affair. It did so in its January 24, 1968, issue in a straightforward, factual piece.[76] A week later, however, it devoted three articles to the story. The first merely restated the facts.[77] The second was based on an interview with Blase Bonpane, the fourth Maryknoller expelled for his participation in the Melville episode. In it Bonpane stressed his belief that violence was institutionalized in Guatemala and made possible by U.S. support. He added that if the U.S. would change its role, violent revolution would be unnecessary.[78]

The third article was groundbreaking. It was written by Thomas Melville, explaining his side of the controversy. He began by remarking that "misery is perhaps the biggest factor in preventing a true growth of Christianity in Latin America."[79] He then accused the Guatemalan church of being part of the problem rather than the solution. Instead of chiding the rich for abusing the poor, the bishops insisted that the clergy adhere to "a legalistic Catholicism, based on rites and sacraments, without any real attempt to translate their significance into daily living."[80] The hierarchy refused to support land reform and catered to the demands of the elite minority, which threatened to cut off financial support if "social-minded priests" were permitted to operate. To back up his argument, Melville pointed out that Archbishop Mario Casariego had instructed his priests to avoid addressing social justice themes because these were controversial. Likewise, when twenty-five clergymen tried to organize agricultural workers on the South Coast, three bishops wrote to them forbidding them to participate, saying that the church had no business involving itself in such concerns. Melville's own congregation did not escape his critique:

> I personally know a good friend and benefactor of the Maryknoll Fathers, a daily communicant, who accused a Christian labor leader who was trying to organize a union on his big sugar plantation of Communism and thus had him shot by the army.[81]

Melville stressed that as Christians he and his fellow conspirators preferred peaceful revolution but that in Guatemala the power structure had made this impossible. In the past eighteen months, the army and their death squad associates had assassinated more than 2,800 intellectuals, students, labor leaders, and peasants who had been working in nonviolent ways to combat the ills of society. Indeed, the headquarters of the Mano Blanca terrorist group was even located in the main police building in downtown Guatemala City. The masses were thus forced to resort to drastic action because, as President Kennedy said, "those who make pacific revolution impossible, make violent revolution inevitable."[82] Melville closed with passion:

> We were accused of being communists. . . . But I say here that I am a communist only if Christ was a communist. I did what I did and will continue to do so because of the teachings of Christ and not because of Marx and Lenin. . . . Our response to the present situation is not because we have read either Marx or Lenin, but because we have read the New Testament.[83]

The actions of the Maryknoll revolutionaries also caused other Catholic periodicals to voice their opinions. In a lengthy article in *Orbis*, Francis X. Gannon accused the expelled priests and nuns of an "inadequate assessment of the pace of economic growth and social change in Guatemala." Predicting that the developmentalist approach of the Alliance for Progress and the Central American Common Market would eventually cure the ills of Guatemala, he painted the Melvilles as naive.[84]

Commonweal remarked that the religious revolutionaries had resorted to drastic action because they "became convinced that little progress towards social justice could be achieved within Guatemala's present political and social structure." Yet "the sad part . . . is that their superiors generally agree[d] on the need for stringent social reform" but realized that foreign missionaries were not free agents since they had to operate under the sufferance of civil authorities. Since Guatemalan government leaders barred them from political action, their efforts to work for social change were restricted. This made their situation different from that of national priests. *Commonweal* pointed out, however, that the Melvilles had raised some serious questions:

> As the Church breaks its traditional ties with the rich, the powerful and the military in underdeveloped areas like Latin America and lines up on the side of the poor and the oppressed, to what extent may foreign missionaries take part in the revolution? Are they, who are often in the vanguard of reform, doomed to stay on the sidelines, forbidding full commitment lest they implicate their religious congregation or nation?[85]

The editorial further asked whether clergy and religious were ever justified in resorting to violent revolution and answered with serious reservations: "The prospect of pistol-packing nuns and gun-running clergy is still a gloomy one."[86]

A second *Commonweal* article took a more radical approach. Author Ralph Clark Chandler questioned the sincerity of those who found fault with the Melvilles but who ignored the fact that other foreign clergy supported the repressive conservative policies of the Guatemalan government. He asked sarcastically:

> Is it political interference of foreign national churchmen that some are objecting to today, or is it that much of the new activity is on the left of the political spectrum and therefore brings into question the church's traditional and unspoken-of ties with the rich and the powerful in Latin America?[87]

Chandler chided the Guatemalan church for blessing as Christian a laissez-faire capitalist society that viewed Indians as cheap labor for plantation owners and forced them into perpetual serfdom. He contrasted this to Thomas Melville's conviction that it was un-Christian for the church to allow Indians to continue to believe that their misery was a punishment from God for past sins and that wealth resulted from God's favor.[88] He conceded that it was prudent for Maryknoll to expel the Melvilles, for not to do so would put in jeopardy the many excellent projects that the congregation had set up to ameliorate the condition of the poor.[89] Nevertheless, he predicted that "out of the strange amalgam of idealism and foolishness" of which the Melvilles were a part, a new and more just Guatemala would eventually be born. Chandler concluded by implying that the church's prudence might well keep it from playing a role in this new birth.[90]

America's editorial on the Melville affair was significant; it represented the first time the Jesuit magazine had opted to criticize U.S. involvement in Guatemala and the Guatemalan church's indifference to the poor and oppressed. It began with the following observations:

> The article by Fr. Thomas Melville . . . in the *NCR* . . . is the moving testimony of a man who can take no more. He pens, from personal experience and direct observation, a scathing indictment of 1) capitalism run amuck in Guatemala, and 2) an impassive Church. . . . Certainly, poverty and low wages are not the Church's doing. But the accusation Fr. Melville makes of the Church's indifference amid the general misery is a telling one. . . .
>
> The abuses listed in the article and even its over-all judgment may be inaccurate. None of that, however, is the real novelty here. What is striking is that at last churchmen are crying out against social evil, "not because we have read either Marx or Lenin, but because we have read the New Testament."[91]

The editorial concluded by prophetically stating that the Melville incident and the dramatic news coverage given to it were indications that "the Maryknollers [had] turned a page of history."[92] One could add that the *America* editorial indicates that the Jesuit magazine had likewise turned a page in its own history.

It is noteworthy that although no Catholic periodical approved of the Melville group's decision to resort to armed struggle, the conspirators were nevertheless treated with sympathy and respect by most of the Catholic media. The *National Catholic Reporter, Commonweal,* and *America* all seemed to agree with the rebel missionaries' charges that the Guatemalan church had been too supportive of the status quo and that U. S. policy in the region was bankrupt. Indeed, it is worth noting that even the fact that two of the conspirators left Maryknoll and married was respectfully reported.

After the Medellín Bishops' Conference, one would be hard pressed to find an article on Guatemala in U. S. Catholic magazines that did not criticize the tiny country's dismal human rights record and U. S. support for the Guatemalan government. A 1969 piece from the *National Catholic Reporter* illustrates this point. Written by Sidney Lens, it postulated that Washington and the Latin American elite class had formed a mutually profitable alliance, which kept the masses marginalized and the region underdeveloped. Lens's discussion of the 1954 Guatemalan coup differed markedly from those in Catholic periodicals in the late 1950s. He talked of a "CIA sponsored coup that brought United Fruit–puppet Castillo Armas to power"[93] and noted that it was no coincidence that after Castillo became president, U. S. investments in Guatemala rose 3,000 percent, bringing immense profits to North American corporations.

A 1969 *Commonweal* article likewise typified the new "revisionist" Catholic journalism. The tone of the piece was set in the opening paragraph:

> The sidewalks of Guatemala City are clogged with the blind, the halt, and the disfigured, selling Chiclets, lottery tickets, or openly begging. Some are homeless; others live in flimsy wood and tin shacks. In the countryside, the rural poor are undernourished, prey to intestinal diseases, illiterate, and if Indian, despised. Fifteen years after the overthrow of the leftist regime of President Jacobo Arbenz, there has been scarcely a single advance in any field even to alleviate misery, much less to mobilize Guatemala's people."[94]

For the first time ever in the U. S. Catholic press, Juan José Arévalo was praised as a reformer, with author Warren Sloat even claiming that he "entered the presidency in modest means and left the same way."[95] How different this was from the 1946 *Commonweal* article that had accused Arévalo of "making tens of thousands of dollars through inflationary conditions he permits to exist."[96] It is also significant that the author labeled the Arbenz government "leftist." This was the first time this term, rather than "communist," was used in reference to this hitherto maligned president in a U. S. Catholic magazine. Indeed, after 1969 one would be hard-pressed to find the "communist" label applied to Arbenz by the Catholic media. Sloat's article concluded by calling the soon-to-be president, Col. Carlos Arana Osorio, a right-wing terrorist and death-squad leader.[97]

A 1970 *Commonweal* article was even more daring. It chastised the U. S. secular press for presenting the assassination of the German ambassador to Guatemala "as an isolated act of violence that leftist extremists perpetrated against a decent government" and for going so far as to portray Colonel Arana as an "antiguerrilla hero."[98] The author forcefully argued that one could understand the ambassador's death only by placing it in the context of the murders of 6,000 peasants by the military regime: under the Arana government "rightist crimes multiply, the social situation worsens, [and] leftist terror appears as a response."[99]

The author referred to the Arbenz regime as "reformist" and called Castillo Armas a "dictator."[100] He wrote off the highly touted Central American Common Market: "Planned and applauded by Washington, [it] profits only American corporations."[101] He also dispensed with the overused "communist" label by glibly remarking that "for a Guatemalan military man a 'Communist' is anyone whose ideas are different from those of the Guatemalan military; in short . . . anyone who has ideas."[102]

During the next decade the U. S. Catholic media had little to add about Guatemala. Only a 1974 *NCR* piece merits attention. It described the national elections of that year as "rigged" and "fraudulent" and reported that eleven U. S. missionaries had been forced to leave Guatemala for supposed "political activities." The apologia of one of the expelled priests encapsulated well the change that had taken place in the U. S. missionary church and the Catholic press that followed its activities:

> The church in Guatemala had been noted for just ministering to "souls" rather than the whole man; the priest's place was in the sacristy, he would baptize and administer the sacraments—not much else. There are still priests that would say that any social-economic activity is completely outside the realm of what the priest should be doing.
>
> Since Vatican II, in my own preaching and the preaching of the other [expelled] men, there has been an emphasis on human dignity, on rights as well as obligations.[103]

Throughout the 1980s, when government-orchestrated violence in Guatemala rose to unprecedented heights, the U. S. Catholic press was especially successful in uncovering and reporting brutal details missed by the secular media. Its effectiveness resulted in large part from the eyewitness accounts it received from the many North American missionaries working in the rural areas of the country. On more than one occasion, Catholic magazines would chide mainstream newspapers for their "erratic coverage of Guatemala,"[104] accusing such media giants as the *New York Times* and the *Washington Post* of minimizing or failing to report human rights abuses.[105] When the Reagan administration attempted to lift the Carter-imposed ban on military aid to Guatemala, the U.S. Catholic media vociferously objected, making their protest more effective by recounting the violent murders of priests and church workers by military-related death squads.[106]

Indeed, when Catholic periodicals in the 1980s referred to Guatemala's past history, they no longer used the word "communist" when mentioning the Arbenz administration. Arbenz's name was now almost always linked with "reform." The 1954 coup was treated as a tragic lost opportunity perpetrated by the CIA. Castillo Armas was condemned as a ruthless dictator who had nipped democracy in the bud. Archbishop Rossell, who had earlier been touted as the real force responsible for the downfall of communism, now went unmentioned, as if he had never existed. Needless to say, the U.S. Catholic press by the 1980s had made a total about-face from its Cold War stance of the 1950s and early 1960s. Even *Catholic Digest,* the most impassioned foe of "communist Guatemala" in the 1950s, was by the 1980s printing articles on the murders of Catholic religious in Guatemala and El Salvador.[107] Indeed, the U.S. Catholic church and its media had become some of the most outspoken critics of U.S. policy in Guatemala. Their sharp criticism was undoubtedly a factor in the Carter administration's decision to terminate U.S. military aid to Guatemala and President Reagan's inability to convince Congress to renew it.

four

The Catholic Press
on El Salvador

P at and Ray Donovan, when speaking publicly about the murder of their daughter, Jean, in El Salvador, liked to point out that they had no idea where the country was located when she told them she had been assigned to a mission team there. The first thing they had to do, they said, was search for a map. The Donovans were certainly not exceptional in their ignorance. Prior to the late 1970s, few Americans knew where El Salvador was, and even fewer knew or cared about its history or current problems. This would certainly change, however, in the 1980s. In no small part due to the Catholic church's option for the poor, this tiny nation would now receive much media attention, and U. S. policy toward El Salvador would be hotly debated.

To understand coverage of El Salvador in the U. S. Catholic press, a brief review of the country's church-state relations should prove helpful. Following a scenario similar to what occurred in most of Central America during the 1870s, Liberal proponents of agro-export took control of the Salvadoran government in 1871 and soon incorporated anticlerical statutes into the national constitution. When church officials complained, they were expelled from the country. But, concluding that internal unity was essential in face of an upcoming war with Guatemala, Liberal leaders in 1876 decided to allow the exiled clerics to return home. According to Jesuit historian Rodolfo Cardenal, their expulsion showed the clerics just how vulnerable they were at the hands of the Liberals. Thinking it was in their best interest, they determined to avoid future political conflict. They soon developed an understanding with the Liberal government. The institutional church would refrain from involvement in political, economic, and social issues, and the state, in turn, would treat it in a more benevolent manner.

This relationship lasted until the episcopal tenure of Archbishop Luis Chávez y González of San Salvador, who, in the 1950s, began to encourage the formation of peasant cooperatives.[1] Influenced by Vatican II and the Medellín Conference, Chávez by 1970 had more fully committed himself and his archdiocese to work diligently on behalf of the poor. Parish schools were opened in poor barrios, a secretariat for social concerns was created, and centers for training lay leaders were set up. Priests and nuns were encouraged to deemphasize their traditional roles and concentrate more on service to the marginalized masses, especially through the formation of Christian base communities (CEBs) and peasant cooperatives. Chávez's efforts were enthusiastically supported by most of his priests and nuns and by his auxiliary bishop, Arturo Rivera Damas. They were unappreciated, however, by the ruling class and the other Salvadoran bishops, who claimed they were tainted with communistic ideology. From 1972 on, peasant and labor organizations grew rapidly in membership, and workers' demands became more aggressive. No doubt this was in part due to the stimulus of archdiocesan efforts. Blaming the unrest on "communist clergy," the state apparatus responded to the demands of the popular organizations with increased repression, which included the arrest and deportation of several sympathetic priests. Feeling he lacked the physical stamina to lead the archdiocese during such trying times, the elderly Chávez decided to retire, but not before recommending that the Vatican replace him with his only episcopal supporter, Bishop Rivera Damas. Rome, however, ignored his request. Sending a message that was clear to all, it selected Bishop Oscar Romero y Galdámez, a critic of Chávez's methods, as the latter's successor.

Romero's story is, of course, well known. While bishop of Santiago de María from 1974 to 1977, he had begun to rethink his conservative position concerning church-state relations, going so far as to publicly denounce the government's expulsion of some foreign priests from his diocese. Nevertheless, it was a surprise to almost everyone when, as archbishop, he elected to continue the progressive policies of Chávez. His homilies articulated so well the cries of the oppressed that he was soon being called by his supporters the "voice of the voiceless." Aired over the archdiocesan radio station, YSAX, these sermons soon became quite popular throughout much of the country. Government-sponsored violence increased even more dramatically. YSAX radio, the Jesuit-run Central American University, and other church facilities were frequently bombed. Thousands of people were murdered or disappeared, and when for the first time priests joined their number, Romero, commenting on the sad state of affairs, showed why he was so loved by the masses:

> It would be sad, if in a country where murder is being committed so horribly, we were not to find priests also among the victims. They are the testimony of a church incarnated in the problems of its people.[2]

As with Chávez, Rivera Damas was the only Salvadoran bishop to support Romero.[3] The others, along with the papal nuncio, complained to the Vatican, accusing the archbishop of fanning the flames of discord instead of working for reconciliation. Warned by Rome to cease his "involvement in politics," he was forced to expend much energy and time defending himself. Nevertheless, he continued to champion the cause of the poor masses. Finally, on March 24, 1980, he was assassinated.

Prior to 1969, the *Catholic Periodical and Literature Index* listed only one article on El Salvador, a piece by a Georgetown history professor published in 1959 in the *Magnificat*. It is of interest only because it typifies the shallow nature of the Catholic press's analysis of Central America in the 1950s. In summary, this article naively depicted El Salvador as a nation with a bright future, one in which a reformist government and the church were working together to eradicate corruption and injustice.[4]

For the next ten years Catholic magazines totally ignored El Salvador. Then, in response to the so-called "soccer war" between this tiny nation and Honduras and the way it was being treated in the secular media, historian Thomas Anderson wrote two articles, one in *Commonweal* and the other in *Continuum*. They are significant for two reasons. First, they demonstrate an understanding of the region that was unmatched at the time in the secular press. Second, they show just how much the U.S. Catholic church and its press had grown in its understanding of Central America since the 1950s. The first explained that the war had resulted from more than a soccer rivalry. Its causes were far more complicated and were rooted in long-standing socioeconomic inequalities. In truth, argued Anderson, the war was fabricated by the reactionary regimes of both nations in order to create a nationalistic fervor, which they hoped would divert attention from the need for internal reform.[5]

In *Continuum*, Anderson accused the secular press, most notably *Time* and *Newsweek*, of treating the "soccer war" flippantly, as if it were a joke or a comic-opera.[6] The U.S. government was also chided for neglecting to undertake serious scholarly research as a basis for the creation of its Central American policy. Skillfully linking the 1969 "soccer war" to the earlier "communist" revolt of 1932, in which thousands of landless Indians were massacred by Salvadoran military forces on orders from the oligarchy, Anderson explained that severe land maldistribution, which resulted in a steady flow of landless Salvadoran peasants into Honduras, was the real reason for conflict in El Salvador. He concluded by predicting that future wars were inevitable not only in El Salvador but throughout the isthmus if the cry of the masses for much-needed reform continued to be ignored.[7]

It is interesting that for all the years prior to the appointment of Romero as archbishop, only four articles were listed on El Salvador in the *Catholic Periodical and Literature Index.* This number would triple in Romero's short three-year episcopal tenure, an obvious tribute to his charismatic outreach. Seven of these appeared in the *National Catholic Reporter.* All were written by June Carolyn Erlick, a reporter living in Central America and therefore able to observe developments firsthand. This is significant because at that time no other U.S. Catholic periodical had a journalist on hand in El Salvador. Because of her presence there, the *NCR* was able to provide details unavailable to other Catholic journals.

Since Erlick was allowed to interview Romero and accompany him on some of his trips to rural villages, she was in a position to observe his rapport with the poor and communicate this to her readers.[8] When she reported on the antigovernment demonstrations she witnessed, she took care to estimate the number of priests and nuns who took part.[9] Such an observation indicated to her readers that not only radicals from the popular organizations but clergy and religious as well were participating in such rallies. Erlick diligently reported security force attacks on peaceful protesters and listed in most cases the approximate numbers killed and wounded.[10] She stated prophetically that many predicted that Romero would eventually be martyred,[11] and she pointed out that the archbishop was careful to condemn all violence, whether from the right or the left.[12] She reported the right-wing bombing of the Catholic radio station YSAX,[13] while explaining that it and the archdiocesan paper *Orientación* were in constant peril, since they were the only sources of truthful news coverage in the country.[14]

Erlick's articles from the late 1970s and early 1980s played an important role in awakening U.S. Catholics to the persecution of the church in El Salvador. They represented a major commitment by the *National Catholic Reporter* to keep North Americans informed on the realities of the Salvadoran crisis. Indeed, throughout the 1980s and 1990s the *NCR* would continually surpass all other Catholic periodicals in the amount of coverage it allotted to this country. In so doing, it contributed substantially to the Catholic church's effort to counteract the positive "spin" of the Carter, Reagan, and Bush administrations concerning El Salvador.

Our Sunday Visitor also began to show more interest in El Salvador during Archbishop Romero's episcopal tenure. In an article profiling Romero, it noted that he was called a saint by the poor and a communist by the rich.[15] A second piece remarked that the Central American ruling class, which so feared communism, seemed to invite its presence by its myopic human rights abuses. Citing statistics from Amnesty International, it claimed that right-wing death squads and off-duty security-force personnel had committed more than 2,000 political murders over the previous twenty months, yet the government refused to investigate these crimes. But the author also lashed out at the Salvadoran left, accusing it of kidnapping and murdering innocent people and intentionally attempting to destroy the country's capitalist economy. The author concluded by stating that violence was also growing daily in Guatemala and Honduras and that therefore the United States had to take positive action before it was too late for these countries. If the United States did not act soon, he warned, it would "continue to watch the dominoes fall toward its own borders."[16] This conclusion is significant. It shows that *Our Sunday Visitor*, a more conservative weekly than the *National Catholic Reporter*, had no problem condemning right-wing violence in El Salvador but was still not ready to abandon the Cold War rhetoric reminiscent of Catholic periodicals in the 1950s.

In 1980 *Origins* also gave new-found attention to El Salvador, translating and publishing Archbishop Romero's call for an end to U. S. military aid to this country.[17] From this time on, *Origins*, along with *LADOC*, would serve as a conduit, making Salvadoran church documents readily available to the U. S. church.

Whereas the *National Catholic Reporter* was primarily concerned with providing the latest news from troubled El Salvador, *America* and *Commonweal* tended to concentrate more on political analysis. Two 1978 articles by John McAward, who wrote under the pseudonym "Ed Moran" while working in El Salvador, illustrate this. One appeared in *America* and the other in *Commonweal*. McAward contended that the U. S. media, believing that El Salvador was insignificant, took little interest in its problems. They routinely accepted the Salvadoran media's distorted depiction of events and repeated it without challenge. Thus, all who opposed the government were erroneously depicted as terrorists. Only the Catholic church under the prophetic leadership of Archbishop Romero delivered the truth to the international community, but his fellow bishops counteracted his efforts. Unfortunately, the Carter White House ignored the archbishop. This sent the wrong message to Salvadoran authorities, implying that the U.S. president's human rights policy was not to be taken seriously.[18]

McAward's articles were the first in Catholic periodicals to take the U.S. government to task for its Salvadoran policy. Except for the two previously mentioned pieces by Anderson, they were also the earliest to declare the U.S. media derelict in its coverage of this country, a charge that the Catholic press would continue to make throughout the 1980s.

Four additional *America* articles that appeared prior to Romero's death merit attention. In a June 1979 commentary, *America* accused the international media of inaccurately portraying Salvadoran bloodshed as a by-product of the government's attempt to defeat guerrilla terrorists. In truth, stated the editorialist, most government violence was directed against peasant, worker, teacher, and student organizations, none of which were guerrilla groups. The small elite class, which controlled the country, saw these popular organizations as a threat to the status quo. Rather than allow much-needed reforms, they violently attacked the opposition. The commentator was also not reticent about criticizing the hierarchy: "To the church's shame, four of the six bishops side with the powers in control. [Only] Archbishop Romero and Bishop Arturo Rivera do not."[19] Like Erlick in the *National Catholic Reporter,* the editorialist was careful to point out that Romero condemned all violence, whether it came from the left or the right.[20] Another *America* commentary lauded the coup by young military officers that had toppled the dictator General Humberto Romero. It optimistically stated that the reformist composition of the new junta indicated that "an honest and sincere attempt to find a political solution" to the country's problems seemed to be finally underway.[21] A third editorial, however, sadly reported the resignation of the reformist members of this junta and their replacement by Christian Democrats, who were still willing to work with its right-wing military members. The piece predicted that the new government would be ineffective in its announced attempt to implement land reform, simply because the landowners and military, the real powers in El Salvador, would not allow it to succeed.[22]

In an article in the same issue, Jesuit Philip Land was much harsher in his appraisal of this second junta. Contrary to what many believed in the U.S. State and Defense Departments, he wrote:

The Christian Democrats are a nonsolution. So long as the C. D. Government cannot extricate itself from allegiance to the oligarchy, it does not hold a political option. So long as it fails to challenge head-on the parallel Government's [oligarchy's] repression it must be repudiated. So long as it disbelieves in radical social, economic and political reform, it has nothing to offer the people.[23]

He further contended that U. S. citizens and their president should reflect soberly on the image they were presenting to the world. It was one of the United States "once again interfering in a small country and coming down on the side of the oppressors of the people."[24] Just two days after the publication of these last two articles, Archbishop Oscar Romero was assassinated.

Up until this time few people in the United States had paid much attention to events in El Salvador. But the assassination of an archbishop, followed by the brutal killing of about forty mourners at his funeral, caused many North Americans, especially Catholics, to take notice. U. S. Ambassador Robert White and Salvadoran junta leader José Napoleon Duarte attempted to separate Salvadoran authorities from the murders by speculating that the execution of Romero was probably the work of a professional hit-man unconnected with the Salvadoran government or military. Both also claimed that leftist terrorists had instigated the violence that took place at Romero's funeral. Such speculation was no doubt intended to assure the U. S. press and public that the Duarte-led government was centrist, dedicated to moderate reform, and the only acceptable alternative to the violence-prone extremists of both left and right.

For their part, the mainline secular media were mostly content to rely on the accounts of White and Duarte. They were virtually unanimous in declaring that Romero was probably killed by a right-wing extremist not associated with the government. Their speculation on the violence at the archbishop's funeral was also colored by White's views. The *Washington Post,* for instance, after reporting that it was uncertain as to who was responsible for the bloodbath, added that leftists with bombs and pistols had been seen setting cars on fire during the funeral. *Newsweek* merely stated that White blamed the left, while the *New York Times,* after repeating White's accusation, noted that both the left and right denied responsibility. *Time,* for its part, reported the following:

Armed leftist militants apparently panicked at the blast [of a bomb filled with handbills] and began firing wildly, sending the crowd surging. . . .

Some witnesses claimed that gunfire also came from soldiers in the government's National Palace.[25]

Whereas the U. S. mainline media were content to accept the accounts of White and Duarte, this was not the case with the U. S. Catholic press. The *National Catholic Reporter,* for instance, challenged the official report concerning Romero's murder by relying on the eyewitness testimony of religious leaders. It quoted, among others, a Franciscan priest who was a former president of the U. S. Conference of Major Superiors of Men and was in El Salvador at the time of Romero's death. He stated emphatically that "there is no question in the clergy's minds that the assassination was committed by the right" and that its immediate cause was the archbishop's homily calling on Salvadoran soldiers to disobey orders to kill their fellow countrymen.[26] This citation typified what was now becoming the modus operandi of the U. S. Catholic press in its coverage of El Salvador. When challenging the statements of the secular media or U. S. government, it would fortify its case by relying on the word of religious leaders who had firsthand experience in the region.

An *America* article by James L. Connor, president of the U. S. Jesuit Conference, not only illustrates this approach but also shows just how skillful some U. S. priests were in using personal testimony to demonstrate the flawed nature of U. S. policy in El Salvador. Connor began by relating a phone conversation he had with a State Department official just after Romero's assassination. The official casually remarked that

> One had to recognize that in a way "the archbishop had been asking for it" by taking a partisan stand with the left and stirring up the people with talk of revolution. After all . . . the church should be playing a moderating, calming and healing role.[27]

But Connor next informed his readers that being present at Romero's funeral had convinced him of just how skewed such interpretations were:

> The U. S. Government's official position towards El Salvador is badly misguided. Of that I am now convinced. Prior to March 30, I would not have said this so confidently. But that day I got a fresh perspective on the question as I huddled with 4,000 terrified peasants inside San Salvador's cathedral while bombs exploded and bullets whistled outside in the plaza where we had gathered to celebrate the funeral of Archbishop Oscar Romero.[28]

The Jesuit next made a telling point in his argument: Aside from priests and religious, most of the others who were present when the shooting occurred were the poor and powerless. Therefore, the official government version blaming leftists for the violence was not based on eyewitness testimony. Those who were there, argued Connor, were certain that government forces were responsible for the bloodshed.[29]

Connor closed with passion:

> In El Salvador, governments come and go. Be it a military dictatorship or a civilian-military junta in form is of little consequence because the real power behind the throne remains the same. It is the wealthy oligarchs who consistently control the government, the police force, the judiciary, the militia, the media and—with much more limited success . . . the church.[30]

To the U. S. State Department's insistence that support for the present government was the best guarantee of peace and stability, Connor offered the following counterargument:

> I know that to support the government militarily is, in effect, to support the dominance and the aggression of the oligarchy. It is to maintain institutionalized violence. We are not, therefore, guaranteeing peace, but are continuing the silent, inexorable warfare of an elite over the peasants whose death toll was over 900 in the past 90 days. Even if there were no actual bloodshed, we are effectively denying access to basic human rights to millions of peasants by supporting the continuance of a social situation which is basically unjust.[31]

Needless to say, such personal accounts by highly respected religious leaders proved to be a most effective weapon in the U. S. Catholic church's attempt to undermine White House efforts to defend its Central American policy. Consequently, the Catholic press would make frequent use of them throughout the 1980s.

America was not the only Jesuit publication determined to present the church's alternative view on El Salvador. *Catholic Mind,* in its September 1980 issue, printed an address that Archbishop Romero had intended to deliver at a meeting of the National Council of the Churches of Christ. The piece was important in that it was an *apologia* directly from Romero, explaining exactly what the archdiocese was attempting to do and why. In it the archbishop outlined the reality of Salvadoran "structural violence" (high infant mortality, malnutrition, inadequate housing, health problems, starvation wages, under- and unemployment, etc.) and the state's use of "repressive violence" to maintain this sad status quo. He further explained that the collaboration of the church in the people's liberation process was not based on class, ideology, or politics. It was grounded firmly in the teachings of the Gospel and the social doctrines of the church. Indeed, he argued, if the church ceased to be the "voice of the voiceless," it would betray its fidelity to the teachings of Christ.[32]

Our Sunday Visitor was also critical of official reports on the violence at Romero's funeral, pointing out that they were contradicted by the testimony of both Catholic and Protestant leaders who were eyewitnesses to what took place. It quoted a Cleveland priest who had been at the funeral and who expressed skepticism at the government's version of events. More interesting, however, was the priest's account of a conversation he had had with several upper-class Salvadoran women at the Miami airport while waiting to board his plane, an account that succinctly illustrated the mindset of the Salvadoran oligarchy. Seething with anger, the women claimed that Romero had ruined their nation and was the cause of all its troubles. "I never experienced such hatred," the priest exclaimed. "They all but said that the archbishop got just what he deserved."[33]

It should be noted that two other Catholic periodicals, *St. Anthony Messenger* and the *Catholic Worker,* turned to El Salvador for the first time as a result of Romero's murder. The former printed a lengthy portrayal of the archbishop, placing his life within the context of Salvadoran poverty and violence. The author, Moises Sandoval, editor of *Maryknoll,* took care to point out that although the prelate was a champion of social and economic reform, he was at the same time a staunch defender of the principle of nonviolence.[34] The *Catholic Worker* piece was by Jon Sobrino, a theology professor at San Salvador's Central American University and a confidant of the martyred archbishop. He attempted to explain the mind-set behind Romero's courageous commitment to justice.[35]

Over the next few months the Catholic press continued to question the logic behind the U.S.'s Salvadoran policy. A *Commonweal* editorial was especially effective at cutting to the heart of the matter. It began by defining the problem:

> Current U.S. policy in El Salvador is predicated on the existence of a moderate center. It is a study in the paranoid style of politics. On the one hand, it is governed by the fear of a right-wing coup and a total massacre of the opposition. On the other side lies the fear of "another

Cuba." The pertinent question is whether the rightist coup hasn't already happened, and whether the fear of a left-wing revolution isn't in great part a phantom.[36]

The collapse of the first junta, followed by a rightist reign of terror, the editorialist argued, made the answer obvious. Real power was already in the hands of the extreme right. The center had not held. Its members had moved to the left and joined the revolution, but they certainly could not be cast in the mold of a Pol Pot or Castro.

The editorial now took on a scathing, sarcastic tone:

Increasingly . . . U. S. policy is based on fictions—of a center that isn't there, of crazy leftists (there are some, no doubt), and of a land reform that serves well to target peasant leaders for assassination. The cathedral and seminary in San Salvador are filled with refugees—refugees from the "land reform."[37]

The piece became even more damning: U. S. policy in El Salvador, and indeed throughout the Third World, suffered from the absence of any long-range planning or support for basic economic, political, or social reconstruction. Moreover, there was no provision for situations when fascists took control, as they had done in El Salvador, and carried out violence so horrific that it "drives the moderate center to the barricades." The United States, as it did in Nicaragua in the last days of Somoza, had again stumbled into backing a rightist reign of terror. It should immediately terminate its commitment to the Salvadoran junta.[38]

In *America* Richard Alan White, a senior fellow at the Council of Hemispheric Affairs who had just returned from a month in El Salvador, expressed outrage at what he had witnessed: "Every morning, brutally tortured corpses—clad only in underwear, their thumbs characteristically tied behind their backs—lie in the streets."[39] Forty to fifty such people were murdered each day in El Salvador, the vast majority by security forces. But the United States, argued White, shared blame for this carnage, since it financed it with foreign aid.

White next turned to the countryside, where he saw dangerous parallels between U. S.-sponsored programs and those that had been carried out in Vietnam.

The resulting dynamic is an old story. Through the strategic hamlet strategy, tens of thousands of peasants are being displaced. Then these people, through civic action programs, are made dependent upon the very government that has uprooted them for food and health care. In turn, these new demands upon a beleaguered and corrupt government create the necessity for even greater assistance from the United States.[40]

White argued that these civic action programs, like those in Vietnam, were primarily aimed at helping the military, not the suffering refugees. He predicted that just as these programs had proved counterproductive in Vietnam, they would also fail in El Salvador.

In November 1980 Salvadoran soldiers murdered six of the country's most prominent opposition political leaders. An *America* editorial took the unprecedented step of accusing the incoming Reagan administration of complicity in the crime, in that it had ignored government violence while promising to increase military aid once the Carter team left office.

> It seems clear that right-wing forces in El Salvador and elsewhere . . . perceived the change in administrations to mean less concern from Washington about whether governments friendly to the United States were scrupulous in the observance of human rights. . . .
>
> Ronald Reagan has criticized Jimmy Carter's approach to human rights as inconsistent, and there can be honest differences. . . . But such differences pale in significance in the light of what is taking place in El Salvador. No President can allow himself to be associated with such ruthless repression.[41]

This editorial is significant. Whereas Catholic periodicals had frequently criticized the Carter position on El Salvador, implying that it was naive and premised on faulty analysis, they never questioned the integrity of this president. This would not be the case with Reagan. The above *America* editorial certainly questioned the morality of Reagan's blueprint for El Salvador. It would not be the last Catholic magazine to do so.

While *Commonweal* and *America* were providing meaningful political analysis, the *National Catholic Reporter* was furnishing, often in graphic detail, a litany of Salvadoran atrocities perpetrated by the military against the church. It related to its readers the murder of a priest and several women, bombings of church property, and searches of parish buildings in which furniture, walls, bathroom fixtures, books, church records, and photographs of Archbishop Romero were destroyed.[42] Erlick, the *NCR*'s Central American correspondent, citing the executive director of the archdiocesan legal aid office, informed her readers that 11,000 people had been murdered in only the first ten months of 1980, while 265 Catholic schools and churches had been bombed or machine-gunned.[43]

Due to the on-site nature of her assignment, Erlick was able to visit the town of San José in Chalatenango, near the Honduran border, just after a military sweep of the area had been completed. She reported that peasants had been murdered and survivors forced to flee to the hills but that what she had found was not unusual:

> The story of San José repeats itself in village after village in El Salvador, in the swollen bellies of malnourished children, in the worn faces of women on the run. A rosary of ghost towns is forming through Chalatenango. In El Salitre, only five or six families are left where 200 formerly resided. In Las Penas, only 50 families remain out of 250 families. The rest are refugees without a refuge.[44]

Erlick was also in a position to visit and report on the archdiocese's herculean work at its seven refugee centers, where it provided for about 2,500 displaced persons. She took pains to point out that the centers cared for refugees "from both sides of the political fence."[45]

In a September article that in hindsight is chilling, she interviewed members of a Cleveland missionary team determined to stay in El Salvador when other foreigners were leaving.[46] Indeed, only three months later, two members of this team, along with two U.S. Maryknoll missioners, would be brutally murdered by Salvadoran National Guardsmen.

Of all the murders in Central America, none has evoked more indignation among North Americans, especially Catholics, than the executions of Sisters Dorothy Kazel, Maura Clarke, and Ita Ford, and lay missioner Jean Donovan. The fact that these religious women were sadistically raped before they were killed, that the Salvadoran military attempted to cover up the crime, and that the new Reagan administration attacked the reputations of the women in a crude attempt to salvage its Salvadoran policy, infuriated large numbers of religious Americans who had previously paid little attention to events in Latin America.[47] Taking their cue from the civil rights and antiwar movements of the 1960s, many of these people now formed ecumenical organizations dedicated to changing their government's Central American policy through educating the public, lobbying, and peaceful protest. The best known were Witness for Peace, the Sanctuary Movement, the Washington Office on Latin America, the Quixote Center, the Pledge of Resistance, the Religious Task Force on El Salvador, and the SHARE Foundation. Other multi-issue social justice organizations, such as Pax Christi,

Network, the American Friends Service Committee, and the Unitarian Universalist Service Committee, began to devote more time and energy to Central American concerns. The same can be said for the U.S. Conference of Catholic Bishops and the National Council of Churches, as well as a variety of Catholic religious orders, several mainline Protestant religious denominations, and a few evangelical Christian groups such as Sojourners.[48] Thus, there can be no doubt that the murders of these four female missionaries served as a defining moment for the U.S. Catholic church and several other Christian churches as well. Henceforth, tens of thousands of U.S. religious people would work actively to change what they considered to be an immoral policy of their government toward El Salvador and Central America in general.

For its part, the U.S. Catholic press increased its coverage of El Salvador substantially, often dovetailing its efforts with those of the above groups. Whereas the *Catholic Periodical and Literature Index* listed only sixteen U.S. articles on El Salvador in the years prior to Archbishop Romero's death and eighteen in the eight months before those of the churchwomen, it included no less than 150 in only the first two years after their murders.

In the three weeks following this tragic slaying, the *National Catholic Reporter* responded with massive coverage of El Salvador written by seven different reporters, an obvious indication that this nation would henceforth receive priority coverage from this periodical. Individual profiles of the four women, each separately written, dominated the December 19 issue. Quite moving, these articles were easily the most thorough to appear in the U.S. Catholic press. They were later published in an abbreviated form in *Catholic Digest*, marking the first time that this rather conservative magazine devoted space to a Central American issue since the 1950s.[49] Other *NCR* reports included a graphic description of the unearthing of the slain women's bodies,[50] as well as a piece in which the vicar general of the archdiocese of San Salvador correctly predicted that the weapons used in the women's murders would prove to have been supplied by the U.S. government.[51] The *NCR* also cited the State Department's refusal to make public its investigative report on the Salvadoran government's involvement in a cover-up of the killings, even though the U.S. bishops had requested that they do so.[52]

America displayed particular anger at the Duarte-led junta's attempt to write off the U.S. women's murders as the work of right-wing extremists unconnected with the government. Pointing out that only a week earlier these same officials had made similar excuses concerning the killing of the six opposition leaders, the Jesuit journal argued that there was "strong evidence" linking the Salvadoran military to both crimes.[53]

A second *America* editorial ridiculed the announcement that Duarte had just been appointed president of El Salvador, thereby becoming the country's first civilian head of state in forty-nine years. Contending that the appointment had resulted from intense Washington pressure, the writer stated that there was no reason to believe that any real change had taken place in the structure of Salvadoran power. This point merits a further comment. Whereas over the next several years the secular media would mostly treat the Duarte-led Christian Democrats as a voice of reason valiantly trying to bring about democratic reform under almost impossible conditions, the Catholic press would view things differently. It would depict Duarte and his cohorts as ambitious politicians with no real power, as marionettes who, although they might desire reform, nevertheless refused to challenge the Salvadoran military or the Reagan administration because to do so would mean probable loss of office.

But *America*'s wrath was especially directed at President-elect Reagan and his advisers: "No signal . . . of the Reagan transition team has been more clear than their thunderous silence about the atrocities that have taken place in El Salvador this past month."[54] The editorial added that there was little doubt that Reagan's passivity had weakened the position of every U.S. advocate of human rights throughout Central and South America.[55] The writer, however, did not spare the Carter administration. Commenting on the lame duck president's decision to lift his suspension of military aid to El Salvador, he called it "a tragic blunder" that would undoubtedly be compounded by the incoming Reagan administration:

> The recent murders of U.S. citizens[56] are only the most dramatic instances of the right-wing violence that goes unchecked and unpunished in El Salvador. For the United States to sponsor such violence by further military assistance is a violation not only of national values but of long-range national interests.[57]

Commonweal treated the incoming administration with even more disdain. In an article bluntly entitled "Green Light for Terror," Richard Alan White wrote with unusual bitterness:

> When election returns on the night of November 4 showed that Ronald Reagan would soon be the president of the United States, El Salvador rightists celebrated "their victory" by firing guns into the air. Ever since, in expectation of the Reagan presidency, they have increasingly been firing their guns into people.[58]

Charging that the Reagan team had encouraged and supported a rightist military solution, White proposed an alternative approach. The Duarte-led Christian Democrats and the military could be convinced that the formation of a centrist coalition government, which would include the Democratic Revolutionary Front (FDR) opposition, would be in their best interest:

> The foundation of El Salvador's export economy rests upon selling coffee and cotton . . . in large part to United States markets. Simple straightforward trade restrictions, tied with pressure upon our allies to implement similar policies, exercising our influence in the international banking world to limit multilateral credits and loans, and, of course, eliminating all bilateral economic and military assistance, would quickly result in this new centrist government.[59]

White pointed out that these were exactly the methods that the United States had used so successfully to bring down the leftist Allende government in Chile, adding sarcastically that we did not seem to have the same resolve when right-wing governments were involved.[60]

America editorials expressed further outrage at the Reagan administration's insistence that the Salvadoran situation necessitated a response based solely on a Cold War, East-West confrontational approach. Arguing that the Reagan view was simplistic and unfair to the Salvadoran people,[61] the editorialist further contended that it was counterproductive to U.S. interests:

> The Reagan-[Secretary of State] Haig policy, largely ignoring the injustice and repression at the heart of the conflict, concentrated its energies and its propaganda on the issue of military aid. The result has unsettled our allies in Europe, antagonized our neighbors in Latin America and even discomfited the junta in El Salvador.[62]

The *National Catholic Reporter* took a similar position, observing that the refusal of Japan, England, France, Germany, and Canada to join the United States in providing military aid to El Salvador was proof that the Reagan administration stood isolated in its views.[63] For its part, the *Catholic Worker* judged the Reagan-Haig blueprint to be "rife with distortions and omissions" and contradicted by the documentation of the human rights organization Amnesty International and the San Salvador archdiocesan legal aid office.[64]

Commonweal, however, was especially sarcastic, declaring, "Haig's sales job for improving the quality of official terror in El Salvador . . . misleading [and] in part downright false." It then asked:

Is the U. S., like the Soviet Union in Poland, really determined to do permanent sentry duty for oppression in Central America? . . . In 1932, when Salvador's military leaders massacred 30,000 peasants, the U. S. government looked the other way. This time, they'll be doing it with our weapons and with our advisors.[65]

The Catholic press's attitude toward the new presidential team undoubtedly was colored by derogatory statements made about the churchwomen by Reagan spokespersons. Soon-to-be U. S. ambassador to the United Nations Jeane Kirkpatrick suggested that the murdered women were not just nuns but political activists for the guerrillas. Ernest Lefever, Reagan's nominee for human rights commissioner, implied that the four could have been "nuns hiding machine guns for the insurgents." Secretary of State Alexander Haig postulated that the religious women might have been killed in an exchange of gunfire with security forces while trying to run a roadblock.[66]

Outraged by such unsubstantiated remarks, the *National Catholic Reporter* charged that they were part of an intentional plan by the Reagan administration to smear the reputation of the Catholic church not only in El Salvador but throughout Latin America. It further pointed out that the Reagan team had produced no credible evidence to support its contentions.[67]

Unlike the feisty *NCR,* most Catholic periodicals chose not to comment on the above remarks, probably reasoning that to do so would only give them greater publicity. What is important, however, is that such caustic statements went far in convincing the Catholic media that the Reagan administration was disingenuous in its approach to the Salvadoran church and poor. Consequently, several periodicals concluded that U. S. Catholics and other religious people had to take the lead in changing U. S. policy toward El Salvador. These publications now began to encourage their readers to become personally involved in activities aimed at educating the public and convincing political leaders to support their views on El Salvador. In so doing, the Catholic press embarked upon a new "activist" phase in its coverage of Central America, a phase that would last throughout the 1980s and into the early 1990s.

An article in the January/February 1981 issue of the *Catholic Worker* perhaps best illustrates this new approach. Author Peggy Scherer complained that the national media were derelict in their coverage of El Salvador. Faced with such irresponsibility, she reasoned, Christians must take matters into their own hands. Indeed, many had already done so. She listed examples: Thousands in Cleveland and New York had signed petitions calling for an end to U. S. aid to El Salvador. Many church members had sent letters of protest to government officials. Groups had been formed to organize marches and rallies and to raise the consciousness of the public on Central American issues. The International Longshoremen's and Warehousemen's Union (ILWU) was given special praise for refusing to load military cargo destined for El Salvador. For those interested in becoming involved, Scherer suggested that they order the organizing packet of the Religious Task Force on El Salvador and listed the group's mailing address.[68]

Other articles in the *Catholic Worker* would continue in the same vein. An editorial from March 1982, for instance, ended with the following: "We beg our readers to take immediate action, in memory of Romero, against U.S. policy—prayer and fasting, letters, demonstrations, educational efforts, and nonviolent direct action are all means of saying no to injustice."[69]

The *National Catholic Reporter* also played a leading role in encouraging Catholic activism by favorably covering a variety of protests, always taking care to highlight the participation of clergy and religious. *NCR* journalist Stephanie Russell commented in a March report, "Widespread opposition to United States foreign policy towards El Salvador has grown quickly in recent weeks among many religious groups, particularly among Catholics."[70] She noted the similarity between the rapid spread of these protests and those of the early stages of the anti-Vietnam war movement. She described the new groups as ecumenically centered but added that Catholic religious orders seemed to be key organizers. Finally, she listed three reasons that explained the origins and rapid growth of the new protest organizations: outrage over the churchwomen's murders, the militaristic approach of the Reagan administration, and the conviction that the national media had failed to provide accurate information on El Salvador.[71]

Like the *Catholic Worker*, the *NCR* discussed the ILWU's work stoppage, pointing out that it was the San Francisco Archdiocesan Commission on Social Justice that had convinced the union to embark on its course of action. It also compared the boycott to that of Solidarity in Poland.[72]

In other articles the *NCR* reported on demonstrations in Providence and Washington and in front of the U.S. embassy in Managua, making special mention of the fact that U.S. bishops, Capuchins, Maryknollers, Dominicans, and Sisters of Loretto had been involved.[73] Another piece told of a five-day fast and sit-in at Holy Name Cathedral in Chicago, in which the protesters, members of the Religious Task Force on El Salvador, demanded that the Chicago archdiocese speak out against U.S. Salvadoran policy. The report noted that the demonstration ended in success when the archdiocese issued a statement calling for an end to U.S. military aid to El Salvador. It concluded by citing the remarks of a Task Force member, who contended that similar pressure needed to be used in other places where the church had been reluctant to speak out.[74]

A January article stated that the *Tucson Citizen* had received numerous angry letters after publishing an editorial suggesting that the murdered churchwomen had been involved in "misguided political activism." It also listed the mailing address of the president and Minister of Defense of El Salvador so that readers could write them to denounce the recent kidnapping of two journalists by Salvadoran soldiers.[75] A piece on 1980 Nobel Peace Prize winner Adolfo Pérez Esquivel highlighted his conviction that U. S. Christians must play a primary role in convincing their government to stop arms shipments to El Salvador and instead initiate peace negotiations.[76] Another report quoted a delegation of priests, nuns, and Catholic laypersons who, upon returning from a fact-finding trip to Central America, urged U. S. citizens to write to the State Department and Honduran government protesting the expansion of violence into the Salvadoran refugee camps in Honduras.[77] The *NCR* likewise informed its readers that two Republican congressmen who decided to break with the Reagan administration on Salvadoran policy stated that they did so only after the "Catholic church and other religious groups" educated them on what was actually taking place in that troubled nation.[78]

Another Catholic publication that merits close attention for its 1981 reports on El Salvador is *Our Sunday Visitor*. In the three months following the churchwomen's deaths, *OSV* printed several articles on this country. All were short, straightforward, and with virtually no commentary. On March 22, however, it ended its cautious approach, issuing two scathing attacks on the Reagan administration. The first, by Judy Ball, accused Reagan officials of intentionally ignoring the truth while orchestrating a massive public relations campaign in favor of the Salvadoran government and military. She was particularly cynical about the administration's claim that it had uncovered massive documentation proving that communists were supplying the Salvadoran guerrillas with military equipment: "Curious, isn't it, that within weeks the Reagan administration was able to unequivocally determine the communist-guerrilla weapons supply link, while the December murders of four American missionaries remain unsolved."[79]

The second article, by Father Vincent Giese, *OSV* editor, argued with passion that the real issue in Central America was not Marxism, Cuba, or the Soviet Union. Contending that this was only a façade used by the United States to mask the truth, he went on to claim that our real concern was the economic interests of a few wealthy families and U. S. businessmen.[80] He continued along the same line in the next issue, telling of peaceful Salvadoran refugees being viciously attacked by soldiers[81] and remarking that the U. S. church—with its "blah liturgies, uninspiring homilies, bland faces [in the pews] . . . on Sundays, [and] obsession with trivial issues"—could learn much from its counterparts in El Salvador and Nicaragua.[82] Future issues of *Our Sunday Visitor* would continue to harshly attack the United States for its Central American policy.

The more aggressive tone of *OSV*'s El Salvador reporting commenced just after Father Giese returned from a three-week fact-finding trip through Central America. By this time most U. S. grassroots church groups concerned with El Salvador were in one way or another involved in organizing such trips as part of their effort to educate churchpeople on the realities of Central America. Participants were formed into delegations, which were then sent to the isthmus, where they spent much of their time visiting war-torn areas and listening to the stories of those affected by violence and poverty. They often met with U. S. missionaries, CEB members, and other churchpeople. When they returned home, they were expected to tell others what they had seen and heard. Some participants would write articles, which were published in Catholic magazines and local city and diocesan newspapers. Needless to say, these fact-finding trips played a major role in raising the consciousness of North American churchpeople. Such was obviously the case with Father Giese, and, as editor of *OSV*, he was in an excellent position to express his convictions to an audience of mostly moderate to conservative Catholics. Giese would make several additional trips to Central America throughout the 1980s, always reporting his findings in the pages of *OSV*. Indeed, as a result of his leadership, *OSV* would throughout the decade remain one of the harshest critics of U. S. policy not only in El Salvador but throughout Central America.

The years 1981–1982 also marked the first time several hitherto unmentioned Catholic publications turned their attention to El Salvador. Robert E. Burns, contributing editor of *U.S. Catholic*, took "our incredibly slothful media," and in particular *Newsweek*, to task for accepting the Reagan administration's ideological explanation for his "simplistic, macho" Salvadoran policy.[83] *New Catholic World*, devoting its entire September/October issue to "The Church in Central America," included three perceptive articles on El Salvador, all of which were highly critical of U. S. policy.[84] *Sisters*, a monthly for female religious congregations, contained three reflective pieces on the suffering and death of missionaries and the poor in El Salvador.[85] The *Sign* included pieces on Sister Maura Clarke and Archbishop Romero.[86] Even the highly specialized *Liturgy* entered the fray, calling on parishes and religious groups to raise the consciousness of Catholics by incorporating the stories of the Salvadoran martyrs into their liturgical services and religious education programs. It listed the addresses of three activist groups, the Religious Task Force, the Quixote Center, and the Oakland Reflection Group, all of which had developed liturgical packets for memorial services for Oscar Romero and the four churchwomen.[87]

In summary, then, prior to the episcopal tenure of Archbishop Romero, the U. S. Catholic press, like its secular counterpart, paid virtually no attention to El Salvador. In the late 1970s this changed, largely due to the attention commanded by the charismatic Romero. The *National Catholic Reporter* was the first Catholic periodical to report extensively on El Salvador. By assigning a correspondent to the region, it was able to provide detailed coverage when other Catholic publications could not. *America,* for its part, led the way with perceptive analysis that was rarely equaled in the secular media. Even in these early articles, Catholic journalists took great pains to emphasize that the vast majority of Salvadoran clergy and religious were supporters of Romero and sympathetic to the popular organizations. Likewise, they had no tolerance for those bishops who were critical of the archbishop, going so far as to call their conduct shameful. They were careful to point out that Romero was an advocate of peace who condemned all violence regardless of whether it came from government agents or leftist guerrillas. They were also quite willing to declare the Carter administration's Salvadoran policy naive, wrongheaded, and counterproductive.

After Romero's murder, the Catholic press redoubled its effort to end U. S. military aid to El Salvador, claiming that such assistance only served to keep a repressive oligarchy in power, an elite class that had institutionalized violence in order to preserve the unjust status quo. It aggressively attempted to refute the Carter administration's contention that the Salvadoran military was not responsible for Romero's assassination and that the Salvadoran junta was moderate, reformist, and the only reasonable alternative to violence-prone extremist government. To make its point, the Catholic press relied on testimony from churchpeople, both Salvadorans and North Americans, who had eyewitness knowledge of what was happening in the region. Some of these people worked in the areas of conflict, while others made fact-finding trips there. Here *America* was especially fortunate, since U. S. Jesuits were able to visit their Salvadoran counterparts in San Salvador and personally hear their analysis of the crisis. Catholic periodicals were also far from reticent in accusing the secular media of shabby journalism when the latter uncritically accepted the explanations of the Carter administration or the Duarte-led regime on El Salvador.

More than any other event, the brutal murder of the four North American churchwomen was a defining moment for the U. S. Catholic church and its press as far as El Salvador was concerned. The sadistic nature of the crime, the Salvadoran military's effort to cover it up, and the new Reagan administration's crude attempt to smear the reputations of the victims led the Catholic press to conclude that it was dealing with a president totally unsympathetic to its position. Whereas Carter's policy had been depicted as simplistic and counterproductive, Reagan's was described as vicious and even immoral. Coverage in Catholic periodicals was now much more widespread and often sarcastic in tone. The Duarte government was characterized as nothing more than a façade kept in place by the U.S. government in order to create a veneer of "respectability," covering up the fact that the brutal military was really in control.

But more significant, the Catholic press, faced with an administration that it saw as adversarial, concluded that it had no choice but to take a more activist approach to the Salvadoran crisis. For the first time in its history, the U.S. Catholic press called on its readers to join grassroots religious-based organizations dedicated to convincing the public that U.S. foreign policy was immoral and therefore needed to be changed. People of faith were asked to participate in protest marches, to sign petitions, to write letters to their congresspeople and to the editors of their local newspapers, to make fact-finding trips to El Salvador, to hold memorial services in memory of Archbishop Romero and the four churchwomen, to speak at church services and to church groups, to conduct educational workshops, and, in short, to use whatever peaceful means were necessary to change their government's policy toward El Salvador and the rest of Central America. Although, as before, *America*, the *National Catholic Reporter*, and *Commonweal* continued to lead the way, now numerous other Catholic periodicals joined the cause. It is no exaggeration to conclude that the U.S. Catholic press had by 1981 embarked upon a peaceful crusade, the likes of which it had never been involved in before.

One final point of much significance remains to be made. In its numerous articles on El Salvador, the U.S. Catholic press showed no support for the Farabundo Martí National Liberation Front. Its aim was to change U.S. policy toward El Salvador and to foster reform there, but always through peaceful means. Consequently, it was careful to note that Archbishop Romero and other progressive Christian leaders condemned violence regardless of whether it came from the left or the right. With the exception of a few conservative Catholic publications that will be treated in a later chapter, the Catholic media remained consistent in their wholesale condemnation of violence in El Salvador throughout the 1980s and into the following decade.

five

Nicaragua to 1980

T he turbulent church situation in Nicaragua in the 1970s and 1980s was extremely confusing. Consequently, one cannot hope to understand the complexities of U.S. Catholic press coverage during these years without first becoming well versed in the history of Nicaraguan church-state relations. In addition, one must also become familiar with the historical evolution of conflicting forces within the Nicaraguan church. For this reason, before treating media reports, a detailed review and analysis of past events is necessary.[1]

It was not until 1893, about two decades later than elsewhere in Central America, that the Liberal Party rose to power in Nicaragua. Following the traditional Liberal pattern, the new government soon passed anticlerical legislation and exiled those church officials who protested. In Nicaragua, unlike elsewhere in the isthmus, however, the Liberals were forced by the United States to relinquish the reins of government in 1909. President José Santos Zelaya, an ardent nationalist, had challenged North American economic hegemony within his country's borders, thereby bringing about U.S. military intervention. The United States was able to place the Conservative Party back in power and, bolstered by American Marines stationed in Managua, keep it there until 1928, even though it had little popular support. Fully realizing the precarious nature of their situation, the Conservatives spent much of their time in office enriching themselves and their relatives, while allowing North American businessmen a major role in running the Nicaraguan economy. The

Conservatives did nullify the Liberal anticlerical laws, however, and the Catholic hierarchy maintained cordial relations with them.

Frustrated by continuous Liberal attempts to overthrow the weak Conservative government, U. S. officials brought the two rival parties together in 1927 for a meeting at Tipitapa, a town just north of Managua. Here they agreed to end their hostilities and accept the results of a U. S.-supervised election set for 1928. The Liberals won this election, and José Moncada became president. The unpopular Conservatives had no choice but to accept a greatly reduced political and economic role, while the Liberals were only too happy to replace them as governmental collaborators with North American power. Thus, it seemed that the United States had strengthened its dominant position in Nicaragua. One Liberal, however, refused to accept the Tipitapa Pact. For the next six years, Augusto César Sandino carried on a successful guerrilla war against the Nicaraguan government, thereby frustrating both the National Guard and the U. S. Marines.

Faced with the results of the Tipitapa Pact, the Catholic hierarchy decided its interests would be best served by suppressing its traditional antipathy for Liberalism and attempting instead to cultivate a harmonious relationship with the Moncada administration. Consequently, at the bequest of government officials, Archbishop José Lezcano y Ortega of Managua and three other bishops issued a joint pastoral letter condemning Sandino's rebellion and calling on his forces to lay down their arms. Lezcano also wrote to the Nicaraguan clergy, requesting its support for the National Guard. Bishop Canuto Reyes y Valladares of Granada even went so far as to publicly bless the weapons of U. S. Marines about to embark on a mission aimed at eradicating Sandino's army.

After Anastasio Somoza García, the U. S.-appointed head of the National Guard, had Sandino assassinated and seized the presidency for himself, the Nicaraguan bishops, overlooking his brutality, provided him with what John Kirk terms "official ecclesial legitimization."[2] In return, Somoza heaped favors on the institutional church and its hierarchy. A mass in 1938, celebrating the fiftieth anniversary of Archbishop Lezcano's priestly ordination, illustrates well this symbiotic relationship between church and state. Somoza was given a special place of honor at the solemn pontifical service, and his soldiers formed an honor guard through which the archbishop processed. In a pastoral letter composed by Lezcano for the occasion, he thanked the dictator for the special attention and kindness he had bestowed on both the church and its archbishop, adding that the church for its part had "sincere and respectful loyalty" for the government.[3]

Such sycophancy toward the dictator became standard fare for the episcopacy. In 1942, using the gold crown from the cathedral statue of the Virgin of Candelaria, Lezcano crowned Somoza's only daughter Lilliam "queen
of the army." In his accompanying speech, he referred to Somoza's National
Guard as a "magnificent institution . . . fundamental to the social order and
well-being of the country."[4] The archbishop was not alone. In 1950 the Nicaraguan bishops issued a pastoral letter in which they warned the people that
"all authority comes from God" and that therefore "when Catholics obey
the government, they do not degrade themselves" but instead act out of "respect for God."[5]

Lezcano's successor, Archbishop Vicente González y Robleto, was also
supportive of the dictatorship. When Somoza was assassinated in 1956, the
prelate buried him with full church honors, declaring him a "Prince of the
Church." After a failed uprising against Somoza's son Luis, led by Pedro
Joaquín Chamorro in 1959, González y Robleto issued a pastoral letter on the
nature of legitimate authority and the proper Catholic response to it. In no
uncertain terms the archbishop declared the Somoza government the legitimate authority in Nicaragua, which therefore had to be obeyed, adding that
to resist authority is to resist God. Even if Somoza was a tyrant, which he
clearly was not, noted González, he would still have to be obeyed. After heaping praise on the government, the archbishop asserted that no one was pun-
ished in Nicaragua unless he was involved in revolutionary activities. Finally
he lauded the Somoza government for being "a benefactor of the Church."[6]

Throughout the Somoza years up until 1970, bishops or their representatives took care to bestow church approval on the government by attending all state ceremonies, usually opening them with a prayer. Little mention was made by church officials of the need for social justice. As the plight
of the masses became increasingly more desperate and the landholdings
and personal wealth of the Somoza family grew enormously, the episcopacy remained almost totally mute. In return for its support, the Somozas
favored the institutional church with land and property donations and
monetary gifts. Expensive cars were even given to some bishops. Although
following the Medellín Conference some prelates, most notably Julian Barni
of Juigalpa and Matthew Niedhammer of Bluefields, began to support pastoral innovation and some distancing of the church from Somoza, only
Bishop Octavio Calderón y Padilla of Matagalpa was outspoken in his opposition to the dictator.

Even though Vatican II's *aggiornamento* had little immediate effect on
most of the Nicaraguan bishops, it did cause a number of churchpeople to

become more socially active. In 1966 Father José de la Jara formed the first Nicaraguan Christian base community in his San Pablo parish in Managua.[7] Soon after, the priest-poet Ernesto Cardenal organized a CEB at Solentiname, a remote island on Lake Nicaragua.[8] Both would serve as models for the more radical CEBs throughout the country. Likewise, by 1970 in Juigalpa and the isolated eastern state of Zelaya, priests and religious supported by their bishops had begun to create an impressive array of CEBs, agricultural cooperatives, and literacy programs.

But, along with the Medellín Conference, it was the death of González y Robleto in 1968 that fully opened the doors for reform. In early 1969, the Nicaraguan church held its first *Encuentro Pastoral* (Pastoral Meeting) to discuss its situation in light of Vatican II and Medellín. Three bishops and over 200 priests and religious attended. After many presentations and much analysis, most participants agreed that the Nicaraguan institutional church left much to be desired. Furthermore, to be a force in the nation's future, it had to implement massive reforms immediately. To push the church in the right direction, Rome, in 1970, in a move that surprised almost everyone, appointed the young auxiliary bishop of Matagalpa, Miguel Obando y Bravo, as the new archbishop of Managua. In so doing, it passed over Donaldo Chávez Nuñez, the auxiliary bishop of the archdiocese, who was more experienced and politically powerful but who also had close ties with the Somozas.

The new archbishop soon made it clear that he was cut from a different cloth than his predecessors. When Somoza sent him a luxury-model Mercedes Benz as a gift, he refused to accept it. He likewise declined to attend state events, thereby sending a public message that the symbiotic relationship between church and state was a thing of the past.

Aided by the appointment of six new bishops, which reduced the episcopacy's pro-Somoza faction to a minority, the Nicaraguan Bishops' Conference was ready by 1972 to follow Obando's lead. In the years that followed, it would issue an impressive series of pastoral letters calling for structural changes and an end to human rights abuses. The new bishops, however, although they adhered for the most part to the Medellín model, remained in many respects traditionalist and anti-Marxist. Consequently, in these pastorals they would also warn the faithful against those who would resort to violence in their pursuit of reform.

In 1974, for instance, after Somoza arrested twenty-seven prominent opposition leaders who had called for a boycott of the upcoming election, the bishops issued an important letter condemning the incarceration and declaring that citizens had the right to dissent when faced with governmental injustice and arbitrary behavior. They qualified their remarks, however, noting that justifiable dissent did not include insurrectional or armed protest. Historian Manzar Foroohar is correct in pointing out that this clarification was aimed at separating the institutional church from the more radical Sandinista National Liberation Front (FSLN), a revolutionary group founded in 1961 by Carlos Fonseca Amador, Tomás Borge Martínez, and Silvio Mayorga, three Marxists who modeled their movement on Fidel Castro's Cuban revolution.[9] But it was also aimed at a second source, radical priests such as the Cardenal brothers, Uriel Molina, and others, who not only were pro-Sandinista but were boldly threatening the traditional hierarchical structure of the church by challenging the authority of the bishops.

The episcopacy's problems with such clerics went back at least to 1970, when Father Fernando Cardenal led about one hundred students of the Christian Revolutionary Movement, a group that he had formed at the Jesuit university, in a hunger strike at the Managua cathedral in protest of the arrest of some radical student leaders and FSLN members. As tensions mounted, Obando and four other bishops, contending that such protests were political and disrespectful of the Blessed Sacrament, condemned the occupation. They also threatened the priests who were involved with suspension of their priestly faculties if they did not immediately leave the cathedral. Seeing growing popular support for the hunger strikers, the Somoza regime decided to capitulate and release the prisoners in question, thereby making the bishops' threat a moot point.

But this was not the end of the affair. Shortly thereafter, several hundred people, mostly CEB members, signed an open letter to the bishops questioning the morality of their actions and lecturing them on their Christian responsibilities. Father Ernesto Cardenal sent a second open letter in which he equated the bishops' conduct to that of the Pharisees and reminded them that "the people of God," not sacred buildings, were the real church.[10] The public nature and disrespectful tone of both letters were undoubtedly intentional and meant as a challenge to the bishops to get with the Sandinista program or face the consequences. In light of the hierarchical structure of the Catholic church, it is no wonder that the bishops viewed the conduct of the Cardenals and their supporters as extremist and a threat not only to themselves but to the very nature of Catholicism. Bishop Pablo Vega of Juigalpa said as much in an article in *La Prensa*, the newspaper published by Pedro Joaquín Chamorro, a major leader of the anti-Somoza forces. After labeling Cardenal a disciple of Fidel Castro and a propagandist for a socialist collectivism that was contradictory to Christian principles, he accused the priest-poet of being the linchpin in a campaign against the bishops.[11]

Torn between a corrupt dictator and a growing minority of pro-Sandinista priests, the Episcopal Conference in March 1972 issued a lengthy pastoral to clarify the church's position. After calling for greater freedom and an authentic social transformation that would incorporate the needs of all citizens, the prelates warned their priests and nuns that they were obliged to abstain from partisan political involvement and must respect and unite behind their bishops.

The caution, however, made little if any impression on the radical clergy. In December 1972 the Cardenals and Molina again challenged not only Somoza but the bishops when they began another student occupation of the cathedral. Conflict was avoided, but only because the cathedral was destroyed by an earthquake that devastated much of the capital. Yet the pro-Sandinista clergy were determined to push further. Ernesto Cardenal and other radical priests began meeting with students from the Christian Revolutionary Movement to study Marxist theory and apply it to Christianity. Eventually almost all members of this pro-FSLN organization joined the guerrilla front as combatants. Understandably, Obando and his fellow prelates were strongly opposed to priests forming Marxist study groups and advocating violence.[12]

The December earthquake proved to be a primary factor in Anastasio Somoza Debayle's downfall. His corrupt conduct in relation to relief efforts turned most Nicaraguans as well as international public opinion against him. Obando intensified his criticism of the government's conduct in his pastorals and his monthly column in the *Boletín de la Arquidiócesis de Managua*. Nevertheless, his words did little to temper the criticism of the radical clergy and CEB members associated with them, who would settle for nothing less than a full endorsement of the FSLN.

A commemorative mass, celebrated by Obando on the first anniversary of the earthquake in the central plaza in Managua, perhaps best illustrates the difficult position of the hierarchy in relation to both the Somoza regime and the so-called popular church. The mass was intended to be a simple memorial for those Nicaraguans who had died in the earthquake. Somoza, however, attempted to take advantage of it. Although uninvited, he attended along with several of his officials, evidently hoping to boost his popularity. But the dictator was not alone in trying to use the religious event for his own ends. As political scientists Michael Dodson and Tommie Sue Montgomery write, pro-Sandinista CEB members decided "to attend [the mass] with the explicit purpose of expressing a theological position different from that of the bishops."[13] They drew up slogans on signs which were not only anti-Somoza, but which also justified revolution in Christian terms. With the help of radical priests and nuns, these were then smuggled into the plaza.

Once the mass began, the signs were displayed, much to the embarrassment of Somoza. Angered not only at the placards but also at the critical comments made by Obando in his sermon, Somoza ordered his national guardsmen to unplug the loudspeaker that was being used for the mass. He then stormed out of the service. Clearly, both the reactionary Somoza and the radical popular church had hoped to co-opt Obando by using the commemorative service for their own purposes. Unlike the president, however, the radicals were successful. Undoubtedly, many who attended the service, seeing the pro-Sandinista Christian-revolutionary signs and hearing Obando's criticism of the government, concluded that the archbishop and the radical groups were on the same wavelength. This is exactly what the episcopacy wanted to avoid.

Sensing that their moment had come, the Sandinistas made a bold move. On December 27, 1974, a commando unit stormed a party at the home of Somoza associate Chema Castillo. Several high government officials and Somoza friends were taken hostage. With the commandos holding all the cards, the shaken dictator had no choice but to call on the archbishop to mediate the crisis. Obando accepted, but Somoza was far from happy with the outcome. After sixty hours of negotiations, Somoza was forced to acquiesce to all the major demands of the Sandinistas. The FSLN received $5 million in ransom and their manifesto was published; fourteen political prisoners, including Daniel Ortega, were released; and all Sandinistas involved received safe passage to Cuba. But much more important was the fact that Somoza had been shown to be vulnerable. Since the FSLN had brought about his degradation, the guerrilla organization's popularity rose enormously. For his part, the dictator felt that Obando had favored the FSLN in the negotiations and therefore held him partly responsible for his humiliation. From then on he sarcastically referred to the archbishop as Comandante Miguel.

Radical Christians, however, remained unimpressed with the hierarchy. Over the next few years they issued several public criticisms of the bishops, claiming that they were failing in their apostolic responsibilities to the people by aligning with the dominant classes and issuing only timid protests against Somoza.

The prelates fought back. In a January 1977 pastoral letter, they displayed their anti-Somoza credentials by strongly denouncing a "state of terror" in which peasants were forced to flee their homes, the government employed torture, executions, and incarceration without benefit of trial or legal representation, and the church was repressed. But they then turned on the "so-called liberating movements," warning that these led to personal revenge.

This pastoral infuriated the Somocistas—so much so that the director of the national police accused Obando of supporting "communist revolution with his inflammatory pastoral letters." The radical clerics, however, remained unmoved. No sooner had the bishops warned against "so-called liberating movements" when they were challenged by their old nemesis Ernesto Cardenal, who openly announced that he and his Solentiname CEB, as part of their Christian commitment, had decided to join the FSLN. This was followed by the much-publicized formation of the "Group of Twelve"—prominent professionals including Fathers Fernando Cardenal and Miguel D'Escoto, who, after publicly dedicating themselves to the ouster of the dictator, warned that the FSLN must not be excluded from the anti-Somoza movement. Next, Sacred Heart Father Gaspar García Laviana disclosed in an open letter that he had joined the *Frente* as a combatant, vowing to fight "with gun in hand . . . until my last breath."[14] Shortly thereafter he was killed in combat and loudly proclaimed a Christian hero of the revolution by the Sandinistas and their clerical supporters. Not surprisingly, such actions did not sit well with the Nicaraguan Episcopal Conference, which correctly viewed them as an intentional challenge to its episcopal authority and, rightly or wrongly, as a Marxist attempt to co-opt the church.

The assassination of Pedro Joaquín Chamorro on January 10, 1978, shocked the country. Publisher of *La Prensa* and longtime leader in the fight to depose the Somozas, Chamorro was an icon to all who opposed the government, regardless of their class affiliation. Thus, his brutal death, obviously the work of Somoza, convinced large numbers of moderate Nicaraguans that the Sandinistas had been right. The violence of the dictatorship could be terminated only by an armed uprising of the people. Taking advantage of the situation, on August 22, 1978, the Sandinistas, led by the charismatic Eden Pastora, pulled off another brilliant commando raid. This time they seized the National Palace, taking most of the nation's congressional deputies hostage. Again Obando was asked to mediate the crisis, and again the episode ended in a clear Sandinista victory and a Somoza humiliation. Fifty-nine FSLN prisoners, including Tomás Borge, were released, and a $500,000 ransom was paid.

Following Chamorro's murder, Obando and his fellow bishops significantly stepped up their attacks on the government. In February 1978 the archbishop stated that, although he favored nonviolence, some theologians taught that collective armed struggle was permissible in situations of grave injustice if all peaceful means had failed. In August the archdiocesan priests' council issued a document, signed by all members, including Obando, which called for Somoza's resignation and the implementation of democratic elections. In September, together with the Conference of Religious (CONFER), it sent a letter to President Carter, asking him to halt all aid to the Nicaraguan government. Likewise, in August the Bishops' Conference denounced the government, but as in the past it again rejected violence, explaining that "the mission of the church is distorted both by those who would confine it to the sanctuary and by those who take up the gun."[15]

In September 1978 the Sandinistas felt strong enough to call for a final offensive. In the fighting that ensued, large numbers of Christians, especially CEB members, participated. Likewise, many priests and nuns, not only from the radical minority but from the moderate majority as well, assisted the rebel forces in a variety of ways. Surprisingly, the bishops also aided the cause. In May 1979 the Episcopal Conference issued an explanation of the church's just-war theory. Moreover, in a major departure from the past, on June 2 the bishops publicly legitimized armed insurrection against Somoza with the following words:

> We are all hurt and affected by the extremes of revolutionary insurrections, but their moral and legal legitimacy cannot be denied in the case of obvious and prolonged tyranny which seriously violates the fundamental rights of the person and harms the common good of the country.[16]

On July 17, however, Archbishop Obando met in Caracas with members of the Venezuelan Christian Democratic Party, along with Nicaraguan businessmen and political moderates, in a futile attempt to add two more non-Sandinistas to the proposed five-person provisional junta, which was being organized to run Nicaragua after the fall of Somoza. Had they been successful, the FSLN would have been outnumbered in the new government four to three. Their failure, however, assured *Frente* domination of the new executive body. On July 19, 1979, the dictatorship fell and the Sandinistas entered Managua victorious. There can be no doubt that the FSLN was the major player in the defeat of the Somoza regime. But it is also true that Obando and the Episcopal Conference played an important role.

Like virtually everyone in Nicaragua, church leaders participated in the widespread euphoria that followed the fall of Somoza. Bishops and priests presided at masses of thanksgiving attended by thousands throughout the country. But all the celebration could not mask the fact that the archbishop and the Episcopal Conference had a critical decision to make, one that they realized could be crucial in determining the institutional church's future in Nicaraguan society. Consistently anti-Somocista but never pro-Sandinista during the 1970s, the episcopacy now had to decide how to respond to the new Sandinista government. The FSLN was immensely popular, not only with the people but also with a considerable number of clergy and religious, including some moderates who considered themselves anticommunist. Realizing this, the new government wisely courted its Christian supporters, publicly praising them for the role they had played in the revolution. But more significantly, it assured them that Sandinismo and Christianity not only were compatible but would be merged together in the building of a new Nicaragua premised on an option for the poor, a mixed economy, political pluralism, and a nonaligned foreign policy. The Sandinista Directorate also took an important step in winning support from political moderates when it allowed two highly respected members of the private sector, Alfonso Robelo Callejas and Violeta Chamorro, widow of the slain publisher of *La Prensa,* to sit on the newly created five-person Provisional Junta for National Reconstruction.

On the other hand, the bishops feared that the FSLN was subtly attempting to co-opt the church in order to negate a potentially powerful foe, thereby making the creation of another Cuba easier. Some parishes were loosely mixing church and revolutionary symbols, as in the celebration of the Misa Campesina Nicaragüense, in which Jesus was depicted as an anticapitalist peasant revolutionary. "Martyrs of the revolution" were also appearing in murals behind altars in some churches. They included Carlos Fonseca, Augusto César Sandino, and sometimes others, such as Father Gaspar García, and were often intertwined with depictions of Jesus and the saints. FSLN founder and Directorate member Tomás Borge would soon go so far as to popularize the slogan "Sandino yesterday, Sandino today, and Sandino always," an obvious paraphrase of Hebrews 13:8, "Jesus Christ yesterday, today, and always." Later in a speech Borge would even claim that when archeologists opened Sandino's tomb they found it empty, because "Sandino had risen."[17] Soon a story was circulating that Borge, upon confronting the national guardsman who had tortured him in prison, had astonished the terrified Somocista by forgiving and freeing him in imitation of Christ who forgave his tormentors from the cross. Word was also spread that the "deeply religious" comandante had a massive collection of crucifixes that he kept on display in his office.

The *Frente* went further. It appointed a number of radical priests to high office who throughout the previous decade had tormented the hierarchy and questioned its authority. Ernesto Cardenal was made Minister of Culture, Miguel D'Escoto Foreign Minister, Fernando Cardenal director of the literacy campaign and later Minister of Education, and Edgard Parrales Minister of Social Welfare. Within a month of Somoza's fall, the Antonio Val-divieso Center was established in Managua and placed under the codirection of Father Molina. Dodson and Montgomery describe it as a "major vehicle for linking the churches and the Revolution," noting that its goals were "to keep the revolutionary spirit alive among Christians, to help Church lead-ers understand the revolution, and to counteract the pressure of rightist businessmen on Church leaders."[18] The center was soon providing training seminars for CEB leaders and publishing books and pamphlets that com-bined Christianity and Marxist theory. The Jesuit Instituto Histórico Centro-Americano, headed by Father Alvaro Argüello, another longtime critic of the bishops, also touted the Christian-Sandinista theme. In September 1979 it organized a week-long seminar on "Christian Faith and Revolution in Nica-ragua" aimed at bringing churchpeople and FSLN members together to dis-cuss ways the church could better accompany the revolution. Proceedings of the meeting were published in a booklet that depicted on its cover a crucified Christ. Superimposed, as if rising out of the dying Savior, was the image of a guerrilla combatant, arms raised and holding a rifle. Likewise, in the coun-tryside the Jesuit-run Comité Evangélico de Promoción Agraria (CEPA) was conducting peasant leadership seminars in which pro-Sandinista comic books, such as one entitled *Cristo Campesino*, were being used.

All this was highly disturbing to the bishops, who, when they weighed the pluses against the minuses of the new government, found it to be want-ing. Yet the prelates were on the horns of a dilemma. The Sandinistas were extremely popular and had the support of quite a few priests as well as the CEBs. They were selling themselves as pro-Christian and moderate and had already inaugurated impressive projects for the poor. Although the bishops believed rightly or wrongly that this was no more than a Marxist ruse, they realized that if they publicly opposed the new government, they would be seen by the majority of the populace as reactionary Somocistas. The fact that this was more or less what the Nicaraguan episcopacy had been for the past four decades before the Medellín Conference did not help matters. The institutional church's questionable past had come back to haunt it. Indeed, when the Episcopal Conference put forth a letter on July 30, warning against the possible imposition of "something foreign" [meaning Marxist] on Nica-ragua, Ernesto Cardenal immediately called their behavior reactionary, but so did the Conference of Religious. Thus, the bishops realized they had little choice. They decided to give qualified support to the new government and hope for the best. Consequently, on November 17, 1979, the Episcopal Confer-ence issued a pastoral letter, "Christian Commitment for a New Nicaragua," which John Kirk terms "unique in the annals of Church history."[19] After distinguishing between "humanistic socialism" and the "spurious" form, which is antireligious, dictatorial, and repressive, it gave its blessing to the Nicaraguan type, noting that it seemed to be original, creative, and in no way imitative—that is, neither capitalistic, dependent, nor totalitarian. The letter also reemphasized the church's option for the poor and attempted to reach out in friendship to the CEBs, indicating that they had a valuable role to play in the new Nicaragua.

The honeymoon between church and state, however, did not last long. Indeed, it would be no exaggeration to say that it was over almost before it started. Before the end of the year, a confidential FSLN position paper was leaked to the press. In it the author argued that the Sandinistas should attempt to undermine and gradually destroy organized religion. Thus, the *Frente* should co-opt prominent Christian holidays like Christmas and turn them into secular celebrations. Needless to say, the position paper seemed to confirm the bishops' darkest suspicions about the new government. The embarrassed FSLN attempted to defend itself by contending that this was only one member's view and had never received Sandinista approval, but the damage was done.

The Episcopal Conference was also wary of the much-touted literacy campaign that had begun in March 1980. Although over 300 nuns and priests participated in it, the bishops were concerned with the large number of Cuban teachers involved. They had also received complaints that Marxist techniques of indoctrination were being employed. Moreover, in May the Episcopal Conference had sent a communiqué to the priests in political office, indicating that it was time for them to resign and return to their priestly duties. When the priests in question responded that they could not do so in good conscience, the frustrated prelates realized that they were in no position to force the matter, for to do so would cause a confrontation that could turn the masses against them. The priests in government had undermined their authority, and they had no real choice but to back off, at least for the time being. Yet in mid-1980, when Alfonso Robelo and Violetta Chamorro resigned from the junta, charging that the Sandinistas had reduced them to mere figureheads, the bishops realized that the resignations meant that the upper and middle classes had decided to break with the revolutionary government. Now that the bishops had powerful anti-Sandinista allies, they felt less compelled to cooperate with the Sandinista government. Convinced that the FSLN was well on its way in its plans to establish a Cuban-like dictatorship, the episcopacy made ready for open warfare. Although the charge later made by critics of the church—that the bishops had never been comfortable with the revolutionary government—is certainly true, it is also correct to say that the Sandinistas from the beginning made no attempts to meet the bishops halfway on any points of contention. Realizing that it was immensely popular, the *Frente* felt it could ignore the complaints of the episcopacy and through its clerical allies challenge its authority. It would prove to be a foolish supposition.

Prior to the late 1970s, very little attention was paid to Nicaragua or the Somoza regime by the U.S. Catholic press. One article, which appeared in a 1962 issue of the *Sign,* however, deserves attention because of its exceptional analysis. Highly critical, it chided the Somoza family for living in splendor while the masses suffered, U.S. Ambassador Whelan for his cozy relationship with the Nicaraguan dictator, and the Nicaraguan bishops for their refusal to crusade for justice. On the other hand, it lauded "Christian revolutionaries" like Pedro Joaquin Chamorro and Gonzalo Cardenal (brother of Ernesto and Fernando) for their willingness to fight and suffer in order to rebuild Nicaragua in accordance with the principles outlined in the papal social encyclicals.[20] The article, written shortly after the failed attempt by the United States to overthrow Castro at the Bay of Pigs, brought home its point in dramatic fashion: "The Nicaraguan revolutionaries find it difficult to understand how the United States can train troops for an invasion of Cuba but not stand up for democracy in Nicaragua."[21]

This *Sign* article stands alone. More typical are the following three pieces from *Worldmission, Sign,* and *America.* The first, published in 1958, pleaded for missionary priests to combat what it termed the three major dangers in Latin America: secularization, communism, and religious superstition. The author's myopic vision was especially evident when he remarked that the greatest problem facing the clergy on the Nicaraguan Atlantic coast was the widespread practice among the laity of common-law marriage. No mention was made of poverty, the suffering of the masses, or the Somoza regime.[22]

The second article, from 1964, harkened back to the missionary reports from the 1930s through the 1950s in its emphasis on the exotic adventures of a European Catholic family living and working in the midst of "vines, monkeys, [and] magic" in the jungles of Nicaragua. Although the author mentioned malnourished children and widespread illiteracy, it was merely in passing. The piece was basically devoid of any socioeconomic or political commentary.[23]

The third article, a 1959 editorial, differed in that it labeled Somoza a repressive dictator. Nevertheless, in classic Cold War fashion, it was careful to add that if Somoza was toppled from power, communists could replace him.[24]

By the late 1970s, the tone of the U.S. Catholic press had changed dramatically. Most publications reporting on Nicaragua were now unified in their condemnation of the Somoza regime and the support it continued to receive from the Carter administration and the U.S. Congress. Likewise, virtually all called for the United States to pressure Somoza into resigning.

America, with its connections to the Jesuits in Managua and with an associate editor, James Brockman, who had over a decade of Latin American experience, including time spent in Nicaragua, was in an excellent position to offer insightful commentary. Brockman's fluency in Spanish and familiarity with Nicaragua allowed him to move easily from Managua to the smaller cities of Estelí, León, Masaya, and Matagalpa, where most of the fighting and destruction were taking place. There, with the help of his contacts, he was able to interview local priests as well as laypeople from both the elite and lower classes. These, coupled with his discussions with opposition leaders and university personnel in Managua, enabled him to offer accurate observations. As early as mid-1978, for instance, he concluded that the fall of Somoza was no longer just a possibility but a certainty that all but U.S. officials seemed to realize, and that the masses would accept no new government which excluded the FSLN.[25] A visit following the September uprising led him to assert, correctly, that few Nicaraguans were willing to accept a U.S.-brokered peace and that fighting would continue until the people were in a position to determine their own fate.[26]

America's articles and editorial were not only anti-Somoza but clearly pro-Sandinista. An October 1978 commentary pointed out that U.S. military aid to Somoza's National Guard made possible its bombing of five Nicaraguan cities in which thousands of noncombatants were killed. Like other Catholic periodicals, *America* also informed its readers of the powerful Somoza lobby in Congress headed by Representative John Murphy (D-NY), which was in large part responsible for the passage of such aid.[27] Another editorial ridiculed President Carter's suggestion that Somoza resign but that his National Guard and Liberal Party be allowed to continue to take part in the political process. The author equated this scenario to a post–World War II Germany in which the Nazi Party was permitted to exist without Hitler. The writer also questioned the veracity of the U.S. charges that Cuban communists were orchestrating the September uprising, stating that it "flies in the face of the facts" and was supported by not "a scrap of proof."[28]

Following the lead of many but not all of the Jesuits in Nicaragua, *America* welcomed the Sandinista rise to power with unbounded enthusiasm. One editorial suggested that the FSLN had elevated tiny Nicaragua into a symbol of hope for millions of oppressed peoples throughout the world who now believed that they too could replace dictatorship with freedom.[29] *America* praised the Sandinistas for passing a Bill of Rights and taking it seriously, outlawing capital punishment, treating captive Somocistas with decency and respect, and implementing a radical restructuring of the sociopolitical system.[30] The Republican Party's charge that the FSLN was fomenting communist revolution elsewhere in Central America was denounced as a lie,[31] and Carter was urged to cease stalling on the deliverance of a Nicaraguan aid package that Congress had already passed.[32] But the following editorial claim perhaps best illustrates the optimism and euphoria of *America:* "Few revolutions have ever acted so swiftly to heal the wounds of strife and to replace brutality, greed and corruption with humanity, generosity and self-sacrifice."[33]

The fear and suspicion of the Nicaraguan bishops concerning the goals and motives of the Sandinistas and the conduct of the radical clergy certainly were not shared by *America*. Indeed, there was no hint in any *America* article prior to mid-1980 of anything but complete harmony and cooperation between the FSLN, the radical clergy, and the episcopacy. Not long before Archbishop Obando went to Venezuela in a vain attempt to put together a plan for a transitional government in which the FSLN would have only a minor role, *America* was chiding the United States for refusing to include the revolutionary group in negotiations aimed at ending civil strife in Nicaragua. Its author went so far as to offer the following assessment:

> The U. S. distrust of the Sandinistas amounts to a certain distrust of the Nicaraguan people who support them. If the United States is to regain any of its damaged prestige in Nicaragua—and in Latin America, which is watching Nicaragua—it must place more trust in its people.[34]

Following Somoza's downfall, a U. S. Jesuit anthropologist working in Panama defended the Sandinistas against the negative charges of the Somoza congressional lobby, asserting that so far "the FSLN has acted credibly and sensibly" and that "there are remarkably few hints that [it] is doctrinaire."[35] Contrary to the bishops, he interpreted the inclusion of priests in important government posts as proof that the revolutionary government was not antireligious. Finally, he asserted that the easy mix of Sandinismo and progressive Catholicism gave hope to the Nicaraguan people for a better future and also for "a new model for other oppressed peoples of Central America."[36] In another article, a U. S. Jesuit theologian went much further, arguing that Christianity and communism could be compatible, while defending Ernesto Cardenal's assertion that he was a Christian communist.[37]

U. S. congressman and Jesuit Robert Drinan, after taking part in a fact-finding trip to Nicaragua, also waxed eloquent concerning the revolutionary government. He termed it unique in that it was socialist yet widely supported and inspired by Catholic activists. He also noted that its cry for a just economic order had convinced many church leaders that what had happened in Nicaragua represented the first fruits of Medellín and could prove to be a model for the rest of Latin America. Remarking that "America's response [to the revolutionary government] may well have an enormous impact on the future of Christian democracy and social justice in Latin America," he urged U.S. Catholics to lobby Congress for Nicaraguan aid.[38]

Commonweal published nothing on Nicaragua in the 1970s. Its two articles in 1980, however, were highly favorable to the FSLN. The first, by Thomas Quigley, Latin American advisor for the U.S. Bishops' Conference, criticized a Republican congressman, who, he claimed, was so anxious to smear the Sandinistas that he neglected to check the veracity of a letter he had received attacking them. The letter, which was read in a House debate over aid to the Nicaraguan government, proved to be a fraud. Quigley concluded with a reminder to his readers that the U.S. bishops were "pressing very strongly for the aid package."[39]

The other *Commonweal* article was by the editor of the liberal Protestant *Christianity in Crisis*. He expressed strong support for the new revolutionary government, praising it for its land reform and literacy programs, for establishing a mixed economy and pluralistic political system, and for limiting human rights violations to "miraculously few." Remarking that the Nicaraguan bishops had expressed a willingness to work with the new government, he noted that the United States by doing likewise could make amends for its past sins in Nicaragua. By passing a generous aid package, he argued, Congress could entice the new government to move toward democracy. However, a refusal of aid could tragically force the Sandinistas to gravitate toward the communist block.[40]

Prior to the fall of Somoza, *Origins* reprinted two episcopal letters that emphatically expressed the church's opposition to his regime and early support for the revolutionary government. The first, by Archbishop John Quinn of San Francisco, who was writing on behalf of the U.S. Conference of Catholic Bishops (USCC), was to President Carter. Quinn made it clear that he was acting in response to the pleading of the Nicaraguan Bishops' Conference. He called on Carter to "express in the most forceful and unequivocal fashion the utter disgust and horror of our nation for the ruthless terror being visited [by Somoza] upon the people of Nicaragua."[41] The second was a translation of the Nicaraguan bishops' extraordinary November pastoral letter, in which the prelates stated their commitment to the revolutionary process.[42] These two letters were far from insignificant. As the official vehicle of the USCC, *Origins* informed the Catholic faithful of the positions of the hierarchy on public policy. The inclusion of these letters made it clear that at that point in time the institutional church looked favorably on the direction that events in Nicaragua were taking.

Of all Catholic publications in the early 1980s, the *National Catholic Reporter* easily provided the most extensive coverage on Nicaragua. Like *America* and *Commonweal*, its point of view was unabashedly pro-Sandinista. This is apparent from its heavy reliance on interviews with pro-FSLN clergy, especially the Cardenals and Miguel D'Escoto. Seldom does one hear the opinions of anti-Sandinista church voices, and when one does, they are almost always counteracted by FSLN-clerical defenders. As with most other Catholic periodicals, *NCR* reports and opinion pieces gave little if any indication prior to mid-1980 that all was not well between the bishops, the Sandinistas, and pro-FSLN priests.

The vast majority of *NCR* articles on Nicaragua from 1978 through 1980 were by on-site journalist June Carolyn Erlick. Her reports, prior to the Sandinista triumph, accentuated Somoza's unpopularity and brutality, while contending that U. S. policy was premised on inadequate and therefore misdirected information. A September 1978 article, for instance, recounted recent atrocities committed by Somoza's *Guardia,* cleverly interjecting that President Carter had just sent a letter to the dictator praising him for improving his human rights record.[43] When discussing the fighting in Nicaragua, Erlick was careful to employ the term "civil war" rather than "uprising" or "revolt," thereby providing the FSLN with greater legitimacy. She also emphasized the courageous role the bishops were playing in the anti-Somoza camp, highlighting, for example, that the *Guardia* had threatened the bishops of Grenada and León.[44]

Writing in August 1978, Erlick gave the impression that an irresistible groundswell had developed against Somoza: "Conservatives, Marxists, business people, students, teachers, and clergy" had all joined forces.[45] She added that some prominent Nicaraguans had formed a group called "Los Doce," which had publicly resolved to bring down the regime, defying arrest.[46] In an interview with one of the twelve, Miguel D'Escoto, his dubious claims that 85 percent of the Nicaraguan clergy and religious were "fully identified with the [Sandinista] cause" and that five U. S. military experts had been assigned to train the *Guardia* went unchallenged. Moreover, Erlick displayed her affection toward D'Escoto by referring to him as "Father Mike."[47]

As the fighting intensified in June 1979, Erlick depicted Somoza as a vicious killer pathetically attempting to cling to power, even though he had no support. Archbishop Obando had declared that the Sandinista effort met the criteria for a just war, she wrote, and several Latin American countries had severed diplomatic relations with Somoza's government. She likewise quoted the damning words of the Secretary General of the Latin American Conference of Religious: "[Somoza] is annihilating his entire people indiscriminately. It is a crime to be young in Nicaragua."[48]

In a piece composed a month after the dictator's downfall, Erlick interviewed Sandinista officials, who declared that the new government was grounded in nationalism, democracy, Christianity, and social justice. No mention was made of Marxism.[49] In a later report she linked the revolutionary process to the Medellín Conference and its option for the poor, citing a Maryknoll priest and nun, both of whom waxed eloquent about "the integration of faith and revolution."[50]

The earliest indication in the *National Catholic Reporter* that church authorities were not in full accord with FSLN policy can be found in a February 1980 article by Bill Kenkelen, which noted Archbishop Obando's concern that Cuban teachers in the Sandinista literacy program "have been ridiculing the religious beliefs of the people."[51] But in the same issue, Erlick interviewed the director of the literacy program, Fernando Cardenal, who belittled Obando's fear: "[The Cubans] have come to help, not to impose value systems."[52] In another report, Erlick put a positive "spin" on the participation of the Cuban teachers. She contended that although some priests and nuns were initially concerned about what they assumed to be professed atheists teaching their parishioners, their worries were put to rest when a group of them showed up for mass. Erlick next quoted an unnamed nun: "They're a good group of people, even if they don't believe in God. . . . Maybe we'll even convert a few."[53] Thus, Obando's negative was cleverly reversed into a positive.

A piece by British journalist Peter Hebblethwaite on Cardenal's arrival at the Vatican to defend his refusal to step down from political office followed the same pattern. On the one hand, Hebblethwaite was one of the first Catholic reporters to point out that the papacy was no friend of the new Nicaraguan government. Indeed, he quoted John Paul II on Sandinismo: "[A]n atheistic ideology cannot serve as an instrument for the promotion of social justice, since it deprives man of his freedoms, of spiritual inspiration."[54] Yet the pope's words were followed by a statement from the Peruvian father of liberation theology, Gustavo Gutiérrez, who countered that the Nicaraguan revolution was the first revolution in history to contain serious Christian participation. Consequently, it provided Latin America with another model for radical change, one that was more significant than the flawed Cuban model and the failed Chilean model.[55] Thus, the pope's atheistic label was countered by Gutiérrez's identification of Sandinismo with Christianity.

It was not until May 16, 1980—almost a year after the Sandinista takeover—that Erlick gave more than a passing indication that serious problems existed between the church and the revolutionary government. In a piece on the controversy over priests in government, she allowed two of the clerics in question to express their views on the matter. She also cited the Maryknoll and Jesuit superiors for Central America, who were sympathetic to these priests. Erlick took care, however, to balance her article by quoting two churchmen on the other side of the issue. Boaventura Kloppenburg, director of the theological seminary of the Latin American Episcopal Conference (CELAM), remarked that "these political priests may be great politicians, but they're not great priests." In a more thoughtful tone, a Spanish cleric added: "I wonder how the clergy can serve on a Sandinista-dominated state council, and serve its parishioners who don't happen to be Sandinistas. . . . I don't think the church should get involved in politics at all."[56] Interestingly, Erlick shied away from stating the bishops' position on the matter. Not until December 1980 did she clearly state that serious differences existed between the bishops and the state, noting that the Episcopal Conference had become "more openly critical of the revolution" by "conservatively" accusing the government of using religion for its own purpose and fomenting class hatred.[57] But even here she took pains to label the Vatican chargé d'affaires in Nicaragua as the key player in the conference's more critical stance. In other words, she indirectly (and incorrectly) implied that Rome was the real adversary of the Sandinistas and that the Nicaraguan bishops' new tone resulted from Vatican pressure.

Of the periodicals studied thus far, *Our Sunday Visitor* was the only one that displayed early reservations about the FSLN. It was alone in reporting on the July 1979 pastoral letter in which the bishops expressed concern over Sandinista ideology and direction. In that piece, the secretary of the U. S. Capuchin mission office was cited bluntly referring to the new government as Marxist.[58] In May 1980 it noted John Paul II's uneasiness with the FSLN's "atheistic ideology."[59] More critical, however, was an article, also from a May issue, by a U. S. priest who had recently worked in Nicaragua. He concluded that Father D'Escoto displayed "Marxist tendencies" and that Nicaragua would probably become a Marxist state.[60]

An August interview with a regional director of the Jesuit Volunteer Corps offered a more positive slant. He argued that the press had grossly distorted the reality of Nicaragua to the detriment of the new government.[61] A December piece by a staff reporter, however, returned to the earlier negative tone. It discussed the widening split between the Nicaraguan bishops and the priests in government. In so doing, it cited Maryknoll Father Albert

Nevins, an *OSV* columnist and a highly respected authority on Catholic missions, who declared that the bishops were on the mark in labeling the new government communist. He further contended that the priests holding government positions did so only to hide the government's Marxism.[62]

Thus, prior to 1981, even though the Sandinistas espoused a form of Marxism and the Nicaraguan bishops had serious differences with the revolutionary government, the U. S. Catholic press was almost unanimous in its enthusiastic support for the FSLN, which it saw as a model for other Latin American nations. Of the publications discussed so far, only *Our Sunday Visitor* expressed reservations concerning the ideology and direction of the Sandinistas. But by early 1981, as will be shown in the next chapter, following *OSV* editor Father Vincent Giese's trip to Central America, even this periodical began to wax eloquent concerning the Sandinista revolution. Moreover, no Catholic periodical seemed to be overly concerned with the conflict between the bishops and the radical clergy.

six

Nicaragua in the 1980s

After Violeta Chamorro resigned from her government post in April 1980, *La Prensa*, the Chamorro family newspaper, began a relentless onslaught against the Sandinistas. Included were charges that they were atheistic and hostile to religion. Realizing that such accusations could cause them problems, the Sandinistas decided to issue an official clarification of their position on religion. Their statement, which appeared on October 7, 1980, tactfully began by praising people of faith, including Archbishop Obando, for their contribution to the revolutionary process. Next came a commitment to religious freedom and an assurance that religious belief would be no impediment to party membership.

Scholars who are sympathetic to the revolutionary government point out that by issuing such a statement, the FSLN was demonstrating its moderation by rejecting the classical Marxist position that religion is the opiate of the masses. Moreover, by welcoming religious people into the party, it was repeating its belief that Christianity and revolution were compatible. Thus, these scholars reason that, through its clarification on religion, the *Frente* was actually making a good-faith attempt to mollify the hierarchy, an attempt that the bishops chose to reject.

Although there may be some truth to this argument, it misses the point. On the basis of their interpretation of past Sandinista actions, the bishops saw the *Frente*'s welcoming invitation to Christians not as a gesture of goodwill and moderation, but as another attempt to undermine episcopal authority and co-opt the church.

In other words, the bishops viewed it as a hostile challenge rather than as a goodwill attempt to mitigate tensions between church and state. Consequently, the Episcopal Conference on October 17 issued a harshly worded letter accusing the FSLN of using Christian revolutionaries and radical priests to create division within the church, adding that the church would "never surrender to any enslaving or idolatrous system aimed at promoting atheism." Nicaragua needs liberation, they concluded, "not a new Pharaoh."[1]

Ronald Reagan's election as U.S. president in November 1980 further complicated an already volatile situation. Throughout his campaign, Reagan chided President Carter for being too conciliatory toward the Sandinistas. Linking the FSLN in typical Cold War fashion to Moscow-directed international communism and postulating domino theory arguments, the new Reagan team made the eradication of the Sandinista government a top priority on its agenda. Shortly after taking office, it suspended Nicaraguan aid previously passed by Congress and began secretly funneling arms and money to Guardia-led counterrevolutionary forces known as contras. Such aid soon enabled the contras to launch raids on rural Nicaraguan villages from bases in Honduras. It was a textbook case of the application of low-intensity warfare, which was soon wreaking havoc on the Nicaraguan economy, diverting funds from Sandinista social programs, and taking the lives of hundreds of innocent civilians. The CIA bombing of Nicaraguan oil storage tanks and the mining of harbors, together with joint U.S.-Honduran military exercises on the Nicaraguan border, brought additional concerns to an already overburdened Sandinista government. No doubt this extra pressure caused the Sandinista leadership to be less tolerant of internal criticism, including that of the bishops. Likewise, increased U.S. hostility toward the FSLN probably influenced the Nicaraguan bishops in their decision to act more overtly in their own negative critique of Sandinista actions. Journalist Penny Lernoux summarized the situation well when she commented: "Had the contra war not occurred, tensions between the government and the traditional church would still have existed, but they might have been dealt with in a different manner. The war brought out the worst in both sides."[2]

Certainly the Reagan administration's strategy included fomenting greater hostility between the Catholic hierarchy and the Sandinistas. Nevertheless, as this chapter will show, the *Frente* played right into Reagan's hands, thereby proving to be its own worst enemy.

Troubles between church and state greatly escalated between 1981 and 1983, and, as Lernoux noted, neither side always acted honorably. Obando's decision to visit the site of a supposedly miraculous sweating statue of the Virgin Mary in late 1981 illustrates the intemperance of church leaders during this time. *La Prensa* had claimed that the statue was a sign of divine disapproval of Sandinista rule, and the archbishop's visit lent not only credence to an obviously spurious miracle but also church approval of ethically questionable journalistic tactics.

For its part, the FSLN's claim that it respected freedom of religion proved hollow when it canceled the weekly televised mass of Obando. The broadcast of the archbishop's Sunday mass on the state network was a Nicaraguan tradition predating the tenure of Obando. The government, however, informed the archdiocese that henceforth the televised mass would be rotated among several clergymen, of whom Obando would be one. Realizing that the other clergy would be pro-Sandinista priests, Obando refused to accept this change. Consequently, his televised mass was canceled by the government.

Church-state relations were further strained over Sandinista-Miskito conflict on the Atlantic Coast. The Miskito Indians had little in common with other Nicaraguans. They had lived in virtual isolation for centuries and were Caribbean rather than Spanish in culture. Most were Moravian Protestants, and those who were Catholic were already involved in reform programs set up in the 1970s by their U. S. Capuchin clergy. Thus, when the Sandinistas attempted to implement their reform projects on the Atlantic Coast, they found little enthusiasm or cooperation. Having no understanding of the Indians' distinctive way of life, Sandinista soldiers overreacted and arrested several Miskito leaders, charging them with subversive activities. Four Miskitos were killed in an altercation in the town of Prinzapolka. After those who were incarcerated had been released, one of them, Steadman Fagoth, led a group of his angry followers across the Coco River, where they joined with contra forces and soon began receiving arms and funds from the CIA. By January 1982, contra cross-border attacks had escalated and about sixty people had been killed. Unable to search out and destroy the Miskito counterrevolutionaries, Sandinista soldiers arrested civilians whom they perceived to be supporters of the combatants. Many were tortured and some executed. To prevent the contras from gaining new recruits and from using the indigenous villages as bases for their operations, the Sandinista government decided to relocate the Miskitos in camps outside the area of conflict. Those who refused to cooperate in the removal process were treated harshly and sometimes violently. Two priests and three nuns who worked with the Miskitos were accused of collaborating with the United States and the contras in a so-called "Red Christmas" operation to form an autonomous Miskito state. Consequently, they were expelled from the country. Sandinista soldiers also destroyed villages that the Miskitos had been forced to evacuate.

The Reagan administration, which had been secretly funding contra operations in the area, now took advantage of the situation it had helped create. As the U.S. Congress made ready to vote on a proposal for $19 million in contra aid, Reagan officials attempted to justify the package by accusing the Sandinistas of religious persecution and genocide against the Miskitos. Their case was bolstered greatly when the Nicaraguan bishops issued a pastoral letter condemning the revolutionary government for destroying the Miskitos' housing and animals and for initiating "forced marches . . . without sufficient consideration for the weak, elderly, women, and children," thereby causing the death of some Indians.

Needless to say, the bishops' statement played a major role in Congress's decision to approve contra aid. Infuriated, the Sandinistas, questioning the motive and timing of the bishop' letter, accused the episcopacy of being in league with the Reagan administration. They further charged that the bishops' critique was based on inaccurate, secondhand information; had the prelates accepted the government's invitation to visit the relocation camps, they would have found that no one had died in the process of removal and that the elderly, children, and pregnant women had all been transported by helicopter, not by forced march. Pro-FSLN clergy rallied around the government. Jesuits, Dominicans, and other priests and religious, as well as CEB leaders, denounced the bishops for neglecting to address the real reason for relocation, namely, contra attacks from Honduras. They also asked why the bishops criticized the government's Miskito policy while speaking not a word concerning the numerous murders, kidnappings, and other atrocities perpetrated by the contras against civilians.

The bishops did not respond to such questions. They did, however, begin a process of removing pro-Sandinista clergy and religious from their parishes. By late 1982, fourteen priests and twenty-two nuns had been so removed. This, in turn, led to protests and church occupations by CEB members. In one such incident, Managua Auxiliary Bishop Bosco Vivas attempted to enter a church that had been so occupied in order to remove the Blessed Sacrament. A scuffle ensued and he was roughed up. The incident received extensive coverage in *La Prensa,* and Obando excommunicated the parishioners involved. He then placed the parish under interdict, a highly unusual punishment whereby parishioners were cut off from mass and reception of the sacraments.

Pope John Paul II, who previously had refrained from openly involving himself in the controversy, now decided to send a strongly worded letter in support of the bishops. His primary target was not the government but prorevolutionary Catholics. Stating that "the most insidious dangers and the most deadly attacks [on the Nicaraguan church] are not those that come from without . . . but rather those that come from within," the pope castigated the so-called "popular church."[3] It was creating division, he charged, and attempting to set itself up as a parallel magisterium in opposition to the institutional church. He concluded by demanding that all Nicaraguan Catholics obey and support their bishops.

Fearing the effects of this popular pope's message on the masses, the government forbade publication of the letter. This was a futile move, for the Vatican then released it. Thus, the media was made aware not only of the contents of the pope's message but also of the Sandinista prohibition. The result was a public relations disaster for the government. Realizing it had made a mistake, it reversed itself and allowed publication, but the damage was already done.

On August 12, 1982, the day after its reversal, the Sandinistas showed themselves to be even more heavy-handed when the state-owned television network and the two progovernment newspapers showed photos of Father Bismarck Carballo, director of Radio Católica, running naked from a house. The Sandinistas claimed that the priest, after being caught in bed with his lover, had been forced to flee for his life by her jealous husband. By coincidence, cameramen just happened to be in the area covering a nearby demonstration and were therefore able to catch him on film. Carballo's version of the event was, of course, different. He told reporters that he had been lunching with a female parishioner at her home when an armed man entered the house, ordered him to undress, beat him, and then forced him to run naked from the house. In other words, he had been set up by the Sandinistas. As Phillip Berryman noted: "The official [Sandinista] version stretched credulity; at the very least, Carballo seems to have been entrapped, perhaps seduced."[4]

At any rate, large numbers of Nicaraguan people were outraged at what they considered the sacrilegious conduct of the Sandinistas. Yet when students from five Catholic high schools staged protests in support of Carballo, they were confronted by members of the Sandinista Youth Organization. Fights broke out and two student protesters were killed. The situation had clearly gotten out of hand.

Tensions cooled, however, as both sides turned their energies to preparing for the upcoming March 1983 visit of Pope John Paul II to Nicaragua. Evidently the Sandinistas naively believed that they could convince the pontiff to condemn contra atrocities and U. S. interference in Nicaragua. John

Paul, however, was concerned with ending division within the Nicaraguan church. In the end, the papal visit proved to be the *Frente*'s most serious public relations disaster.

Nicaraguan president Daniel Ortega set the negative tone when he welcomed the pope at the airport with a long, inappropriate harangue on U.S. imperialism. Next, Father Ernesto Cardenal, one of the four priests who refused to step down from public office, genuflected before the pope to kiss his ring. Soon cameramen were photographing the pontiff shaking his finger in the face of Cardenal while scolding him. Later, in his sermon, as he celebrated mass in the Plaza of the Revolution, the pontiff criticized the popular church and demanded that Nicaraguan Catholics unite under the authority of their bishops. This caused frustrated FSLN supporters to interrupt him with revolutionary slogans. Three times the pope shouted "*Silencio!*" but to no avail. The chants continued, and now some Sandinista officials joined in. The disruption persisted throughout the mass. Never before had the globe-trotting pope been treated in such a disrespectful manner. The next day the episode merited front-page coverage throughout the world. It was also the topic of numerous, mostly negative, editorials. Sandinistas tried to excuse the incident, arguing that it was an unfortunate, spontaneous cry of a frustrated people, angered because the pope had refused to condemn contra atrocities. But the damage was done. The papal mass was a disaster for the Sandinistas, and their image would never fully recover from it. Large numbers of Catholic clergy and laity throughout the world who had not previously been hostile to the Sandinistas now turned against them. More importantly, the Reagan administration was able to use the incident to pressure its opponents in Congress to authorize more aid to the contras.

Taking advantage of the new sympathy for their cause resulting from the papal mass, the Nicaraguan bishops and their clerical supporters became more aggressive in their attacks on the government. The Sandinistas responded in kind. In June 1984 the government accused Father Amado Peña of smuggling guns for the contras. Two videos were produced as proof. In one, Peña could be heard speaking in rather vulgar language of having people killed in order to create panic. In the other, he was filmed delivering a suitcase filled with explosives, which, according to the government, were meant for the contras. Peña claimed that he had been framed, and the bishops supported him. A few days later a Sandinista mob attacked parishioners at Peña's church. Ten priests who had taken part in a protest march in support of the accused cleric were expelled from the country.

The church fought back. In late 1984, Fernando Cardenal was expelled from the Jesuit order for refusing to step down as Minister of Education. In February 1985, after Maryknoll refused to expel D'Escoto, the Vatican suspended him from the priesthood, along with Ernesto Cardenal and Edgard Parrales. Two months later, John Paul II made Obando the first cardinal in Nicaraguan history, thereby giving him more prestige for his leadership role in the anti-Sandinista crusade. Consequently, he became even more outspoken in his criticism of the Sandinistas, going so far as to meet with and say mass for contra leaders in Miami and to call on Nicaraguans to disobey the military draft.

Hostilities reached their high point in 1986. With a crucial vote on contra aid set for the U. S. Congress in June, Father Carballo embarked on a speaking tour of Europe and the United States in which he accused the Sandinistas of massive religious persecution. In March, Bishop Pablo Vega appeared, along with three major contra leaders, on a panel organized by the conservative Heritage Foundation in Washington, D. C., and falsely claimed that the Sandinistas had murdered three priests. Finally, in April in a column in the *Washington Post,* Cardinal Obando wrote that the Nicaraguan bishops would not oppose U. S. aid to the contras.

Such conduct obviously played a role in Congress's decision to grant $100 million to the Nicaraguan counterrevolutionary forces. Thus, the Sandinistas responded to the vote by informing Carballo that he could not return to Nicaragua and by expelling Vega from the country. But now the Vatican, growing uneasy with the Nicaraguan imbroglio, decided to quietly intervene. It sent a new papal nuncio to Managua with a message to the bishops that it was time to replace combative behavior with dialogue. The government agreed, and a church-state commission was established to look for ways to resolve differences. This, coupled with the exposé of the Iran-contra scandal, the end of the Reagan presidency, and the creation of the Arias Central American peace plan, put church-state conflicts on the back burner. Little progress, however, was made toward resolving the differences between the bishops and the government.

Beginning in 1981, with hostilities between the FSLN and the hierarchy now out in the open and daily becoming more bitter, the U. S. Catholic press faced a much more difficult task in its coverage of Nicaragua than it had with Guatemala and El Salvador, where the situation was more black and white. Nevertheless, throughout the 1980s, publications such as the *National Catholic Reporter, America, Commonweal, Our Sunday Visitor,* and the *Catholic Worker* held firm to their primary focus, that is, to demonstrate their belief that U.S. policy toward Nicaragua was illegal and immoral and therefore needed to be changed.[5] Thus, they constantly pointed out, for instance, that the U.S. Conference of Catholic Bishops (USCC), as well as Catholic clergy and religious, opposed contra aid and U.S. intervention in the region.[6]

They also remained, at least until about 1985, mostly unwavering in their support for the revolutionary government, often making excuses for its questionable behavior. For this reason, they never ceased to publicize the always sanguine conclusions concerning the revolution declared by U.S. Christian-based fact-finding groups returning from Nicaragua, even when these groups had little expertise concerning Central America.[7] This is not to say, however, that they were blind to the excesses of the Sandinistas. Indeed, one also finds in these publications a considerable amount of criticism of the FSLN,[8] but there is far more praise.

During this decade, the above publications showed little empathy for the Nicaraguan bishops' struggle to maintain the traditional hierarchical power structure of the church, a structure that seemed too undemocratic and deferential for their North American taste.[9] Thus, although the Vatican was deeply troubled over the radical clergy's and laity's lack of respect toward the bishops, most U.S. Catholic publications were willing to excuse all but the worst excesses. The Catholic popular press, for instance, with a few exceptions, said little concerning the humiliation of Father Carballo. It likewise expressed much less outrage at the Sandinistas' rude behavior at the papal mass than one might have expected. It was for the most part sympathetic to the priests in political office who had refused to step down when ordered by the bishops. It felt that Bishop Vega had caused his own expulsion by his excessive behavior. But perhaps most significant, whereas the Reagan administration, the Vatican, the Nicaraguan hierarchy, and La Prensa were especially disturbed by the Marxism of the FSLN, the above-mentioned Catholic periodicals had little problem with this at least up to 1985 and to some degree even thereafter. To them, Sandinista ideology seemed to be a mixture of Marxism, nationalism, and Medellín-based Catholicism. It had little in common with Russian communism. The new revolutionary government had implemented an impressive array of reforms which were benefiting the poor, something that no previous Nicaraguan government had attempted to do. Contrary to what the Nicaraguan bishops and the pope said, these Catholic publications did not believe that the FSLN was really persecuting or attempting to co-opt the church. Most conceded that the Sandinistas had made "mistakes" and at times displayed despicable conduct, but considered them better for Nicaragua than any of the alternatives available at the time. Thus, until 1985 most of the U.S. Catholic popular press sympathized with the Sandinistas, and several periodicals continued for the most part to do so throughout the decade. Indeed, much had changed in its mode of analysis since the Cold War years of the 1950s.

The extensive reporting on Nicaragua in *Our Sunday Visitor* after the early 1981 visit of its chief editor, Father Vincent Giese, illustrates the above points. As stated in an earlier chapter, Giese lauded the progressive element of the Central American church, including that of Nicaragua, going so far as to comment that the U. S. church could take a lesson from it.[10] On the Miskito controversy, he stated:

> The Sandinistas made a lot of mistakes in the beginning that embittered the Indians. . . . [But] politically . . . the Miskitos have not always been on the side of the angels in their dealings with the new revolutionary government. Mistakes and mistrust on both sides have contributed to the polarization.[11]

Giese accepted without question the government's claim that its decision for removal stemmed from the so-called Red Christmas plot, in which some Miskitos, Moravian pastors, and Catholic priests supposedly collaborated with the United States in a plan to create a separatist contra state in northeastern Nicaragua. He dismissed Miskito leader Steadman Fagoth as "a shadowy figure in collusion with counterrevolutionaries in Honduras and the United States."[12] He accused the bishops of making false statements in their letter on the removal, statements which he said were taken directly from U. S. State Department reports and had since been refuted by independent human rights observers.[13] He claimed, for instance, that children, the elderly, and pregnant women, contrary to the bishops' account, were not force-marched to relocation sites but were taken by plane.[14]

Giese contended that human rights observers, U. S. congressmen, religious leaders, and journalists who had visited the resettlement villages agreed that the Indians were well treated there.[15] An interview by *OSV* reporter Jim Castelli supported his claim. In it, a Capuchin priest and six Indians from the new villages stated not only that conditions were good but that the Sandinistas provided excellent education, agricultural training, and health care for residents.[16] Giese contrasted this positive picture with the Miskito refugee camp in Honduras that he had personally visited, dubbing the latter "a God-forsaken mud hole" where the Indians were forced to live in squalor.[17]

In other reports Giese lauded the Sandinistas' health and literacy programs, their humanitarian treatment of prisoners, and their attempts to craft a nonaligned foreign policy, a mixed economy, and political pluralism.

While he admitted that there was some press censorship, he excused it on the grounds that the anti-FSLN newspapers were "careless with the truth."[18]

Giese maintained that the government's problems with church authorities resulted from a lack of dialogue, which he blamed solely on the bishops. He disagreed with the hierarchy's contention that there were two parallel churches: there was only one, but a "pluralism of Christologies and ecclesiologies." He admitted that the government was building a large military, but he insisted that it was not for war against its neighbors but only for self-defense.[19]

In November 1982, Giese was part of a U.S. team invited by the Nicaraguan Conference of Religious (CONFER) to investigate charges, made by the U.S. government and the Nicaraguan bishops, that the Sandinistas were persecuting religion. The team's report, which was summarized in *Our Sunday Visitor,* fully exonerated the FSLN. It concluded that although both church and state had at times acted imprudently, "we found no instances of imprisonment, torture, or killing of people by the government." There was also no interference with religious education nor with worship by Catholics or Protestants. The charge that CEBs were more political than religious was declared unfounded. Likewise, the team was unwilling to affirm the negative assertions concerning the "popular church" found in John Paul II's pastoral letter to the Nicaraguan hierarchy. What it did conclude, however, was that contra attacks and the danger of a U.S.-sponsored invasion from Honduras were Nicaragua's most serious problems.[20]

In a longer article, Giese repeated the above conclusions in more detail. But he also accused the bishops of aligning themselves with conservative business organizations and upper- and middle-class charismatic Catholics in Managua.[21]

A similar apologetic tone can be found in the text of a photo essay written by Giese following the tumultuous papal visit. The piece contained no criticism of Sandinista conduct. Instead, Giese attempted to excuse the rude behavior at the papal mass by attributing it to the trauma resulting from a state funeral the day before for seventeen young soldiers ambushed by the contras.[22]

Thus, *OSV* articles by Giese totally supported the positions taken by the FSLN and the pro-Sandinista clergy. Charges by the U.S. government, the Nicaraguan bishops, and even the pope were declared to have little or no validity. Even the problems resulting from the pope's mass were blamed on the contras rather than the Sandinistas. Indeed, the FSLN could not have had a better apologia had they written it themselves.

Yet surprisingly, several *OSV* articles compiled from wire services presented a very different picture of the Sandinistas. One described the pope's suspicions and fears concerning the popular church, priests in government, and the FSLN, without any rebuttal from pro-Sandinista defenders.[23]

A second, on the Carballo incident, gave only the priest's version, adding that it was corroborated by Archbishop Obando. Sandinista police were depicted as responsible for the violence following pro-Carballo demonstrations, while the archbishop's version of the beating of Bishop Bosco Vivas was also presented without FSLN rebuttal.[24] In another piece, Archbishop John Roach, president of the USCC, was cited as soundly criticizing the Sandinistas. References were made to media censorship, Sandinista interference with the church's role in education, and Sandinista attacks on bishops and other church personnel.[25] In these wire service reports, several prominent anti-Sandinistas were cited, but no defenders of the FSLN.

The commentaries and articles found in *Commonweal* at this time were not unlike those written by Giese in *Our Sunday Visitor*. They depicted the Reagan administration's Nicaraguan policy as totally immoral and showed little tolerance for the views of the Nicaraguan bishops. One editorial charged the State Department with producing position papers on the Miskito situation, press censorship, and the Catholic church that were "highly misleading if not plainly false."[26] It further accused the United States of attempting to bait the Sandinistas into crossing into Honduras so that American soldiers would have an excuse to invade Nicaragua.[27] A second editorial blamed Washington for using the Miskitos as sacrificial pawns in its Cold War strategy.[28]

While *Commonweal* did concede that the Sandinistas had been harsh in their dealings with the Miskitos, it asked sarcastically why Washington was concerned with the well-being of only these indigenous peoples; why did the United States not also speak out on the mistreatment of Guatemalan, Colombian, Brazilian, Chilean, and Peruvian Indians?[29]

A Thomas Quigley article described a White House pamphlet, "What Central American Bishops Say About Central America," as intentionally misleading and dishonest, full of misquotes, quotes out of context, mistranslations, and other erroneous information.[30]

A piece by Catholic socialist John Cort, following a fact-finding trip to Nicaragua, gave short shrift to the bishops. Cort contrasted the filled churches of prorevolutionary priests with the near-empty churches of pastors in sympathy with the hierarchy. He spoke disapprovingly of Obando for centering the archdiocesan chancery in an upper-class suburb. He wrote that when he arrived there at one o'clock, hoping to interview the arch-bishop, the building was closed and the gate locked. He then quipped that he could not help thinking: "Your Eminence, you'll never beat the Sandi-nistas with those working hours, or in a place this remote from the poor sheep of your flock."[31] He accused Obando of lobbying for contra aid and of shamelessly saying mass in Miami for contra leaders upon his return with a cardinal's red hat from Rome. He condemned the bishops' pastoral that called for resistance to military conscription, as well as Vega's trip to Wash-ington on behalf of contra aid. He asked how the United States would have responded during World War II if there had been pro-Nazi American bish-ops subverting the policies of the U.S. government. Indeed, he added, such actions "in any other country would be considered treasonous."[32] Cort, how-ever, was not totally uncritical of the Sandinistas. He admitted that some of their responses to the bishops had been extreme. He also pointed out that al-though they made much of the Christian elements of their revolutionary process, only one of the nine comandantes was a practicing Christian.

A similar line of argument was followed by the *Catholic Worker,* which contended that U.S. official statements on Nicaragua presented "a biased and distorted view of the situation." Far from being a totalitarian nation in league with Cuba, Nicaragua was a country working hard to meet the needs of its poor. After lauding its reform programs, the *Catholic Worker* defended government censorship of *La Prensa,* contending that irresponsible reports, such as false claims of food shortages meant to cause panic, made such short-term closings necessary.[33]

America's perspective on Nicaragua was succinctly encapsulated in a 1983 editorial in which it declared that "the current policy of the United States towards Nicaragua is simply indefensible, either on political or moral grounds."[34] An article by Arthur McGovern, a Jesuit philosophy professor and authority on liberation theology, took this a step further. McGovern noted that if Nicaragua did become another Cuba, it would in part be because the bellicose policies of the Reagan administration gave it little choice but to move toward the Soviet camp for survival.[35] Another piece by a different au-thor employed similar logic: Reagan's actions to destabilize Nicaragua only forced the Sandinistas to lessen their commitment to democratic freedoms, pluralism, and a mixed economy. Moreover, they gave the *Frente* little alterna-tive but to increase the size of its army and go to the Soviet bloc for arms.[36]

James Brockman took a different approach in arriving at a similar con-demnation of Reagan policy. He provided *America* readers with a grim pic-ture of how U.S. tax dollars were being spent in Nicaragua. Following his early 1985 visit to the small town of Ocotal on the Honduran border, the Jesuit described the rubble that was still visible following a June 1984 contra mortar attack. He told of people who were taken off and executed and of two thirteen-year-old boys who were kidnapped and brought to Honduras by the counterrevolutionary forces in order to force them to become contra soldiers. He described the infamous CIA sabotage manual, which the contras accidentally left behind and which provided undeniable proof of U.S. complicity in contra atrocities.[37]

Washington journalist Margaret Wilde defended the Sandinistas' Miskito policy against the negative claims of the Reagan administration and the Nicaraguan bishops.[38] In separate articles, both McGovern and Stephen De Mott, the associate editor of *Maryknoll* magazine, attempted to excuse the censorship of *La Prensa* on the grounds that the newspaper intentionally printed false information with the intent of damaging the revolutionary government. McGovern pointed out that, when in Nicaragua, his fact-finding group "gave a carefully worded statement to *La Prensa* only to find a fabricated and very misleading quote" attributed to them the next day.[39] De Mott described *La Prensa*'s irresponsible coverage of the sweating statue of the Virgin Mary. To his journalistic credit, however, he noted that the two pro-Sandinista newspapers, *Barricada* and *El Nuevo Diario*, were also far from responsible in their reporting.[40] A piece by Gary MacEoin, a longtime observer of Latin American religion, attempted to depict Obando and the Episcopal Conference as hostile to the Medellín-based church and as part of a long, continuous line of reactionary Nicaraguan bishops.[41]

But *America* was no shill for the Sandinistas. Humberto Belli, a Nicaraguan sociologist and contra sympathizer, was allowed space to defend the prelates from the charges of MacEoin.[42] A 1981 *America* editorial, after heaping praise on Sandinista programs, criticized the *Frente* for arresting several Nicaraguan businessmen who had criticized the government, for refusing to set a date for elections, and for censoring *La Prensa*. It concluded with the following warning:

> The Sandinista Front has made a serious mistake by not respecting the fundamental rights of free speech, free press and the right to form a political opposition.
>
> Such actions make it impossible for their friends to defend them in the United States and elsewhere. . . . Nicaragua should listen to its friends before it is too late.[43]

Critical *America* commentaries, however, frequently contained some form of qualification. A January 1982 editorial expressed concern over the large buildup of the Sandinista army, as well as over Cuban and Soviet advisors in the country, Soviet military aid, and the training of Nicaraguan fighter pilots in Bulgaria. It noted, however, that if the Reagan administration would shut down its "terrorist" training camps in Florida and renounce the use of military force against the Sandinistas, the *Frente* would have no excuse to justify the above questionable policies.[44]

A November 1983 commentary piece chided the Sandinistas "for not respecting human rights" and for failing to live up to their promise of implementing democratic procedures. It pointed out, however, that "they are not notably worse than many other Latin American dictatorships," and added that the "Reagan administration's war on Nicaragua is becoming more and more indefensible on both moral and political grounds."[45] A July 1984 editorial called the revolutionary government's expulsion of ten foreign priests who had participated in an anti-Sandinista demonstration another example of the FSLN's failure to respect freedom and democracy and to realize that such actions were counterproductive. It then noted, however, that, unlike El Salvador, Nicaragua at least did not have death squads hunting down and murdering opponents of the government.[46] Finally, a November 1984 commentary dubbed the recent Nicaraguan elections "so flawed as to be meaningless." But it went on to warn that Reagan's anti-Sandinista policies, far from preventing the creation of another Cuba, would more likely help bring about exactly what they were meant to prevent.[47]

The *National Catholic Reporter*'s coverage of Nicaragua throughout the 1980s was the most detailed of all Catholic publications and also the most tenacious in its condemnation of U.S. policy and its support for the Sandinistas. A 1982 editorial declared that the United States' "outrageous and immoral" interference in Nicaraguan affairs made its protests of Soviet intervention in Poland less credible.[48] A 1985 article pointed out that the recently imposed U.S. embargo on Nicaragua was counterproductive in that it would undoubtedly force the Sandinistas to move closer to the Soviets to survive.[49] Another piece asked why a contra land mine explosion that had killed thirty-two civilians received prominent coverage only in the *Washington Post*. It then charged the U.S. media with running only stories involving abuses by the Sandinistas.[50]

Among Catholic papers, the *NCR* was alone in revealing the embarrassing fact that the U.S. government's supposedly bipartisan National Endowment for Democracy funneled $100,000 to *La Prensa*.[51] It showed, point by point, how Bishop Pablo Vega collaborated with the contras and spoke before Congress in behalf of contra aid. It revealed that while in Washington he had publicly accused the Sandinistas of murdering three priests, even though this was untrue.[52] This was a significant exposé, since the revolutionary government had just expelled Vega from the country and since the Reagan administration and Cardinal Obando were claiming that the expulsion proved the FSLN was persecuting the church. The NCR likewise contended that although Obando complained about priests and nuns who had been deported by the Sandinistas, in reality twice as many clergy and religious had been expelled by the cardinal because they supported the revolution.[53]

The NCR was quick to publicize the activities of all U. S. grassroots Christian organizations that worked to counteract the Reagan administration's Central American policies. A 1985 piece announced that 55,000 people had signed the "Pledge of Resistance," thereby promising to take part in peaceful civil disobedience should the United States invade Nicaragua. It added that the signees had already protested at congressional district offices in all fifty states in light of an upcoming contra aid bill.[54] A 1986 report stated that the Maryland-based Quixote Center had embarked on a "Quest for Peace" campaign to send $27 million in humanitarian aid to Nicaragua to offset the $27 million Congress had just approved in contra aid.[55] Former Washington Post reporter Christopher Dickey's book With the Contras, which depicted the counterrevolutionary forces as psychopathic killers, was discussed to highlight Reagan's ludicrous description of them as "freedom fighters."[56] When former contra leader Edgar Chamorro sent a letter to Congress calling for an end to U. S. aid for his former colleagues, it was reported in the NCR.[57]

In its zeal to condemn U. S. policy, however, some NCR articles displayed a blatant bias. A 1985 report, for instance, which told of a New Yorker's suit against the U. S. government over its Nicaraguan policy, was titled "Citizen Is Fed up with Reagan's Bull."[58] An article by Peter Hebblethwaite chided the international media for their anti-Sandinista bias, contending that they refused to listen to the Nicaraguan government's side on the issues. But when Hebblethwaite asked what had made the hierarchy turn against the Frente, he did not seek an answer from the bishops. Instead he turned to Father Molina, the pro-Sandinista head of the Valdivieso Center, for an opinion. Indeed, it seemed that Hebblethwaite was guilty of the same lack of even-handedness for which he chided the international media.[59]

An NCR interview of Quixote Center founder Father Joseph Callahan made no attempt to question his rather dubious claim that whereas the Sandinistas had expelled about thirty priests and religious from Nicaragua, Cardinal Obando had forced upwards of one hundred prorevolutionary clergy and nuns from active ministry.[60]

Three articles on the pope's visit were extremely one-sided. One claimed that John Paul's "confrontational attitude" was primarily responsible for the conflict that took place.[61] Another stated that his refusal to mention the funeral of young Sandinistas killed in a contra attack was the cause.[62] Still a third blamed the pope's "highly charged, political homily." Indeed, the last piece went so far as to call on John Paul to apologize to the Nicaraguan people, who had "asked their father for bread and had received a stone."[63]

Most extreme, however, was a 1985 NCR piece by Andrew Reding, in which the author all but canonized Sandinista founder Tomás Borge. After chiding the Reagan administration for portraying the comandante as a Marxist terrorist, Reding assured his readers that "the Bible is among [Borge's] most treasured books. He reads it and quotes from it liberally in his speeches, revealing a depth of scriptural understanding seldom encountered in public figures."[64]

Reding spoke glowingly of the Sandinista founder's collection of over a hundred crosses, which he displayed in his office. He repeated the story of how, rather than seeking an eye for an eye, Borge had chosen to show mercy on the captured national guardsman who had raped and murdered his wife. By so doing, Reding wrote, Borge hoped to transform him. Finally, NCR readers were told that it was commonplace to see the comandante attending mass at Uriel Molina's parish church.[65] This was a far cry from John Cort's account in Commonweal that only one of the nine Sandinista comandantes was a practicing Christian. Although Cort did not mention it, that one was not Borge.[66]

On the whole, however, NCR reports on Nicaragua were surprisingly even-handed. A case in point was the paper's coverage of the controversy over priests in the Sandinista government, a topic that most progressive Catholic periodicals shied away from, doing no more than reporting the basic facts without commentary. An early report by Erlick cut to the heart of the matter by pointing out that the controversy revolved around the larger issue of the attempt by the Nicaraguan government to blend Christian and Marxist elements.[67] In a second piece, after a temporary compromise agreement was worked out that was acceptable to both the priests in question and the prelates, Erlick was effusive in her praise of the bishops, citing "observers" who lauded the Episcopal Conference for its pragmatism and continued commitment to the Medellín and Pueblo Conferences' preferential option for the poor.[68] An opinion piece by Michael Garvey in the same issue was especially interesting and insightful. It began by castigating "Catholic apologists for U. S. foreign policy in Latin America" who were incapable of believing that the motives of the priests in office could be anything but base. But Garvey next remarked that the church would be well served if the priests heeded their bishops and resigned their government posts. The hierarchy's request, he argued, was doctrinally correct and premised on the historically proven fact that Christians must be careful lest the state co-opt them.[69]

Jesuit Father Tennant Wright, on the other hand, saw the controversy differently. To him it was part of a larger, more important question: Would a new Christianity similar to the bottom-up model of the early church be allowed to emerge, or would the top-down European model of the bishops stay in effect? Unlike Garvey, Wright never broached the question of whether the government might be attempting to use the priests in government to co-opt the church.[70]

NCR reports on the Miskito controversy were also relatively balanced. A March 1982 piece by *America*'s James Brockman was especially sympathetic to the Sandinistas. While admitting that the government had made mistakes in the course of trying to deal with a complex situation, he reminded his readers that the removal would not have taken place had it not been for contra attacks. Arguing that the bishops' charges against the FSLN lacked concrete proof, he insinuated that they were merely part of a propaganda campaign aimed at replacing the revolutionary government with a reformist one.[71]

J. H. Evans and Jack Epstein in one article exposed the petty power struggle between the two major Miskito factions, while connecting them to U. S. and Honduran officials and ex-Somoza guardsmen.[72] In a second article on the same page, however, they did not shy away from negative aspects of the Sandinistas. They called a fabrication the FSLN's claim that the CIA had drawn up plans for a Miskito secessionist movement. They further charged that it was concocted to justify the Sandinistas' forced relocation policy. Proof of this, they asserted, came from the fact that the revolutionary government refused to release the documents that it claimed proved its accusation.[73]

An article by Penny Lernoux, longtime critic of U. S. policy in Latin America, was especially telling. She began by establishing her anti-contra credentials: "I thought Somoza a bum, and I said so—for which daring Ronald Reagan called me a communist. It goes without saying that I believe the CIA-backed contra war a disgrace." But she added that she was also troubled by leftists "who excuse revolutionary violence against those who do not share their politics." A case in point was the Sandinista treatment of the Miskitos. "How, I've been asked, could I bring up such a question when the Nicaraguan government is fighting for its life." She then castigated the FSLN in no uncertain terms for bombing three Miskito villages after publicly claiming that they had learned from their past mistakes and now wanted to do better.[74]

Even Peter Hebblethwaite, after commenting that an impartial observer could not distinguish between the Soviets in Afghanistan and the contras in Honduras, noted that the Sandinistas had lost the sympathy of most Europeans and Latin Americans who had initially admired them because they were neurotic, suspicious, and bite the hands of those who try to help them.[75]

Other *NCR* articles were far more critical of the FSLN. Erlick noted that political pluralism in Nicaragua was in decline and that some Sandinistas would have liked to make their state of emergency permanent.[76] De Mott, after pointing out the achievements of the revolutionary government, added that pressures had caused it to overreact by limiting personal freedoms, censoring *La Prensa,* arresting some businessmen who had criticized the government, prohibiting strikes, and oppressing the Miskitos.[77]

Former ambassador to El Salvador Robert White had by the end of 1980 become an outspoken critic of Reagan's Central American policy. Nevertheless, he wrote in an *NCR* opinion piece that the Sandinistas' record of curtailing press freedom and civil rights, forming an army far too huge for only defensive needs, and importing two thousand Cuban military advisers made the belligerent response of the United States and the other Central American governments seem legitimate.[78]

Mary Ann Lambert, in a 1983 opinion piece, presented a long list of reasons for her disappointment in the Nicaraguan revolution: the FSLN military buildup, the neighborhood Sandinista cells and cell members' ridicule of those who did not join them, threats on the lives of Protestant missionaries, the Marxist curricula imposed on Protestant primary schools, and the suspension of various freedoms.

> Unfortunately the trends I have observed lead me to the deep conviction that the men in power in Nicaragua always intended to create a military totalitarian system. . . .
>
> I believe the opportunity for Nicaraguans to determine their own future has passed. It ended when the moderate voices in the post-Somoza government were silenced and when appearances of freedom and pluralism were abandoned.

All this, she concluded, had given Reagan and other reactionary elements in the United States an excuse for their disastrous military strategy. The Sandinistas had thrown away a chance to create a model social experiment for Latin America, opting instead to adhere to "a Marxist-Leninist ideology."[79]

Writing in 1984, Chris Hedges was even more critical: The war between the traditionalist and popular churches transcended religion. It had become a war between "Western mores and the socialist agenda of the Sandinista government." The FSLN had "adeptly closed out the opposition and formed cadres loyal to the wishes of the nine-member junta." Consequently, the church was the only remaining institution powerful enough to challenge the Sandinistas. Ernesto Cardenal openly called himself a Marxist and a Christian. In the parish church of Maria de Los Angeles, the statues of the saints had been removed and replaced with murals glorifying the Sandinista revolution.[80]

> The new regime has publicly ridiculed the church hierarchy, is attempting to control church schools and has sent out groups of Sandinista thugs, known as *turbas,* to break up services and paint the word "counterrevolutionary" on church walls. . . . These *turbas,* nicknamed the "divine mobs of the revolution" by . . . Daniel Ortega, have stoned the archbishop's car. . . . In the town of El Sauce, nearly 300 *turbas* tried to break up a mass officiated by Nicaragua's nine bishops.[81]

The revolutionary government had been forcing Catholic schools to hire teachers whose ideology was approved by the state. It was also demanding that they use a curriculum that was little less than a primer for Sandinista ideology.

> In many state run schools, religion itself has become a forbidden topic. The Sandinistas have begun to use a tactic that was popular in Cuba in the early years of the Cuban revolution. Teachers tell their pupils to bow their heads in prayer and ask God for a piece of candy. When the pupils raise their heads their desks are empty. The students bow their heads again and are asked to pray to the revolution for a piece of candy. With their heads bowed, the teacher places a piece of candy on each desk.[82]

The author concluded by noting that traditionalist church services were now "overcrowded and electric" and that the people cheered the archbishop when he entered church.

Alan Gottlieb, in a 1987 report, confirmed this last assertion: "Fewer priests are associated with the popular church than with the nation's conservative Catholic hierarchy. And popular church events consistently draw smaller crowds than masses celebrated by traditional church leaders." Moreover, 15 to 20 percent of those in attendance at popular church liturgies were foreigners, and "it is at times difficult to separate the religious from the political during these services."[83]

To summarize, the progressive U.S. Catholic press throughout the early 1980s staunchly held to its condemnation of the Reagan administration's Nicaraguan policy. It had little or no sympathy for the Nicaraguan bishops and cavalierly wrote off their claims of persecution at the hands of the Sandinistas as typical overkill by pre–Vatican II churchmen who craved influence with the wealthy. Although at times quite critical of Sandinista "mistakes" and misdeeds, it too often made excuses for revolutionary excesses, especially in the first half of the decade. In other words, the Catholic periodicals wanted to see the best in the revolutionary government, even at times when it required quite a stretch of the imagination to do so. In conclusion, then, one is forced to concede that the vast majority of U.S. Catholic popular periodicals displayed a leftist bias in their coverage of Nicaragua. This is not to imply, however, that taken as a whole their reporting was not of first-rate quality, for it was. Nonetheless, there was a need for a few Catholic publications to confront the overall U.S. Catholic press on its biases. Such a challenge, if done properly, could have made a positive contribution to the Central American debate. A small minority of conservative Catholic periodicals did indeed attempt to challenge their pro-Sandinista counterparts. The next chapter will be devoted to them.

seven

The Conservative
Catholic Press on
Central America

Following the 1980 presidential victory of Ronald Reagan, a small group of conservative Catholic periodicals, seeing the new president as a philosophical soul mate, took it upon themselves to defend his policies from Catholic critics. Since the U. S. Conference of Catholic Bishops (USCC) and the Catholic press were particularly hostile to the new administration's Central American policy, these publications intensified their coverage of this region, attempting to justify U. S. policy on the grounds that it was fully within the parameters of traditional Catholic moral teaching. Reagan's policy was in keeping with the church's traditional opposition to atheistic communism, argued the conservative element of the Catholic press; it was the U. S. bishops, some religious orders and congregations, and the more liberal Catholic media that had strayed from church teaching. Seduced by situation ethics and liberation theology, which was nothing more than veiled Marxist-Leninism, U. S. church leaders had allowed themselves to become useful dupes of international communism. By so doing, they had become "the enemy within," placing not only Christianity but all of Western civilization in jeopardy.

The most vigilant advocates of this line of reasoning were *Crisis* (originally *Catholicism in Crisis*), the *Wanderer, Social Justice Review,* and the *National Catholic Register.* Their attempt to redefine the U. S. Catholic position on Central America will be treated at length in this chapter.

Before moving on to particulars, however, two general observations are in order. First, the conservative Catholic press was in full accord with all dimensions of the Reagan Central American policy, whether it pertained to Nicaragua, El Salvador, or elsewhere. Second, it failed in its attempt to play an important role in defining the U. S. Catholic position on Central America largely due to its extremist mode of argumentation. Unwilling to debate issues in a restrained manner, it more often than not resorted to smear tactics and unsubstantiated charges. In so doing, just like the Sandinistas, it proved to be its own worst enemy.

A case in point is *Crisis,* a periodical created in 1982 because its originators were "dissatisfied with existing Catholic journals."[1] A 1983 commentary by Ralph McInerny, one of its founders, well illustrates its attack mentality. As will be shown, the author not only disagreed with Archbishop John Roach, president of the USCC, but also maligned the prelate, treating him rudely and with disrespect. What had upset McInerny? Roach had stated that the Bishops' Conference opposed U. S. military intervention in Central America and favored a diplomatic, rather than a military, solution to the region's problems.

McInerny began by asking why a church leader from a landlocked midwestern state would feel a need "to pontificate" on distant Central America. He then attempted to answer his own question: "Archbishop Roach can be numbered among those who regard the United States as the source of trouble in the world."[2] Moreover, since Roach was archbishop of St. Paul, Minnesota, perhaps he was attempting to curry favor with liberal Minnesota Senator Fritz Mondale.[3] McInerny continued: The USCC should stop issuing declarations on Central America. It was offensive for its president to make a tendentious statement as if it were an official Catholic position, when it was not.

> A great many intelligent and informed Catholics believe that the U. S. Catholic Conference has fallen into the hands of a small group of ideologues who manage to foist their opinions on the bishops and have them issued, not as their personal views, but as the views of the Roman Catholic Church in the United States. . . .
>
> Archbishop Roach's statement on Central America is a narrowly partisan viewpoint parading as the Roman Catholic position. Those of us who disagree with it would like to be free of the onus of apparent disrespect to successors of the Apostles when we call it bunk.[4]

It is sufficient to note that nowhere in his commentary did McInerny concede the possibility that Archbishop Roach might be well intentioned. Instead he impugned his integrity by suggesting that he was anti-American and was currying political favor with the Democratic party's soon-to-be presidential candidate.

In a 1984 piece, *Crisis* columnist Philip Lawler used the same modus operandi in attacking another USCC president, Bishop James Malone. Following a luncheon at the White House at which Reagan officials briefed the leaders of the USCC on several topics of mutual interest, Malone read a statement, noting that the bishops were pleased with the president's position on abortion but opposed his stands on Central America and nuclear weapons. To Lawler, however, Malone's statement was disingenuous and offensive. Contending that the bishop should have limited his remarks to the "cordial and productive" tone of the luncheon, he added:

[W]hy did Bishop Malone have a prepared, typed statement in his pocket? Obviously his impromptu press conference had been planned in advance. No matter what had occurred during those few hours inside the White House, he would have said the same thing.[5]

The appearance of Bishop Thomas Gumbleton on the MacNeil-Lehrer News Hour as an opponent of U.S. aid to the contras did not go unnoticed by *Crisis* writer Terry Hall. As one would reasonably expect, he was especially critical of Gumbleton's refusal to support Cardinal Obando's claim that the Sandinistas were persecuting the Nicaraguan church. But rather than challenge Gumbleton's interpretation of the facts, Hall degenerated into a tirade of unsubstantiated charges: "The bishop was saying, in effect, that he didn't care about Cardinal Obando—that he didn't care about the persecution of a brother bishop. What he did care about was stopping aid to the contras."[6] Indeed, Gumbleton and his "co-religionists" were "apologists for an increasingly repressive regime." As such, they represented the "fringe element in the national debate on Nicaragua." They were "the irresponsible extreme against which everyone else may define themselves."[7]

In a 1986 article, *Crisis* writer Michael Schwartz contended that the USCC proved it was blatantly biased by its unconditional condemnation of contra aid and its support of the Contadora peace talks. In contrast, he argued that the Nicaraguan Episcopal Conference, by refusing to speak out against the passage of contra aid and in support of Contadora, had actually demonstrated its neutrality. Thus, unlike their North American counterparts, the Nicaraguan bishops had chosen the high ground.[8] *Crisis* held

Thomas Quigley, the USCC's chief advisor on Latin America, especially responsible for what it considered the U.S. bishops' naiveté on Central America. Consequently, its writers were particularly hostile to him. Columnist Lawler went so far as to suggest that Quigley might be intentionally withholding from the U.S. bishops anti-Sandinista information sent by their Nicaraguan counterparts. As for proof, Lawler noted that Quigley was on the steering committee of the Religious Task Force on Central America and other pro-FSLN organizations.[9] In another piece Lawler expressed outrage because Quigley had recommended a congressman who held a pro-choice position on abortion to the bishops of Ireland as an expert on Central America.[10] In still a third article, Lawler sarcastically commended a delegation of American bishops who had gone on a fact-finding trip to Central America for leaving Quigley behind in Washington. The implication was, of course, that without Quigley choreographing their trip, they might actually learn some truth about the region.[11] Another *Crisis* writer, Dinesh D'Souza, derided Quigley by referring to him as the USCC's "resident Sandinista,"[12] an "inside-the-beltway Sandinista," and a "True Believer in radical causes."[13]

Religious orders opposed to U.S. policy in Central America and sympathetic toward the Sandinistas were also special targets of *Crisis*. But rather than debate their differences of opinion, *Crisis* opted to impugn their integrity through sarcastic name-calling and innuendo. Its April 1988 issue was especially scurrilous. On its cover was a drawing of a man with a gun in one hand, a bomb in the other, a knife between his teeth, and two hand grenades hanging from his belt. Under the drawing were the words "Maryknoll's Social Gospel." Inside was an article that disputed a Maryknoll statement that it had decided to close its seminary for economic reasons. Citing unnamed sources for its proof, *Crisis* claimed that the Vatican had ordered the closing because "Maryknoll was doing an excellent job training Marxists but a terrible job training priests."[14]

The author further declared that Rome was concerned with the possibility that Maryknoll seminarians could be having sexual relations with female lay-missionary students, since the latter resided in a Maryknoll house nearby and shared a common dining hall on Sundays. The author at least added that no such cases were known and that such conduct was unlikely to have occurred.[15] Before closing, she delivered a parting jibe, which typified the tone of her entire piece and the modus operandi of almost all *Crisis* reports on Central America: "Among orthodox Catholics, among those who love the church, you aren't going to see a lot of tears over [the closing]....[But] You may have a memorial Mass in Managua."[16]

With similar sarcasm, another reporter accused Maryknoll of abandoning the ideals of its founders for a trendier image, one in which beer was on tap in the refectory, Roman collars were scarce as hen's teeth, and embroidered peasant shirts, leftist politics, and liberation theology were in.[17] She claimed that Maryknoller Miguel D'Escoto had "led the protest that disrupted John Paul II's Mass in Managua."[18] Evidently she did not check her sources, for D'Escoto had discreetly arranged to be away on a diplomatic mission during the pope's visit.[19]

But Maryknoll was not the only recipient of this reporter's wrath: The White Fathers and the North American bishops were pronounced just as trendy. The latter, in their encyclical letter *To the Ends of the Earth,* had been so rash as to proclaim the four U.S. churchwomen murdered in El Salvador examples of "heroic witness."[20]

Geraldine O'Leary De Macias, a favorite Central American "expert" on the conservative talk circuit, also attacked Maryknoll in the pages of *Crisis.* A former member of the congregation who had spent a year working with her fellow nuns in Nicaragua before leaving to marry, Macias claimed that Maryknoll missionaries, along with other foreign clergy and religious, encouraged the masses to link up with Marxists. She termed their leadership "politically ignorant" and "criminally naive" and claimed that they had negatively affected the Nicaraguan people.[21] But she went further, assuring her readers that true Christians in Nicaragua had joined the contras to fight for real democracy. Nowhere did *Crisis* inform its readers that the author was affiliated with the Democratic Revolutionary Alliance (ARDE)—contra forces fighting in southern Nicaragua.[22]

Finally, a *Crisis* author attacked Maryknoll-based Orbis Books for the exclusiveness of its titles:

> You will look in vain on this list for any title in the mainstream of Western theology. Orbis apparently regards such work as culturally conditioned and provincial. In Christ there may no longer be Jew and Greek, but Orbis is doggedly determined that there shall still be African and Latin American. In the West we seem only to have made ourselves idols for destruction. The cultures of underdeveloped areas, even when these are full of practices that would have been termed idolatry in the Scriptures, are for Orbis today's oracles.[23]

The author did not mention that Maryknoll, being a missionary congregation, founded Orbis specifically for the purpose of bringing Third World culture and theology to Western readers. Had he done so, Maryknoll's concentration on Third World topics would have been understandable. He did, however, complain of the overuse of such words as "revolutionary," "innovative," and "challenging" in Orbis titles, quipping that words like "retrograde," "hackneyed," and "dull" would seem more suitable.[24] The author ended his diatribe by declaring that Orbis's concern for solidarity with the oppressed and with the people of Nicaragua smelled of Marxism.[25]

Like the USCC and Maryknoll, the Jesuits were also objects of Crisis's wrath. A piece by Scripps-Howard editorial manager William Burleigh accused the Jesuits of abandoning their traditional role as educators in favor of radical political intrigue. He argued that rather than imparting traditional Catholic values to their students, as they had done for centuries with impressive results, the Jesuits now worked to advance the cause of Third World revolutionary movements like that in Nicaragua. He concluded with a plea for the Order of St. Ignatius to listen to the many voices imploring it to reject its anticapitalist, pro-Marxist agenda and return home to its glorious past.[26] Suffice it to say, Burleigh did not address the possibility that by reaching out to the poor who previously had had little opportunity to receive a Catholic education, the followers of St. Ignatius were actually expanding their traditional role as educators.

So anxious was Crisis to defame the Jesuits that it even published an amateurish assessment of the order's religion classes by a disgruntled student who had just graduated from a Jesuit high school. The young writer charged that her Jesuit instructors taught liberation theology and situation ethics under the guise of social justice. She claimed, without explaining how she arrived at her conclusion, that social justice classes were especially hated by the students. Why? Because the teachers were pro-Sandinista, pro-FMLN (Farabundo Martí National Liberation Front), and anti-American. Indeed, in one course she had received a poor grade on her term paper—an attempt to prove that Guatemalan guerrillas were financed by the Soviet Union, Cuba, and the Sandinistas—only because she refused to use the sources suggested by her teacher. Perhaps revealing something about her own agenda, she complained that her instructors put Martin Luther King and Gandhi on the same pedestal as Jesus and that "Muslims are allowed to be as abusive and insulting about Christianity and Christians as they wish, but if any student wishes to stand up for his religion or his 'white race' he is denounced as prejudiced."[27] Her suggestion for improving her high school "and making it the best in the state": overhaul the religion department and replace courses dealing with social justice with such classes as "Apparitions and Miracles of Mary."[28] The argumentation in the article can only be described as sophomoric, but, in justice to its author, such is what one would expect from a typical high school student. One can only wonder, however, at *Crisis*'s decision to publish it.

Since *Crisis* was founded because its editors were dissatisfied with other Catholic periodicals, it is not surprising that its writers would be especially critical of the Catholic press. Humberto Belli, in a relatively restrained piece, chided *Our Sunday Visitor* and *Maryknoll,* as well as Father Bryan Hehir of the USCC, for refusing to concede that the FSLN was persecuting the church.[29] *Crisis* editor, Michael Novak, however, was not so temperate. He accused the *NCR* of being more leftist than the left wing of the Democratic party when it came to the Sandinistas.[30] He added that "if the *NCR* were operating in Nicaragua, [its writers] Tom Fox and Dawn Gibean [sic] ... would already have been placed in jail or forced to flee."[31] He did not state how he had arrived at this conclusion, which, at any rate seems somewhat curious, since the *NCR* had several writers operating in Nicaragua and none of them had been arrested or deported. This article, by one of *Crisis*'s best known scholars, typifies the cavalier use of unsubstantiated charges that so permeated the pages of this periodical.

Crisis went so far as to assign a special reporter, Tom Bethell, to write a regular column, "Press Watch," which was intended to expose the chicanery and foibles of the Catholic media. (Philip Lawler's "USCC Watch" was expected to do likewise for the Bishops' Conference.) Bethell began one column by commenting that for two thousand years external forces have attempted to destroy the church but had proven ineffective. Today, however, the church faced a far more serious threat, one that came from within. He followed with denunciations of *Our Sunday Visitor,* the *National Catholic Reporter,* and *America.*

Bethell accused *OSV*'s Washington editor, Jim Castelli, of harboring "a deep and abiding animus against the Catholic Church,"[32] but made no attempt to provide evidence to support his contention. *NCR,* a "purportedly Catholic newspaper," was attacked for an article by Sister Jane Boyer, which sarcastically called Mother Teresa of Calcutta "the patron of the status quo" because of her refusal to fight for land reform and an end to structural injustice. Bethell was especially disturbed by the fact that "poor Boyer ended by offering for our consideration a U.S. saint. Ita Ford."[33]

Such a suggestion set Bethell off on a tirade against liberal Catholics, who rebelled against God by stubbornly refusing to tolerate injustice:

> What we find on the U.S. Catholic left today is apostasy, rage, and above all rebellion: rebellion at God's creation, and rebellion against God for tolerating Man's fallen state. So they want to sweep away God

(who permits injustice and inequality to persist) and to set up their own state.[34]

He ended by postulating that left-wing Catholics might actually be communists trying desperately not to reveal their true identity.[35]

Conservatives were certainly justified in challenging the views of *OSV*'s Vincent Giese on Nicaragua, but a commentary by Bethell bordered on the ludicrous. He began by accusing *OSV* and its editor of corrupting unsuspecting orthodox Catholic families through doctrinal misrepresentation and political bias. He then charged Giese with excusing the rude behavior of the Sandinistas at the papal mass in Managua, with attempting to justify the abusive treatment of Father Carballo, and with whitewashing the divisive, anti-Catholic behavior of the base communities. These last three accusations were certainly reasonable. But then Bethell launched into a curious harangue because Giese and his Nicaraguan delegation had not worn clerical garb when having their photograph taken for *OSV*: "[Giese] is shown wearing sun glasses and an open-neck shirt, beaming broadly at the camera. All the others are likewise dressed in what appear to be picnic clothes." Bethell next informed his readers that for the remainder of his article he would refuse to address Giese as Father, since Giese refused to dress like a priest. He would merely be referred to as Giese. Such silliness seems self-defeating in that-it served only to obscure the valid points of Bethell's article.[36]

In another column, Bethell lamented the fact that *America* had not changed under its new editor, but "continues along the grey path of genteel apostasy." There was no doubt, he added, "that *America* is on the side of heresy rather than orthodoxy."[37]

But *Maryknoll* magazine was no better:

What a curious thing is *Maryknoll*... filled always with pictures of those oddly androgynous-looking "missioners" who go to far-flung lands, and preach what amounts to socialism decked out in vaguely religious terminology.... The latest Maryknollword is "option" and it can be simply translated as "socialism"; as in "option for the poor."[38]

The "Press Watch" columnist was not finished. He next added more publications and the American bishops as well to his list of retrograde Catholics:

In general the leftist drift among U.S. Catholic publications, a drift matched by the U.S. hierarchy as a whole, is a remarkable development. *Commonweal, Our Sunday Visitor,* and of course the *National Catholic*

Reporter should be added to the list. In my opinion this drift expresses a loss of faith more than anything else.[39]

The Sanctuary Movement, which provided refuge in U.S. churches for Salvadorans and Guatemalans fleeing persecution in their homeland, was a controversial movement certainly open to responsible criticism as well as support. Thus, it is not surprising that *Crisis* would oppose it, just as the more liberal Catholic press supported it. What stands out, however, in M. Holt Ruffin's lengthy critique of the movement in *Crisis* is the author's viciousness, his refusal even to concede that leaders in the Sanctuary Movement might be well meaning but wrong. Instead, Ruffin declared the movement an exercise in selective compassion, public deception, and irresponsible rhetoric—in short, a scam. The author stated that the movement's leaders were liars who were not really concerned about refugees. Their real motive, he argued, was "a profound conviction that the United States is the real 'evil empire.'"[40]

Sanctuary advocates, argued Ruffin, cried that near-genocide was being committed against illegal immigrants returned to El Salvador by the Reagan administration. In reality, refugees came to the United States for economic reasons, not because of persecution. It was the Salvadoran guerrillas, not the government or military, who were responsible for most of the murders in this tiny country. For proof, Ruffin cited statements from the U.S. embassy in San Salvador and, incredibly, from "reports in the Salvadoran press."[41] Data from Tutela Legal, the Salvadoran archdiocesan human rights organization, and from Americas Watch, Amnesty International, and other similar prestigious organizations, which concluded that the Salvadoran military and its death squad associates were responsible for the overwhelming majority of killings, were ignored by Ruffin.

Understandably, liberation theology was a favorite target of *Crisis* authors. Most took a black-and-white approach to it, equating it with Marxism and even heresy. They also discussed it almost exclusively within a Nicaraguan context.

Typical was an article by the Nicaraguan poet and essayist Pablo Antonio Cuadra. He termed it a "reactionary heresy" that was contrary to the tenets of Vatican II.[42] He argued that it was actually atheistic in that it transformed the poor, with their hope in the resurrection, into Marxist proletariats with nothing but a vague faith in the future. He likewise charged that it required its adherents to replace God with Marx and provided the Sandinistas with the religious cover they needed to persecute the church with impunity. U.S. and European clergy had been especially susceptible to its lure. Their self-centeredness and superiority complex made them unwilling to take the Nicaraguan bishops seriously when the latter claimed religious persecution at the hands of the FSLN.[43] In another article, Kenneth Craycraft also linked liberation theology to the Sandinistas and Marxism and postulated that the defeat of the FSLN in the 1990 elections was tantamount to the defeat of this theology.[44]

Disciples of Christ minister David Hartman noted that in Nicaragua poor campesinos, seduced by the message of liberation theology, were led to support the FSLN and, after the Sandinistas came to power, it was liberationists who sanctified the FSLN's oppressive behavior.[45] But he took his contentions further: In Latin America, "If a government can claim Marx as its progenitor, that evidence is sufficient for the militant liberationist. Such a government is obviously on the side of the poor, the oppressed, and God."[46]

Conservative Catholic journals sometimes granted like-minded congressional leaders space to argue their partisan positions on Central America. In this vein, Congressman Henry Hyde (R-IL) took to the pages of Crisis to warn readers that Nicaragua represented a textbook case of how Marxists exploited Christianity to advance their goals in the developing world. To prove his contention, he offered the words of three "liberation theologians," J. Guadalupe Carney, Ernesto Cardenal, and Gustavo Gutíerrez. The first two wrote of the connection of Christianity and Marxism; the third did not. Gutíerrez was quoted as stating that Latin America needed to be liberated from the domination of the great capitalist countries, especially the United States.[47]

In truth, of these three writers, only one, Gustavo Gutíerrez, was actually a liberation theologian. At most, the other two could be described as radical priest-activists who were influenced by this theology.[48] Thus, it is fair to say that Hyde did not seem to recognize the difference between a theological scholar and an activist, or that if he did, it was irrelevant to him.

An article by Scott Walter deserves mention because it inadvertently contradicted the claims of almost every other Crisis author who had written about liberation theology. Liberal Protestant theologians Harvey Cox and Robert McAfee Brown, in reviews of a Michael Novak book critical of liberation theology, had dismissed Novak's study as no more than another facile attempt to prove that liberation theologians were Marxists. Walker, in an effort to defend Novak, noted that the latter stated several times in his book that most liberationists were not Marxists and that many had "explicitly criticized Marxism."[49]

Only two other Crisis articles were willing to deny that liberation theology and Marxism were interchangeable. Both merit careful attention because, as exceptions to the rule, they serve as examples of how *Crisis* could have made a positive contribution to the debate on Central America and liberation theology if it had limited itself to analyses of ideas instead of attacks on individuals who held different views. The first piece, by an Irish Franciscan philosophy professor, Colin Garvey, was an analytical critique of the liberation theology of Leonardo Boff. In short, Garvey explained why he was uneasy with Boff's all-encompassing use of the term "social class of the poor," as well as with his overuse of revolutionary rhetoric. He also saw the absence of the transcendent aspect of Christianity in Boff's writings as a weakness. Nevertheless, Garvey took pains to treat Boff in a dignified, respectful way, limiting himself to a discussion of the theologian's ideas. Garvey actually went out of his way to chide those who had "tried to smear Father Boff as a Marxist," adding that the charge was untrue.[50]

The second article, by Princeton political science professor Paul Sigmund, adroitly explained the growth of liberation theology from a Marxist-influenced revolutionary theory, which saw class conflict as inevitable, to a more moderate, democratically leaning commitment to the poor. Sigmund ended his analysis by speculating that liberation theologians were at the crossroads between Marxist revolutionary theory and Rousseau-based democratic theory and would have to choose one or the other. He avoided simplistic condemnations of liberation theology, presenting it instead as a complex mode of thought with the potential to be a positive force in Latin America. He took care to point out that although some liberationists had championed aspects of Marxism, particularly in the 1960s and early 1970s, others, like José Comblin, had been quite critical of it. The tone of Sigmund's piece was scholarly and avoided "cheap-shot" rhetoric.[51]

Very few articles appeared in *Crisis* dealing with El Salvador and virtually none with Guatemala. Those that did, without exception, supported Reagan administration policy. Furthermore, they implied that the prevalence of negative views in the United States on El Salvador resulted from widespread misrepresentation of the truth by leftists.

A May 1984 speech by Ernesto Rivas-Gallont, El Salvador's ambassador to the United States, was reprinted in *Crisis*. Its inclusion is telling in that the speech had nothing to do with religion. Simply put, it argued against the Salvadoran opposition's proposal for a peace plan based on the creation of a provisional government in which all groups in Salvadoran society would have representation. Instead, the ambassador argued that El Salvador was already a democracy, but one under siege from communism. He called for more U. S. military aid to El Salvador and a military solution in which the FMLN and its allies were destroyed.[52]

An article by Philip Lawler in the same issue reported on a Washington speech by Bishop Marco Revelo, president of the Salvadoran Bishops' Conference. Lawler began:

> Almost everybody seems to think that the Salvadorean Church opposes the government there, and wants an end to U.S. military aid. The opposite is true. Bishop Revelo, speaking on behalf of the entire bishops' conference, explained that the Church opposes the guerrillas, and wants U.S. military aid continued.[53]

Lawler further told his readers that Revelo had been upset when the USCC stated that the United States should withhold military aid to El Salvador until death squad activities ceased. The bishop had claimed that the Salvadoran government did not control the death squads and therefore could not eliminate them. Lawler concluded by remarking that "journalists and politicians learned something about El Salvador from [Bishop Revelo,] an unimpeachable witness."[54]

What Lawler neglected to tell his readers was that Bishop Revelo had been a bitter foe of Archbishop Oscar Romero, and in 1979 had accused him in writing of imposing a politicized, Marxist pastoral plan on the church, blessing terrorism, defaming the government, and interfering in the business of other dioceses.[55] It is also interesting to contrast Lawler's statement that, as president of the Salvadoran Episcopal Conference, Bishop Revelo spoke for the Salvadoran church with the statement of *Crisis* author Ralph McInerny that USCC president Archbishop Roach, when making pronouncements on Central America, spoke not for the U.S. church but only for himself.[56] Thus, one gets the impression that the staff of *Crisis* perhaps believed that Episcopal Conference presidents spoke for their national church only when the views they expressed coincided with those of *Crisis*.

Two articles on El Salvador by the *National Catholic Register*'s Central American correspondent, Joan Frawley, appeared in *Crisis*. In the first, she remarked that the 1984 presidential election of José Napoleón Duarte was a major victory in the Reagan administration's plan for the evolution of a working democracy in El Salvador. She claimed falsely that the 1979 reform junta had fallen apart because "it did not move quickly enough [with its reform program] for the country's leftists."[57] In truth, it had dissolved when its civilian members resigned in protest because the military blocked their reform program and did nothing to stop the escalating repression.[58] This is a well-documented and indisputable fact. Frawley also cited Bishop Revelo's call for continued military aid. She noted his exasperation with U.S. officials, who were pressuring the Salvadoran government to identify and prosecute Romero's assassin.[59] Like Lawler, however, she neglected to mention Revelo's long history as an enemy of Archbishop Romero and an apologist for the Salvadoran government and military.

In her second article, Frawley argued that liberation theologians, "frozen in time," refused to see that there was a difference between the violent El Salvador of 1980 and that of 1987, where there were free elections and a sharp reduction in death squad killings. Why? Because such positive changes challenged their "static vision and Marxist dialectic."[60] The author next launched into a diatribe on liberation theology, replete with the old charge that it was synonymous with Marxism. Interestingly, she now used the term "radical liberation theologians." She did not, however, define what nonradical liberation theologians were, nor did she shed light on who she thought were radicals and who were not.

In a June 1989 interview piece, Dinesh D'Souza remarked that "the Maryknoll nuns [the four U.S. churchwomen] . . . were killed because of their support of the Salvadoran guerrillas."[61] Suffice it to say, as is so often the case in the pages of Crisis, he made no attempt to substantiate his charge.

In the November 1989 issue of Crisis, Richard Rodriguez postulated that Latin Americans were becoming Protestants because the Catholic church had abandoned its rich prayer life in favor of social work carried out by priests and religious in plainclothes.[62] A second piece in this same issue, a negative review of the movie Romero, chided the director for presenting the Salvadoran reality as static when it had been "constantly edging towards democracy and land reform."[63] The reviewer also insinuated that priests murdered in El Salvador had been killed because of their involvement in socialist politics.

Ironically, these two articles appeared in November 1989, the month that the six Jesuits, along with their housekeeper and her daughter, were murdered by the U.S.-created and trained special Atlacatl Brigade of the Salvadoran army. It is indicative of Crisis's bias that it made no mention of these murders until September 1990, and then only in passing in an editorial aimed at supporting continued U.S. military aid:

> Recently, Catholic "social justice" groups have been sending a spate of letters to Congress that urge an immediate cessation of U.S. aid to the democratic government of El Salvador. . . .
>
> We support U.S. efforts to press the Salvadoran government to complete its investigation of the murder of Jesuit priests in El Salvador, a heinous crime which President Alfredo Christiani has repudiated. At

the same time, the fledging democracies of Latin America deserve U.S. assistance—military aid to defeat the anti-democratic Marxists . . . and political assistance to enable them [to] set up viable human rights institutions. . . .

A "negotiated settlement," the prevailing buzzword, is a grave mistake.[64]

In truth, the "U.S. efforts to press the Salvadoran government to complete its investigation" of the Jesuit murders were far from impressive. As has been documented in numerous publications, the FBI attempted to compromise the testimony of Lucía Barrera de Cerna, the only eyewitness to the murders. Likewise, U.S. military authorities in San Salvador tried to conceal the testimony of Major Eric Buckland, a U.S. military advisor in El Salvador, who had been told by a Salvadoran colonel that Col. Guillermo Benavides had been responsible for the murders. Yet none of this information was mentioned in this *Crisis* editorial.[65] Such omissions, along with selective and exaggerated use of information, only served to undermine the credibility of *Crisis* in the eyes of responsible church leaders.

Like other conservative Catholic publications, *Crisis* vigilantly emphasized the shortcomings and brutality of the Sandinistas, as well it should. The censorship of *La Prensa,* the communique advocating a deemphasis of the religious celebration of Christmas, the use of Marxist theory in the literacy crusade, the attacks on anti-Sandinista priests such as Father Carballo, the violent treatment of the Miskitos and the incarceration of their Moravian pastors, the expulsion of Catholic and Evangelical religious leaders, the heavy-handed treatment of Mormons, Adventists, and Jehovah's Witnesses, and more could be found in the pages of this periodical. But such responsible reporting was almost always followed by half-truths, exaggerations, and innuendos that undermined *Crisis*'s credibility. For example, a piece by "Quidam" (a pen name for a Nicaraguan who said he feared reprisals if he used his real name), which outlined the mistreatment of Catholic leaders, was followed by an accusation that the Vatican was appointing new Nicaraguan bishops who preferred to capitulate to the Sandinistas, rather than support Obando.[66] Along with numerous articles accusing the FSLN of brutality were articles that lauded the Salvadoran government for deescalating death-squad activities, holding honest and free democratic elections, and stifling communist expansion. *Crisis* never addressed human rights abuses in El Salvador and Guatemala. Indeed, from reading its pages one would think that they seldom occurred, and that when they did, the governments diligently worked to see that they were not repeated and that the perpetrators were brought to justice. Claims of Sandinista mistreatment of Evangelicals, Mormons, Jehovah's Witnesses, and others were followed by an inaccurate attack on the Evangelical Committee for Aid and Development (CEPAD), the largest humanitarian and development organization in Central America, which preferred a policy of cooperation rather than confrontation with the FSLN: Humberto Belli accused CEPAD of defending the Sandinista occupations of churches of the above religious groups, when CEPAD actually had intervened quietly but successfully in convincing the Sandinistas to return these places of worship to their owners.[67]

If *Crisis*'s extremism undermined its credibility, the same was even more true of the *Wanderer*. The general thrust of this newsweekly concerning Central America seemed to be that Nicaragua and El Salvador had to be viewed in terms of an international, Moscow-led communist conspiracy to take over the world. Thus, Catholics should support the anticommunist forces in Nicaragua and El Salvador without qualification. A May 1980 commentary by *Wanderer* columnist John Metzler illustrates well this point. He called the Carter administration's plan to provide economic aid to the new revolutionary government of Nicaragua "one of 1980's biggest cases of tomfoolery." In typical Cold War fashion, he termed Nicaragua "the cutting edge of Castroism in Central America." He then warned that the FSLN was far more than the amateur revolutionary nationalists and agrarian reformers that they claimed to be. They were hard-core Marxists who had successfully established a "bridgehead" for future Marxist subversion into the rest of Central America.[68]

An article from the following month demonstrated the same mind-set. Author Paul Scott warned his readers that the Sandinistas marched to the drum of communist Cuba, which, in turn, received its orders from Moscow. The plan was to use "Nicaragua as a Central American beachhead for the eventual Castroite conquest of the petroleum fields of southern Mexico." El Salvador was already under siege and Guatemala was targeted. Why? Because "whoever controls the Caribbean can strangle the U.S. by choking off the petroleum life-line." Instead of helping the pro-U.S. governments in these countries, however, the Carter administration undermined them by cutting off or limiting U.S. aid. The president did not understand that "Castro would never have undertaken such a wide-ranging operation in Nicaragua without the backing of the Soviet Union."[69]

One cannot help but notice that the rhetoric used in the above two articles sounds exactly like that employed by the mainline Catholic press in its commentary on Guatemala in the 1950s. No mention was made of poverty in Central America, of Somoza brutality, or of atrocities perpetrated by the

Salvadoran and Guatemalan militaries and death squads. Indeed, this held true for all *Wanderer* articles. Even the assassination of Archbishop Romero received no more than a short twenty-three-line news report in the *Wanderer*, taken directly from the Religious News Service. Buried on page 3, it was devoid of commentary, presenting no more than the very basic facts.[70]

A 1984 column by Metzler equated the North Americans and Western Europeans who had traveled to Nicaragua to help with the coffee crop with leftists who had fought against Franco in the Spanish Civil War and with Americans who had picked sugarcane in Castro's Cuba. Although such a comparison was not without some justification, Metzler resorted to hyperbole when he claimed that "the coffee crop comrades" were being "scouted" by the Sandinista and East German secret police as potential spies. Not surprisingly, he provided no supporting evidence to back up his assertion.[71]

Exaggerated rhetoric and unsubstantiated accusation permeated Paul Fisher's report on a White House briefing on Nicaragua given by Geraldine Macias and Humberto Belli. These two, who were the most heavily cited "experts" on Central America in conservative Catholic publications, claimed that liberal churchpeople, who were the most vehement supporters of the Sandinistas, no longer believed in personal sin—they believed only in the sin of the capitalist system. Other outlandish claims by the two were also repeated by Fisher without challenge. The Sandinistas were accused of insisting that religious "faith should not be judged from the Gospel, but the Gospel should be judged from the revolution," and that "Christ is not enough" for Christians. Christians must also understand Marxism, since it is "the bridge between God and reality." Belli was cited as adding that the U.S. bishops refused to accept the truth about the situation in Central America because they were under the influence of Father Brian Hehir and Tom Quigley, who were completely biased in favor of the FSLN. Fisher interjected that there was no compelling evidence linking Roberto D'Aubuisson to the murder of Archbishop Romero, and that such a charge was wholly based on the less-than-persuasive evidence of former ambassador Robert White. The article implied that D'Aubuisson should not have been denied entrance into the United States or prohibited from speaking at Georgetown University.[72]

A 1986 piece, citing as its source Elliott Abrams, Assistant Secretary of State for Inter-American Affairs, claimed that a car that had crashed in Honduras immediately after crossing from Nicaragua was found to contain in secret compartments enough ammunition to support 250 to 500 Salvadoran guerrillas for a month. This, according to the *Wanderer*, proved that Father D'Escoto had lied when he told the International Court of Justice that Nicaragua was not providing arms for the Salvadoran guerrillas. The *Wanderer* did not attempt to explain how one car could hold so much ammunition in secret compartments, nor did it discuss the veracity of Abrams, who would later be shown during the Iran-Contra hearings to have provided false information to Congress.[73]

One could continue to discuss numerous additional reports on Nicaragua found in the *Wanderer* that were likewise filled with innuendos, exaggerations, and unsubstantiated charges, but, there is no reason to belabor the point further. Another piece on Nicaragua, however, does deserve mention. An article by John Boland effectively took to task the naive conclusions of Father Phil Land, who had just returned from a seven-day fact-finding trip to Nicaragua sponsored by the Jesuit-affiliated Center for Concern. Boland began by sarcastically noting that, according to Land, the three most highly placed church figures in the country—Archbishop Obando, Bishop Vega, and the papal nuncio—were wrong when they said there was religious persecution in Nicaragua. How had Land reach this conclusion? He had asked Daniel Ortega and other Sandinista leaders and Jesuits like Fernando Cardenal, and they had told him so. With obvious mockery, Boland next used Land's own words against him:

> While it is true, Fr. Land goes on, that Nicaragua's trade union movement is affiliated with the Marxist international trade unions, there is a good explanation for this: "When the Communist international early on visited Managua, the government, in its ignorance of such matters, did not know that there existed another—free—international" and signed up. "To cancel membership now," says Fr. Land, "would be an affront to states upon which the Sandinistas rely—indeed are forced to rely—for help."[74]

On the interruption by Sandinista demonstrators of the pope's mass in Managua, Boland again effectively used Land's words against him:

> It was because the Holy Father did not talk about "rights acquired in the revolution" but insisted on condemning the "popular church" as "absurd and dangerous" that the crowd's "reaction boiled over" and thus the "terribly unfortunate sequence of events" at the Papal Mass.[75]

Lest the point be missed, Boland added that Land had neglected to mention that television cameras showed Sandinista leaders leading the crowd with bullhorns.

Such an article was effective because its author limited himself to an attack on the statements of Father Land, clearly demonstrating their bias and Land's gullibility. He avoided malicious name-calling and unsubstantiated accusations that he could not back up. Thus, by employing reasonable argumentation and abstaining from extremist rhetoric, the author was able to showcase the naive nature of his opponent's argument. Articles of this type undoubtedly did contribute to the Catholic debate on Central America and scored points for the conservative case. Few such articles, however, are found in the pages of the *Wanderer.*

Like other conservative Catholic publications, the *Wanderer* was critical of the pronouncements of U.S. bishops concerning Central America. For years it had demonstrated particular hostility for Cardinal Joseph Bernardin of Chicago's "seamless garment" approach to human rights. (It felt that this approach deemphasized the importance of the pro-life movement.) Thus, when the cardinal spoke at the University of Chicago on the USCC's position on Central America, the *Wanderer* expressed its indignation in a column by Joseph Gill. The columnist began in a disrespectful tone, unbecoming to a professional journalist:

> One can hardly turn the pages of a newspaper these days without being informed of the latest opinion of Joseph Cardinal Bernardin on whatever subject happens to capture his attention that day. And little seems to escape his attention as long as it is outside his jurisdiction. On Jan. 17th it was not even necessary to open the paper to learn that he is not pleased with the Reagan Administration's Central American policy. "Cardinal Rips U.S. Policy," shouted the streamer on page one of *The Chicago Tribune.*
>
> With a ring of self-assured expertise, which has become his special trademark, he told an audience . . . in the University of Chicago's Rockefeller Chapel, "The Catholic Bishops have opposed the basic direction of U.S. policy in Central America since 1980. We have never been convinced of the wisdom of that policy and I remain unconvinced of it today." He spoke as though there was no possibility of disagreement by Catholics. . . . But I, for one—and I am far from being alone—do disagree most emphatically. Moreover, I resent his speaking as though he spoke for all Catholics, including me, without exception.[76]

Gill went on to attribute the formulation of Bernardin's opinions on Central America to the USCC bureaucracy and liberation theology–minded missionaries in the isthmus, especially Maryknollers and Jesuits. He closed by calling on the cardinal and other bishops to refrain in the future "from using their sacred office to propagandize in favor of their personal political agenda."

Gill's argument followed the same mean-spirited pattern as that of McInerny's attack on Archbishop Roach in *Crisis*. It viciously attacked the prelate merely because he had restated the position of the U. S. Bishops' Conference on Central America. In short, Gill's article was frenetic and inaccurate. It may have pleased those conservatives who already supported U. S. Central American policy. Its discourteous tone, however, made certain that it would be largely ineffective in winning religious-minded converts for the Central American policy of the Reagan administration.

Whereas other U. S. conservative Catholic periodicals tended to steer away from El Salvador, this was not the case with the *Wanderer*. It stood out as the most daring Catholic journal—or the most extreme, depending on one's interpretation—in its defense of this country's oligarchy. Such was obvious from as early as the end of 1980. As already stated, the March murder of Archbishop Romero received no more than one short, factual notice, buried on page three. More startling is the fact that the *Wanderer* completely ignored the December 1980 murders of the four U. S. churchwomen; instead, in its Christmas issue, the dubious accusations of a captured Salvadoran guerrilla against the Jesuits received 148 lines of headline coverage. This article reported that Julian Otero, the captured guerrilla, confessed that Jesuits throughout Central America were involved in buying weapons for the FMLN. He revealed to his captors that the Jesuit-run Central American University (UCA) served as a recruiting station for rebel forces and that guerrillas were permitted to operate several clandestine printing presses on its campus. He also disclosed that the most influential members of the FMLN were priests, and that Catholic parishes played a major role in recruiting peasants for the guerrillas.[77] Amazingly, the *Wanderer* took no account of the possibility that Otero might have made this startling confession under duress. Instead, it assumed that his revelations were truthful, noting that Otero's "statement confirms many points made elsewhere in this issue of *the Wanderer* by Orlando De Sola, one of El Salvador's leading businessmen."[78] The *Wanderer* likewise did not seem to be troubled by the outlandish nature of the captive's claims, or by the fact that other conservative Catholic periodicals had declined to publish them. In this same issue, the *Wanderer*, using the interview technique, provided an open forum for Orlando De Sola, a rich Salvadoran landowner and businessman, to make equally outlandish declarations. Answering questions provided by *Wanderer* reporter Paul Fisher, De Sola claimed that the so-called Fourteen Families, which were said to control El Salvador, did not really exist. Indeed, there was no oligarchy in his country.

Its existence was only a myth created by communist enemies of the state. He further stated that the church, since the ascendancy of Romero as archbishop, had lost credibility with the Salvadoran people. De Sola told *Wanderer* readers that Romero could just as well have been murdered by the left as by the right and that many priests used their clerical role to disguise their real work of subversion. Some had even taken up arms as guerrillas and were now killing Salvadoran people. Finally, he claimed falsely that UCA rector Ignacio Ellacuría had come to El Salvador only after being expelled from Spain for subversive activities.[79] One need only remark that it is quite surprising that a Catholic newspaper would allow such serious accusations to go unchallenged, especially following so closely the brutal rape and murder of the four North American churchwomen.

The *Wanderer* went even further in its support of the oligarchy, providing four key officials of the National Republican Alliance (ARENA), whose founder was allegedly responsible for the assassination of Romero, with a forum to express their views without challenge. Again, in response to questions, the ARENA team complained how unjust it was that other Salvadoran presidential candidates were allowed to visit the United States, while Roberto D'Aubuisson, its candidate and founder, was banned. *Wanderer* interviewer Paul Fisher concurred, noting that United Nations Ambassador Jeane Kirkpatrick had recently told a Senate committee that there was no definitive link tying D'Aubuisson to the death squads. One of the ARENA spokesmen then added that the left, along with former U.S. Ambassador Robert White, had smeared D'Aubuisson with unsubstantiated charges of death squad involvement and responsibility for the murder of Archbishop Romero. He remarked that only the Salvadoran guerrillas were in a position to benefit from the archbishop's murder, so perhaps they were responsible. Fisher did not ask him to explain why he had concluded that only the left could benefit from Romero's death.

The ARENA spokesmen soon attacked Socorro Jurídico, the Salvadoran legal aid organization founded by Archbishop Romero, claiming that it had been established by international leftists who had no interest in human rights, just "human Lefts." Fisher seemed to agree when he added that the Salvadoran bishops had recently stated that Socorro Jurídico did not speak for them. He neglected to mention, however, that Bishop Rivera had replaced it with Tutela Legal as the official archdiocesan human rights center and that both of these human rights organizations had independently compiled massive evidence linking the Salvadoran oligarchy and military to murders, disappearances, illegal incarcerations, and torture.

After declaring that attempts at land reform had destroyed the economy, the ARENA group concluded by warning that the Catholic nation of El Salvador was in a battle to save itself from Soviet communism, which, if successful, would spread throughout South America and threaten the United States. Even more important, its success would mean the destruction of Western Christian thought.[80]

Countless other articles of a similar nature appeared throughout the 1980s in the pages of the *Wanderer*. There is no need to further scrutinize them. What perhaps best illustrates the extremism of the *Wanderer*'s attitude toward the conflict in El Salvador, however, and toward Central America in general, is its response to the murders of the six Jesuits in November 1989. Columnist Gary Potter's words speak for themselves:

> This is pure commentary. It concerns the recent killing in El Salvador of six Jesuits.
>
> Let's abstract from it that the massive publicity given their death obscured the simultaneous killing of hundreds of ordinary Salvadorans by the Marxist insurgents (see also Pat Buchanan's column on that point in this issue of *The Wanderer*). Let's also refrain from the obvious. That would be to quote Scripture—"As ye sow, so shall you reap"—and say no more.[81]

But Potter did say more. According to him, North American conservatives claimed that the right could not be responsible for the Jesuit murders because this would only serve to create negative public opinion toward them in the United States. This claim was stupid, he reasoned:

> At the moment of this writing we don't know who did the killing. However, . . . nobody's going to be afraid of outraging or offending the opinion of anyone except a friend. . . . [W]ho and where are the friends in the U.S. of the Salvadoran rightists? It is the Marxist rebels who have friends here, especially in the influential circles of government, the churches, media, and the academy. . . .
>
> There exist in Latin America many real conservatives who simply do not care about U.S. opinion anymore because they've seen us abandon too many allies: Diem, Thieu, the Shah, Somoza, Marcos, and more recently the Nicaraguan contras and the Argentines who were training the contras for us at our behest. These Latin Americans believe the U.S. is not reliable.[82]

Obviously such contorted thinking placed the *Wanderer* in a class by itself, even among conservative Catholic periodicals. No one could expect such reactionary reasoning to be taken seriously by Catholic leaders. Thus, the viewpoint of the *Wanderer* on Central America played no role in shaping U.S. Catholic thought on the crises in the isthmian region of the Western Hemisphere.

Of all U.S. Catholic publications, the little-known *Social Justice Review* perhaps came closest to providing solid evidence for a conservative case against the prevailing view of U.S. Catholic leadership concerning Nicaragua. But, like its conservative counterparts, *SJR* proved unable to limit itself to constructive pieces. The majority of its articles on Central America were replete with the same innuendos and unsubstantiated accusations found in other conservative Catholic magazines. But let us first look at the constructive articles, for they demonstrate how responsible reports could contribute to positive dialogue in the Catholic press.

The Social Justice Review was most convincing when it reprinted information from other sources. The earliest article of this type was a short piece by the future Nicaraguan president Violeta Chamorro. It was a passionate plea against Sandinista press censorship, in which Chamorro noted that "the ultimate limit on this lack of freedom" was the three-time refusal of FSLN censors to allow *La Prensa* to publish Pope John Paul II's June 1982 letter to the Nicaraguan bishops. The editors of *SJR* make the piece even more effective by pointing out that the Sandinista censors actually forbade the insertion of this Chamorro article in *La Prensa*.[83]

Three additional pieces were even more telling. The first was a reprint of a four-page statement given before the Organization of American States by Berkeley geography professor Bernard Nietschmann on the mistreatment of the Miskito Indians by the Sandinistas. The author, a highly respected, published expert on Miskito culture, based his report on the two and a half months he had spent interviewing Miskito Indians in Nicaragua, Honduras, and Costa Rica. He presented devastating testimonies from countless Miskitos who had witnessed murders or had been tortured, raped, or robbed by Sandinista soldiers. He further noted that there had been no attempt by FSLN authorities to punish the perpetrators of such crimes. Nietschmann's testimony was especially convincing in that he was not a conservative. He had favored the revolution and had even served as a consultant to the Sandinistas concerning the creation of a national park.

Nietschmann presented ample proof of a classic case of government soldiers abusing civilians in retaliation for guerrilla attacks. Unable to capture and destroy the enemy, the soldiers turned their wrath on noncombatants whom they perceived to be sympathetic to the guerrillas.[84]

The second article was a reprint of a *Wall Street Journal* report by J. B. A. Kessler. Kessler's credibility was based on eight years as an advisor to the Moravian church, a service that required him to make numerous visits to Miskito villages in Nicaragua and Costa Rica.

Among other things, Kessler told of an incident in the Miskito town of Prinzapolka, where Sandinista soldiers entered a Moravian church during a service and, while attempting to make an arrest, without provocation opened fire on the worshippers, killing four. In retaliation the Miskitos attacked the soldiers, also killing four, and then fled to the jungle. This incident, Kessler explained, was the spark that set off the violence, which would escalate and undermine future Sandinista-Miskito relations.[85]

The above two articles graphically illustrated that Sandinista actions on the Atlantic Coast before 1984 were far more serious than "the few mistakes" to which more liberal Catholic journalists referred. As such they were quite valuable.

The third inclusion was a report by William C. Doherty, executive director of the American Institute for Free Labor Development (AIFLD). It was a devastating exposure of the Sandinista government's attempt to destroy the country's two independent union movements and force all labor groups to affiliate under the Central Sandinista de Trabajadores. Point by point, Doherty documented arrests, beatings, and deportations of union leaders who had refused to affiliate. His data were quite convincing and painted a picture of a government unwilling to allow unions to exist outside its control, a picture not highlighted in the mainstream Catholic press and quite different from the views of Father Land and the Center for Concern.[86]

The Social Justice Review also published an address by Oscar Rodríguez, auxiliary bishop of Tegucigalpa, Honduras. Rodríguez was critical of the Sandinistas, charging that there was "real persecution of the Church in Nicaragua" and that it was grounded in a strategy that had begun with the creation of a "popular church" led by a small group of priests who were more concerned with ideology than with the faith.[87] Rodríguez, however, was careful to point out that the Nicaraguan situation "is not clearly black and white." Rather, "there are many shades of gray."[88] He accused the FSLN of disseminating misinformation about the situation in Nicaragua but also noted that its revolution had accomplished positives such as the reduction of the illiteracy rate.

More important, he explained how right-wing military governments in Central America had created great social injustice, thereby spawning revolutionary movements that eventually were "taken over by the Left and then by Communism."[89] He added that the ever-growing gap between the very few rich and the great majority of poor created conditions ripe for violence. Thus, Rodríguez was placing blame for the problems of Central America on both the right and the left.

He was not reluctant to tell of the Honduran military's part in the massacre of Salvadoran refugees, and added that Guatemalans had fled to Honduras to escape the oppression of their military regime. He stated that about 40,000 Nicaraguan refugees had entered Honduras, some fleeing the violence of the Sandinista-contra war and others, mostly male students, escaping compulsory military service. He was careful to note that these young men did not want to fight for either the Sandinistas or the contras.

Rodríguez's balanced presentation of the complexities of Central America was nothing novel. His analysis was similar to that found in some mainline Catholic periodicals. It was nevertheless important because such a nuanced presentation could not be found in other conservative Catholic journals. Indeed, Rodríguez's was the only article in the conservative Catholic journals so far discussed that said anything positive about the Sandinistas and that criticized the conduct of the Central American right.

The above five *SJR* articles presented strong evidence of the use of violence and heavy-handed tactics by the Sandinistas, but did so in a restrained way. The facts were allowed to speak for themselves and were convincing. There was little use of incendiary rhetoric.

Unfortunately, these five articles stood alone. Other *SJR* contributions on Central America contained the same highly questionable charges and extremist rhetoric found in *Crisis* and the *Wanderer*. They presented their case in simplistic, black-and-white terms, ignoring data that did not support their agenda. An example of this last point is a four-page chronology of religious persecution in Nicaragua. Even the most questionable claims of Sandinista persecution were included. Crucial information in support of the FSLN position was ignored. For instance, the expulsion of Bishop Vega was listed. There was no mention, however, that shortly before his expulsion he had publicly stated on a trip to Washington, just before a congressional vote on contra aid, that the Sandinistas had murdered three priests. The charge proved to be a fabrication. The *SJR* chronology also omitted atrocities committed by the contras against pro-Sandinista religious people. It ignored, for example, the kidnapping, torture, and murder of Felipe and Mary Barreda, two long-time church workers in Estelí who had supported the FSLN. This brutal episode had received wide coverage in progressive U.S. Catholic journals and therefore was well known.[90]

A report by Dick Goldkamp took to task those scholars who had written criticisms of the "Ratzinger Report," which had harshly criticized liberation theology. Instead of challenging their arguments, Goldkamp accused them of harboring "ethnic prejudice" against a Polish pope and a German cardinal. He also subtly tried to link the concepts of this theology to the Marxism of the Peruvian Shining Path guerrilla movement, a connection that was totally unjustified by the facts.[91]

Another article referred to priests who supported the Sandinista revolution as "clerical freaks" and lambasted Father D'Escoto for remaining silent while his Sandinista Party carried out a "brutal anti-Semitic campaign," which "drove the entire Jewish community—numbering 50 families—into exile" in 1979. This supposed anti-Semitic campaign has been shown to be unfounded or at best highly exaggerated. The author of this article should have researched his topic more thoroughly before making such serious charges.[92]

Articles reprinted from *Diario Las Americas* were equally unrestrained in extremist rhetoric and unsubstantiated charges. One accused Jesuits in El Salvador and Nicaragua of heresy and of officiating at "the altar of Lenin instead of in [sic] the altar of Jesus Christ." It further charged Maryknoll with "destroying the moral formation of many youths."[93] A second *Diario* reprint referred to pro-Sandinista U. S. Catholics as "useful fools" who supported communism in the name of social justice and human rights.[94]

Since fact-finding trips to Nicaragua comprised a major part of the agenda of pro-Sandinista U. S. Christians, American groups opposing the revolutionary government understandably tried to undermine them. The *Social Justice Review* was no exception. It included in its pages a lengthy report by two women who had taken part in a Lutheran-sponsored trip to Mexico, El Salvador, and Nicaragua. In light of other commentary in conservative Catholic publications, their conclusions were not surprising:

> The travel seminars sponsored by the American Lutheran Church Women and organized and conducted by the Center for Global Service and Education, Augsburg College in Minneapolis, are not objective educational experiences designed to acquaint women with the problems of Central America as they are purported to be. They are instead two weeks of intensive anti-United States pro-Sandinista indoctrination.[95]

And they were successful. Fed with massive doses of liberation theology and Marxist propaganda, exposed to forty-five speakers of whom only seven spoke from a pro-U. S. perspective, and conditioned by trip leaders to distrust these seven, ten of the women in the seminar succumbed to the pro-Sandinista spell. Most were leaders in their churches; all were sincere and generally concerned about Central America, but they had little background knowledge about the region, its history, and U.S. policy there. In short, they were putty in the hands of the seminar leaders. Only the two authors were strong enough to resist, and had they not had each other to talk to, they too might have begun to question their own positions, even while fully realizing what the seminar was trying to do to them. Indeed, stated the authors, "we feel it is virtually impossible for anyone who is naive and uninformed, and trusting . . . not to succumb to this type of brainwashing."[96]

Familiar with Humberto Belli's *Christians under Fire,* the two authors were able to remain "objective." Unlike their ten fellow travelers, they realized that the vendors in the public market in San Salvador were happy and showed no signs of social unrest. What a dramatic contrast this was to the vendors in Managua, who seemed apathetic and indifferent.

Of the four refugee camps they visited in El Salvador, one was poorly run. "The uncharitable thought crossed our minds," they informed *SJR* readers, that this may have been intentional, "that perhaps miserable conditions made better revolutionaries."[97] This being the case, they did not explain why the other three camps were so well run.

Although the trip directors tried to keep the group from conversing with people who were not on the seminar agenda, this tactic did not work with the authors. Friends of the family of one of them had arranged beforehand for them to meet with Nicaraguans who were unconnected to the tour. These people informed them that what they were being told was all lies.[98] It is sufficient to comment that although the two authors were correct in stating that fact-finding trips of this type to Nicaragua had a pro-Sandinista bias, they themselves obviously had a preconceived agenda, one which was far from objective.

An objective, scholarly analysis from a conservative-based Christian fact-finding trip could have proven valuable for the Catholic debate on Nicaragua. The *Social Justice Review* did report on one such trip, but its questionable conclusions were far from objective and were therefore meaningless. The article's author concentrated on an interview that he had conducted with the leader of a Miskito refugee camp in Honduras. His source claimed that the United Nations was "deliberately underfeeding" the refugees to force them to return to Nicaragua. He contended that "the Communist-Bloc is directing or influencing" the United Nations and that U.S. reporters who came to the camp to interview the Miskitos refused to report what they were told, since they "are being manipulated by the Communists."[99] Needless to say, such outlandish charges could not be expected to change the views of U. S. Catholic leaders on Nicaragua.

Only one article appeared in the *Social Justice Review* that concentrated primarily on El Salvador. It centered on the 1985 presidential victory of Duarte and the comments of Rabbi Morton Rosenthal, a member of the Reagan-appointed U. S. election observation delegation. According to Rosenthal, the election represented "a clear rejection of the revolutionary left and its program." He predicted that Duarte's victory would "reduce and ultimately eliminate murders perpetrated by right-wing extremists and military personnel."[100] He added that the democratic advances in El Salvador "could not have been done without the United States' economic and military assistance." Finally, the author of the article pointed out that the delegation's report "lauded the impartiality of the Salvadoran military" during the election.[101]

It is important to note that this article contained the only mention in *SJR* of right-wing death squad and military killings. Whereas *SJR* showed great vigilance in listing every accusation of Sandinista human rights abuses in Nicaragua, it showed little to no concern for violations perpetrated by the Reagan-backed governments of El Salvador, Guatemala, and Honduras or by the contras. Needless to say, this unevenness detracted from its credibility.

Of all U. S. conservative Catholic periodicals, the *National Catholic Register* published the largest number of articles on Central America. Most tended to be relatively short reports and therefore less analytical than their counterparts in *Crisis* and the *Social Justice Review*. The vast majority followed the same line of reasoning found in the other conservative magazines and newsweeklies already covered in this chapter. Indeed, some *Register* authors—Philip Lawler, Joan Frawley, Michael Novak, and Charlotte Hayes, to name a few—published pieces in *Crisis* that were similar to their *Register* articles. Consequently, to avoid repetition, we will refrain from commenting on most *Register* articles, since these are similar to those already covered in *Crisis*, the *Wanderer*, and the *Social Justice Review*.

In perusing the pages of the *Register*, one quickly notices that there is less of the rudeness and disrespect which so permeated other conservative periodicals, especially where the U. S. bishops were concerned. A report on a Cardinal Bernardin speech on Central America, for instance, was taken directly from National Catholic News Service. The report merely noted that the prelate stated that the USCC was opposed to a military solution in the region and believed that isthmian problems were local in nature, having as their causes long-standing patterns of injustice and human rights violations.

There was no outraged commentary, no rhetoric on how the cardinal had no right to speak for American Catholics.[102]

A report by Frawley was quite critical of Thomas Quigley, advisor for the USCC on Latin America. It revealed that Father Bismarck Carballo had sent a letter to the general secretary of the USCC, complaining that Quigley was hindering the Nicaraguan bishops in their struggle against Sandinista-based religious persecution. This having been said, Frawley next reported on her telephone interview with Quigley, who noted that he had done no more than uphold the bishops' position condemning U.S. covert aid to the contras and the mining of Nicaraguan harbors and that he had never criticized the Nicaraguan bishops.

Frawley next attempted to support Carballo's contention and undermine those of Quigley by pointing out that at a White House briefing the latter had clashed with Nicaraguan dissidents who charged the Sandinistas with persecuting the church. She added that he had also refused to respond to a request from Congressman Connie Mack (R-FL), who had asked for his assistance in supporting the Nicaraguan bishops' claims of church persecution. She repeated Geraldine Macias's contention that Quigley had told her to stop criticizing the Sandinistas because it helped Reagan. She then listed pro-FSLN lobby groups that Quigley was associated with, adding that these organizations criticized abuses of right-wing governments but ignored those of the Sandinistas. Finally, she quoted a spokesperson from Freedom House's Center for Caribbean and Central American Studies who chided the USCC for not showing solidarity with the Nicaraguan church.[103]

Although this article was highly critical of Quigley, it did not contain any smear-type phrases like the ones in *Crisis* that referred to him as the USCC's "resident Sandinista" or an "inside-the-beltway Sandinista." In short, the author presented her case against Quigley and let her facts speak for themselves. She even gave the USCC advisor the opportunity to defend himself.

Another Frawley report admitted that in Nicaragua "every apparent truth has a twin that seems to cancel it out." For every trade unionist, churchperson, and human rights commission that condemned the FSLN, there was another that praised it.[104] Thus, this piece at least conceded that finding truth in Nicaragua was complicated. A third Frawley piece, on Melba Blandón, the chief government censor of *La Prensa*, cited Blandón's contention that censorship was necessary because of distortions of the truth in the anti-Sandinista media.[105] This was the only article I have found in the conservative Catholic press that mentioned the possibility of distorted reporting in *La Prensa*. This is not to say, of course, that Frawley agreed with Blandón, for she did not. Nevertheless, she deserved some credit for at least allowing the Sandinista censor to make her case.

Perhaps the most even-handed and perceptive report in the *Register* was a piece by Terry Mulgannon. It contrasted the feelings of two men who had initially supported the Nicaraguan revolution. One had become disillusioned and disappointed. He and his family had "less than before." The other still enthusiastically supported the revolution. He and his family had a two-bedroom home, something they could not have dreamed possible before the revolution. Mulgannon's analysis was not what one was accustomed to finding in U. S. conservative Catholic magazines:

> Is life any better for the average citizen of Nicaragua in the post-revolutionary climate? In the divided land that is Nicaragua, the answer depends on whom you talk to and whether they have more or less than before. But one can make comparisons to neighboring Central American nations.
>
> There is an opposition newspaper in Nicaragua which, in spite of censorship, still often criticizes the government, as do many of its unhappy citizens. They survive, if not without harassment and sanctions. But those who criticize in Guatemala and El Salvador, and increasingly in Honduras, disappear.[106]

Many *Register* articles, however, did contain the innuendos and unsubstantiated charges that so permeated the conservative Catholic press. An interview of Geraldine Macias by Richard Bodurtha was one such piece. In it Macias claimed that the Maryknoll sisters wanted "a revolution for revolution's sake" and that the Sandinistas took orders from the Soviet Union.[107] Without realizing the irony of her words, she even complained that the FSLN oppressed other Nicaraguan Marxist parties. Bodurtha, however, never asked Macias to provide evidence to back up the accuracy of her statements.

A Frawley article on the Sandinista mistreatment of the Miskito Indians was another such piece. After claiming that few independent groups had been permitted by the Sandinista government to inspect Miskito relocation camps, Frawley noted that there was now documentation proving reports of "the persecution, mass relocation, imprisonment and killing of thousands of Miskito Indians."[108] She then turned to the findings of Jim Stieglitz, a former Green Beret medic from the Vietnam War, who, she said, had decided to go personally to the camps to investigate them for himself. Frawley did not explain why the Sandinistas had allowed Stieglitz to enter and inspect the camps, except to say that his ability to speak Russian and

German got him past the Russians and East Germans, who he maintained were ubiquitous in the area. She likewise did not bother herself with such questions as who paid for or sponsored the former medic's trip. Although Stieglitz's assertions would probably seem highly questionable to more than a few impartial observers, Frawley blindly accepted them as truth. The residents lived in squalor, the former Green Beret reported. The camps contained three times the number of people they were designed to hold. Food was guarded by armed Cuban soldiers. They and the Sandinistas were fed first, so there was not much left for the Indians to eat. Health conditions were appalling; since people did not get enough food, they got sick and died in great numbers. The camps were actually concentration camps where the Indians were forced to do slave labor harvesting and processing sugarcane and palm oil under Cuban overseers. The Miskitos were routinely beaten, tortured, and kept in "tiger cages." In other words, they were treated in the same fashion as the prisoners of the communists in Vietnam.[109] One wonders why Frawley made no attempt to check the veracity of Stieglitz's startling claims by comparing or contrasting them with the findings of others who had visited the camps. She might have at least checked to see what organizations he might have been affiliated with.

In another article, Frawley claimed that "liberation theology priests celebrate 'campesino Masses' in which bullets that will be used by the Sandinista militias are consecrated along with the Eucharist."[110] She provided no evidence to support this serious charge. When the Sandinistas published a secret memo from the W. R. Grace Company, which stated that the firm was providing "financial support" to Cardinal Obando to use against the FSLN, Frawley expressed outrage, not at Obando or Grace, but at the Sandinistas for stealing the memo.[111] Just prior to the 1984 Nicaraguan elections, Frawley wrote that Sandinista law restricted campaigning by opposition parties. She insinuated that if a fair election was allowed, the FSLN would lose. For her source, she cited a report from Freedom House. She made no mention of the numerous other human rights organizations that held views on the election contrary to that of Freedom House.[112]

Frawley was not alone. E. Michael Jones commented on a speech at the University of Notre Dame by Reagan aide Robert Reilly, entitled "Why Are the Sandinistas Persecuting Christians in Nicaragua?" But his report focused only on the fact that the speaker was heckled by the audience. Jones also attempted to undermine the credentials of one of the questioners, political science professor Scott Mainwaring, an expert on the Brazilian Catholic church, by sarcastically noting that the professor admitted he had never been to Nicaragua but said he hoped to travel there in the near future. The contents of Reilly's speech received virtually no attention.[113] Had Jones chosen to focus on the points made by this Reagan official and the counterpoints made by Mainwaring and other Latin American scholars in attendance, his article might have contributed positively to the Catholic debate on Central America. Unfortunately he opted not to do so.

Like other conservative Catholic periodicals, the *Register* was quite critical of the fact-finding trips to Nicaragua sponsored by progressive Christian groups. Frawley compared them to the "Potemkin Village" tours during the time of Catherine the Great, which were aimed at deceiving travelers to Russia.[114] In a second article, she discussed the Nicaraguan trip of 150 U.S. pacifists. She gave their travel agenda: a visit to a barrio community center, where there were slogans stating that there was no contradiction between revolution and Christianity; then a sojourn to Jalapa, a frontier town where the fighting between contras and Sandinistas was heavy. Other activities included a pro-Sandinista vigil at the American embassy and discussions with supporters and opponents of the Nicaraguan regime. She sarcastically referred to the Americans as "pilgrims" and said that for some it was their first visit to Nicaragua, but for others it was not. She added that thirteen of the 150 group members were nuns, who planned to offer reflections at masses in their local areas and before their local peace groups on what they had seen and learned. Finally, she noted with irony that most in the pacifist group felt that, while it was wrong for the contras to fight in Nicaragua, it was moral for the Salvadoran guerrillas to fight in El Salvador.[115]

The piece, although not directly saying so, gave the impression that "the pilgrims" naively allowed themselves to be used by the Sandinistas and came to Nicaragua not so much to find the truth as to confirm what they already believed. It also implied that "the pilgrims'" moral outrage at violence in Central America depended on whether that violence came from the right or left. On the whole, though, the article was effective and relatively fair.

The same was less true for Paul Hollander's commentary on "political pilgrimages" to Nicaragua. Hollander equated the fact-finding trips of U.S. Christians to Nicaragua to the earlier visits of Western clergymen and others to Stalinist Russia and Maoist China, from where they returned home praising the communist "experiment." The author maintained that "political pilgrims" were easily duped because Marxist governments allowed them to see only favorable things and to talk only to people supportive of the regime. The fact that such Christian groups routinely visited political opposition parties, the U.S. embassy, anti-Sandinista business organizations, and opposition church leaders did not cause Hollander to rethink his assumptions. These visits were permitted, he assured his readers, only because the FSLN had not yet consolidated its power. Once it had done so, such freedom would be terminated.[116]

Hollander ignored the fact that the United States had a century-long, disreputable history of involvement in Nicaragua, which certainly would seem to play a motivating role in the decisions of U.S. Christians to travel there on fact-finding trips. Those who earlier had traveled to the Soviet Union and China would not have had such a motivation. He also overlooked the fact that the United States was conducting a surrogate war in Nicaragua, one in which it recruited, trained, and financed a counterrevolutionary army, which had been accused by many reputable human rights organizations of kidnapping, torturing, and murdering innocent civilians. Thus, those religious people who embarked on fact-finding trips to Nicaragua might have been motivated more by concern over the morality of their own nation's conduct than by a fascination with Marxism.

Whereas the *Register* contained a profusion of articles dealing with Nicaragua, outside of a few pieces taken directly from the syndicated National Catholic news service (NCS), there was little coverage of El Salvador. Indeed, aside from a rather insignificant twenty-four-line mention of the murder of the four U.S. churchwomen from NCS, there was absolutely no coverage of this watershed event in the *Register*'s four December issues. This is especially surprising since the December 21 issue contained a long front-page piece on the murder of singer John Lennon, which took place a few days after that of the churchwomen. Evidently this Catholic newsweekly deemed his murder more newsworthy than that of churchwomen killed by national guardsmen from the U.S.-backed Salvadoran government.

Another report in the same December 21 issue, on a recent bombing of the San Salvador cathedral, remarked that Archbishop Romero was the most prominent church figure killed in El Salvador. The four U.S. women were not even mentioned.[117]

Indeed, a reading of the few *Register* articles on El Salvador makes it quite apparent that the Catholic weekly fully supported the Reagan administration's Salvadoran policy and therefore made every effort to play down the significance of right-wing violence, which was seldom mentioned. When it was, the *Register* presented it in a way that was least harmful to the incoming Reagan team. A case in point was a report on the December 1980 assassination of six leftist labor leaders in the capital city. Mention of the killings was quickly followed by a statement that terrorist acts had also been committed against rightists and government officials.[118]

Another piece from 1986 cited a survey by the Intergovernmental Committee for Migration, which concluded that Salvadorans came to the United

States for economic rather than political reasons. The article noted that the survey contradicted the claims of members of the Sanctuary Movement.[119]

Michael Novak defended Reagan policy when he contrasted the president's comment—that U. S. involvement in El Salvador amounted to a moral struggle against Soviet evil—with that of the U. S. bishops, who declared Reagan's policy immoral. Ironically, Novak, the founding editor of *Crisis*, began by chiding the bishops for the harsh tone of their condemnation, which he claimed made "reasoned disagreement . . . less and less easy."[120] He soon got to his central point: "[T]he bishops speak with no more authority than any other citizen," and Catholics are not bound to agree with the way they apply moral principles.[121]

Nowhere in his argument did Novak mention the murder, torture, or disappearances of Salvadorans, including priests, religious, and an archbishop. Nowhere did he mention oppressive state structures that kept the vast majority of the population in dire poverty, while the few lived in extreme luxury. From reading this article one would not realize that socioeconomic injustice was even part of the problem in El Salvador.

Finally, a *Register* report by Joop Koopman on an address delivered by Bishop Pedro Aparicio, vice president of the Salvadoran Episcopal Conference, deserves special attention. The thrust of the bishop's speech was that the United States should commit troops to El Salvador if other means failed to stop the guerrilla insurgency. He contended that the FMLN rebels dressed in Salvadoran military uniforms and committed atrocities to discredit the army. He stated that reports of government repression by the archdiocesan human rights center in San Salvador, although supported by Archbishop Rivera Damas, were exaggerated by priests, mostly Jesuits, who sympathized with the FMLN.[122]

Needless to say, Aparicio's statements were both serious and startling. They were also highly suspect. Yet Koopman made no attempt to further investigate or challenge these claims. She did not mention that Aparicio was a longtime enemy of both Archbishops Romero and Rivera and that he had written Vatican officials claiming that these prelates were imposing a Marxist blueprint on the Salvadoran church. Indeed, whereas all reputable authorities have attributed the murders of Fathers Rutilio Grande, Alfonso Navarro, Rafael Palacios, and Alirio Macías to right-wing Salvadoran death squads, Aparicio long contended that the priests had been involved with Marxist groups who had killed them when they tried to sever their relationship.[123] The bishop provided no evidence to support his claim, just as he provided no evidence for his accusations in this article. Yet Koopman ignored this.

Perhaps the best way to understand conservative Catholic press coverage of Central America in the 1980s is to realize that it was almost identical to mainline Catholic press coverage of Guatemala in the 1950s. As noted earlier in this study, by the 1970s several factors had caused most U.S. Catholic leaders to replace their anticommunist fixation with a more complex global outlook. They now came to see communist Third World revolutions as outgrowths of poverty and oppression. Create justice, they reasoned, and the communist danger will die in the process. This new mind-set caused most American Catholic bishops and the Catholic media to oppose a U.S. policy toward Central America that was exclusively premised on Cold War assumptions. Whereas the United States backed oppressive governments in El Salvador and Guatemala and counterrevolutionary forces in Nicaragua primarily because they were anticommunist, U.S. Catholic leaders and the Catholic press were no longer willing to follow suit. The North American institutional church had outgrown the Cold War reasoning of the 1950s, but the U.S. government, especially under the Reagan administration, had not.

Some U.S. Catholics, however, held tenaciously to the anticommunist Catholic mind-set of the past. To their way of thinking, Western Christian civilization was in greater peril than ever before. Not only was it still under siege from atheistic communism, but now Marxist-Leninists were being assisted by a new pseudo-Catholic "enemy within"—"fellow travelers" intoxicated by modernist concepts of utopian liberation theology and situation ethics. To this conservative Catholic minority, the Reagan administration actually came closer than the U.S. institutional church to upholding traditional Catholic values. A few conservative Catholic periodicals, all with relatively small circulations, became the means through which this small band of Catholic traditionalists called their church back to what they saw as reality. Just as the U.S. Catholic bishops and the North American Catholic press had joined forces with the Eisenhower administration in the 1950s to destroy communism in Guatemala, the small conservative Catholic remnant would ally with the Reagan administration in an attempt to destroy communism throughout Central America and thereby preserve Christian civilization. In this war between Christian good and communist evil, the stakes were too high for these traditionalists to adhere to the niceties of journalistic etiquette. Catholic "fellow travelers" had to be exposed and removed from positions of leadership from which they could destroy not only their church but the entire free world.

On the basis of its Cold War, anticommunist way of thinking, the conservative Catholic press saw the Central American imbroglio as part of a larger East-West confrontation. The Sandinistas and revolutionary forces in El Salvador and Guatemala were merely surrogates of Moscow. If, through them, Moscow gained a Central American beachhead, all of the Western Hemisphere would be in jeopardy. Since the Reagan administration was the only force with the will and power to destroy the isthmian communist insurgency, it must be totally supported. Thus, the conservative Catholic press concentrated almost exclusively on Nicaragua, emphasizing both real and perceived abuses of the Marxist Sandinistas. Obsessed by its Cold War agenda, it was unable to concede that the FSLN was capable of any positive reforms. On the other hand, human rights violations perpetrated by the Reagan-supported governments of El Salvador and Guatemala were ignored. The conservative Catholic media's reasoning went as follows: Such governments were oppressive, but they were anticommunist. If Marxist regimes came to power, they would by their very nature be far more oppressive than the current regimes. Thus, it was best not to publicize abuses by the U.S.-backed anticommunist governments, lest this provide ammunition for Moscow.

By their very way of thinking, however, the conservative Catholic periodicals assured their own failure. Unwilling to debate in a restrained manner, resorting to smear tactics and unsubstantiated accusations not only against the Sandinistas but against bishops, priests, nuns, and the progressive Catholic press, unable to compromise or make even the smallest concession, the traditionalists would have no chance to play an important role in defining the U.S. Catholic position on Central America. They spoke to each other and perhaps impressed officials in the Reagan administration, but the USCC, U.S. Catholic missionaries, and the rest of the American Catholic press did not take them seriously and therefore ignored them. A more reasonable and evenhanded conservative voice in the Catholic media could have served to temper the bias of some journalists in the mainline Catholic press. That traditionalist Catholic periodicals failed to make a contribution to the Catholic debate on Central America can only be attributed to their own rigidity.

eight

The Progressive
U.S. Catholic Press
on Central America
in the 1980s

GUATEMALA

hereas the secular media showed much attention throughout the 1980s to events in Nicaragua and El Salvador, Guatemala by contrast tended for the most part to be ignored. When President Carter terminated military aid to this troubled country in the late 1970s due to its horrendous human rights record, he indirectly relegated it to near-irrelevance in the eyes of U.S. journalists and the American public. Nicaragua and El Salvador were intimately intertwined with U.S. foreign policy, since the contras and the Salvadoran military received massive American aid. Consequently, the secular media deemed developments in these two countries more newsworthy than those in neighboring Guatemala.

Yet human rights abuses escalated in Guatemala throughout the first half of the 1980s and remained a serious problem for the rest of the decade. Military and other security personnel killed over 70,000 civilians, mostly Indians, in an attempt to destroy a guerrilla force of about 2,000. More than 600,000 Indians were driven from their homes and forced to live in squalor as refugees. About 70,000 more were compelled to relocate in government-created "model villages," where they lived as virtual prisoners under the watchful eye of the army. Here they were made to serve as unpaid "volunteers" in civilian patrols, supposedly protecting their region from guerrilla insurgents. Indeed, many human rights monitors believe that the violent record of the Guatemalan government during the 1980s was the worst in all of Latin America. Nevertheless, despite such an assessment, President Reagan throughout his eight years in office attempted to convince Congress to renew the aid that the Carter administration had cut.

To its credit the U. S. Catholic press, along with a few Protestant publications, refused to allow Guatemala to be ignored. It meticulously reported Guatemalan atrocities and commented on the horrendous conditions of its displaced Indians.

Although one would not have realized it from the news accounts of the secular media, more priests were murdered in Guatemala than in any other Latin American country. Between 1978 and 1982 alone, thirteen priests and one religious brother were killed.[1] The U. S. Catholic press not only reported these deaths but took pains to provide details emphasizing that the victims all had one thing in common: they worked with the poor and seemingly for this reason were massacred by right-wing death squads.[2] Catholic periodicals were also careful to emphasize that the murdered clergy were only a minuscule fraction of the tens of thousands who had died or disappeared in Guatemala.[3] Further stress was placed on the suffering of the hundreds of thousands of Indians who were forced to live in refugee camps or in the so-called "model villages."[4] Also underscored was the fact that, unlike in El Salvador, the Guatemalan episcopacy, at least after 1983, was united in its condemnation of violence and its defense of the poor and oppressed.[5] Furthermore, whereas the secular media focused almost exclusively on the Nicaraguan part of the pope's 1983 trip to Central America in which he clashed with the leftist Sandinistas, the progressive Catholic press highlighted John Paul's visit to Guatemala as well, emphasizing his condemnation of government-sponsored violence there.[6]

Finally, the Catholic press was vigilant in its demand that the U. S. arms embargo on Guatemala be continued. In a 1983 article, for instance, Olivia Carrescia and Robert Dinardo, after reporting on the horrible conditions faced by Indians living in refugee camps in Chiapas, noted that the situation would be even worse if President Reagan was successful in renewing Guatemalan military aid.[7] Isabel Rogers (pen name) in a 1984 commentary likewise related stories of "terrorism beyond belief" told to her by Indian refugees in Mexico, ending with the following plea: "We in the U. S. . . . can offer our support by speaking out and insisting that Washington not renew military aid or support the government of Guatemala that is causing its people to flee their homeland in terror."[8]

Rather than highlighting the many articles in U. S. Catholic periodicals dealing with Guatemala, this chapter presents a detailed discussion of a few. These should sufficiently illustrate the nature of the overall reporting of the Catholic press on the country.

Our Sunday Visitor devoted the entire magazine section of its February 14, 1982, issue to a discussion of the church in Guatemala. Three of its four articles were by Robert Holton, its Latin American correspondent, who had recently returned from a lengthy stay in that country. His analysis was sophisticated and perceptive and had one dominant theme: the church and the vast majority of the poor were caught between a repressive government willing to violently squash even the mildest reform and a group of Marxist revolutionaries equally wedded to brutality. They sympathized with neither side in the civil war and prayed that both the military and the guerrillas would just leave them alone.[9]

In one of his articles Holton presented the story of a priest who had been traumatized by the civil war. Since this method of focusing on the suffering of a particular victim was frequently used in the Catholic press to illustrate the intensity of injustice in Central America, this piece, which exemplifies this effective journalistic technique, will be covered in detail.

The author began by noting that the unnamed priest "had all the hallmarks of those who have suffered and they told his story well—the drawn face, the haunted eyes, the shaking hands, the two-day stubble of beard."[10] By keeping his own commentary to a minimum, Holton skillfully allowed the priest to portray his intense mental anguish in his own words. The cleric started his story after failing in an attempt to light a cigarette because his hand shook so violently:

> Just last week . . . the army came into one of my villages and killed 20 men. . . . They used machetes to hack them to pieces. They always do that, these bastards, just to show the people that they can do any damned thing they please. . . .
>
> I don't know how much more of this I can take. They kill, they rape, they rob—the army and the guerrillas—both sides do these things. And all I can do is get up in the church and say words about it. I say hard words. But they are only words. I feel so helpless. So useless. So frustrated. . . .

I am in constant danger of being killed for what I say. . . . I speak
against both sides in church and I am in danger of being killed by either
side—the army or the guerrillas.[11]

So fearful was the priest that he had not slept in the same residence for
more than two consecutive nights over the previous three months. His misery was made worse by the knowledge that the Indian families who allowed
him to stay in their huts placed their own lives in jeopardy. He knew that the
church had to continue to speak out for human rights, justice, and freedom,
but he saw little hope that these ideals would ever become a reality for the
poor. He claimed that weapons sent by the United States and other countries to the military and the guerrillas only compounded the people's misery. He ended his story in deep despair: "Oh, I'm so tired. I can see only
more and more killing and hurt and pain. I don't know how long I can go
on. I don't know how long the other priests can keep this up. I don't know
how long the people can stand it."[12]

Equally impressive was a 1984 *Commonweal* article by political scientist
Gordon Bowen. In it he discussed the death squad murders of priests and
lay catechists and the large-scale destruction of churches and church-run
schools, clinics, and cooperatives in the Guatemalan province of Quiché.
Bowen was especially effective when he cynically contrasted the success of
army roadblocks in impeding the flow of weapons to guerrilla forces with
their total failure to hinder the transportation of the ten to fifteen victims
kidnapped in the country each day.[13] Also effective was his inclusion of a
sidebar containing two contradictory quotations. The first was from Reagan's own Kissinger Commission on Central America:

> An even more serious obstacle in terms of the ultimate containment of
> armed revolt in Guatemala is the brutal behavior of the security forces.
> In the cities they have murdered those even suspected of dissent. In the
> countryside, they have at times killed indiscriminately. . . . Such actions
> are morally unacceptable. They are also self-defeating.[14]

The second was from a televised speech by President Reagan: "In
Guatemala, political parties and trade unions are functioning. An election is
scheduled for July there, with a real prospect that that country can return to
full constitutional government in 1985."[15] The sidebar's title—"Another
Country?"—cleverly brought out the contradiction in the two statements
and as such spoke volumes.

A second piece by Bowen from 1985 was even more telling. It began by contrasting a recent police raid at the University of San Carlos with the Reagan administration's call for Congress to lift its ban on aid to Guatemalan security forces. The author followed with a two-page list of well over a hundred students, professors, and administrators killed, wounded, or abducted by police on the USC campus over the previous year. Bowen then asked why, in the light of such brutality, the White House was requesting $5 million from Congress for Guatemalan security forces.[16] But Bowen was not through. He offered a sidebar that chided the *Washington Post, New York Times,* and *Chronicle of Higher Education* for shirking their responsibility by neglecting to provide accurate coverage of the violent actions of police at USC. He closed with the following pithy observation:

> It is not only Guatemalan academics and students who are invisible. When the Polish priest Father Jersy Popieluszko vanished in 1984, the *Washington Post* ran thirty-one separate stories (five on the front page) and 550 column inches about the crime in the first six weeks after his abduction; *New York Times* coverage was initially even more extensive, over ninety column inches in the first week. Catholic missionary Felipe Balán Tomás has been missing in Guatemala for eight months now, but not one column inch in the *Post* or *New York Times* has been devoted to any of the circumstances surrounding his abduction while saying Mass in February 1985.[17]

Obviously U. S. newspapers had concluded that the disappearance of a priest in a communist country was worthy of attention, while that of a cleric in a right-wing dictatorship was not. To Bowen and to the progressive Catholic press in general this was shabby journalism, and they were intent on making it an issue for public debate.

An *America* article from 1988 by Warren Holleman adroitly encapsulated the thrust of the U. S. Catholic press's message concerning Guatemala in its first paragraph:

> There has been a lot of talk in recent years about human rights in Central America. Republicans talk about the Sandinista regime. Democrats counter with the Somozans, or the Salvadoran reality. While the media and the politicians focus their attention on Nicaragua and Salvador, one other Central American nation has quietly racked up what is, arguably,

the worst human rights record in the Western Hemisphere. That country is Guatemala.[18]

The author went on to list a frightening array of statistics to prove his contention: well over 50,000 civilians killed by the military in the previous ten years; the destruction by the army of 444 Indian villages in a two-year period; a million displaced Guatemalans forced to live as refugees; 70 percent of the arable land owned by 4 percent of the population; nearly half the population unemployed or underemployed; 300,000 children dying each year from hunger; a forty-one-year life-expectancy average in rural areas. He commended the U.S. media and politicians for publicizing the fact that 9,000 Argentines had disappeared in that country's "dirty war" but asked why they now ignored the 35,000 who had disappeared in the much smaller country of Guatemala.

Holleman argued that the much-touted 1985 election of a civilian president was no more than a public relations event permitted by the military to upgrade the nation's image so that the armed forces could again receive overt U.S. aid. He claimed that because the generals permitted the election, the Reagan administration was able to break the Carter-imposed arms embargo. The military actually increased its effectiveness, since it now received $316 million in U.S. aid. Although human rights conditions did improve in the cities after the election, in the countryside they remained as bad as ever.

Holleman further claimed that even from 1981 through 1985, when military aid was forbidden by U.S. law, the Reagan administration secretly shipped tens of millions of dollars worth of arms to Guatemala. He states that in 1982 alone clandestine aid far exceeded all the military aid Guatemala had received in the previous thirty-two years.[19]

Before closing, the author is careful to balance his commentary by noting that the guerrillas had only compounded the problems of the rural Indians:

Guatemala's Indians remain in a no-win situation—between the Scylla of the guerrillas and the Charybdis of the army. Guerrillas continue to enter villages; they rob, harass and recruit at gunpoint. The army continues to follow in the guerrillas' wake: Soldiers enter the village, accuse the peasants of collaborating with the guerrillas and destroy the village.[20]

Like Holton who wrote six years earlier, Holleman pointed out that the hapless Indians had little sympathy for the army or for the guerrillas. Time may have passed, but the sad situation of the suffering Mayans was unchanged, and to its credit the U. S. Catholic press remained indefatigable in attempting to make North Americans aware of this reality.

EL SALVADOR

Throughout the 1980s, the overwhelming majority of Catholic publications continued to condemn government-sanctioned violence in El Salvador while contending that U. S. aid made such oppression possible. Reports from Christian-based fact-finding groups remained a favorite means of conveying this message. An *America* article from 1984 reflected this technique well. The author claimed that her delegation conversed with people from all walks of life who expressed fear of police and military terror. And with good reason, for members of the Salvadoran Human Rights Commission informed them that 47,000 civilians had been murdered over the past four years alone. Four officials of the commission itself had been assassinated, while three others had disappeared. The delegation met with Salvadoran President Alvaro Magaña, who bluntly admitted that the forthcoming elections were being held only to placate the United States.[21]

Recollections from those returning from fact-finding trips were even more effective if they were composed by clergymen. Thus, throughout the 1980s such reports could be found almost weekly in Catholic periodicals. Like those written by laypeople, some were composed by Sandinista advocates whose conclusions seemed to have been reached before they arrived in Central America. Most, however, came from clerics who were critical but objective.

After a 1984 visit to El Salvador, Father Giese provided *Our Sunday Visitor* readers with a sympathetic overview of the courageous work of Tutela Legal, the archdiocesan legal aid office. Most notable, however, was his interview with Father Octavio Cruz, head of the archdiocesan Social Directorate, who told him that a million Salvadorans, 20 percent of the population, had been forced to flee their rural villages as a result of indiscriminate military bombings followed by army sweeps. He added that the government's strategy was to blame the plight of the *desplazados* (the displaced ones) on the guerrillas and then to appear as their benefactor by offering them material assistance provided by the United States.[22] Father Brockman of *America* likewise related to his readers after a 1985 trip that little had changed in El Salvador since the death of Archbishop Romero.[23]

Needless to say, when the personal testimony came from a bishop it was especially effective. An article written by Archbishop John Quinn of San Francisco for *America* following his 1986 visit well illustrates this point. The U.S. State Department had cited his trip as proof that repression in El Salvador had virtually disappeared and that U.S. policy was therefore beginning to work. Quinn responded to his government's positive "spin" with the following: "I am sorry to report that, in my view, very little has changed in any substantial way in El Salvador."[24] Death squads continued to operate with impunity, while bombing in the countryside had intensified. Half the population was unemployed, and those that did find work received slavelike wages. Only the oligarchy, the military, and the U.S. government refused to support a dialogue aimed at achieving peace. As for the government's invocation of his trip: "Such claims do not conform to my experience or observation," he wrote, "and are attributed to me without foundation."[25]

Quinn's article not only contradicted the State Department's rosy picture of Salvadoran reform but also exposed the disingenuous nature of U.S. governmental claims concerning El Salvador. Indeed, so devastating was the archbishop's article that following its appearance Salvadoran authorities placed his name on a list of people who were henceforth to be denied entry into the country.[26]

A short *America* editorial appeared in the same issue with Quinn's article. It noted that the archbishop's Salvadoran experience corroborated the claims of the eleven members of the Sanctuary Movement then on trial in Arizona for illegally smuggling Salvadorans into the country. The defendants argued that Salvadoran and Guatemalan refugees entered the United States primarily to escape violence and not, as the United States Department of Justice contended, only to better themselves economically. Nevertheless, solely on the basis of the government's premise, the trial judge declared that the case could only include evidence on whether or not the defendants had aided the refugees. No defense based on moral or religious grounds would be allowed. *America*'s editorial strongly disapproved of the judge's decision: "As more and more evidence comes in—such as that of Archbishop Quinn— the cause of Sanctuary seems more and more justified and the disallowing of all such evidence in the Tucson trial correspondingly unjustified."[27]

Indeed, this editorial typified the overwhelming support for the Sanctuary Movement found in most Catholic periodicals. The *National Catholic Reporter,* for instance, related the tragic story of Felipe and Elena (not their real names), who, together with their five children, escaped death in Guatemala with the help of Sanctuary workers who smuggled them into the United States, where they declared sanctuary at a Benedictine monastery in Vermont.[28]

In an article titled "On Trial in Texas: Is It Legal or Not to Help Refugees?" which treated the case of Sanctuary worker Stacy Merkt, *NCR* reporter Patricia Scharber Lefevere emphatically argued yes.[29] In another piece, the *NCR* noted that several members of the jury were crying as they declared Merkt guilty. It then explained that although these jurors obviously sympathized with the defendant, since the judge had ordered them to decide the case purely on whether or not she had helped the refugees, they had no choice but to convict; hence the tears.[30]

When President Duarte decided to move his family to the United States for reasons of safety, *America* asked why humbler Salvadorans far less able to protect themselves in their home country were not given the same right. Since they were not, the editorialist reasoned, the Sanctuary Movement was obviously necessary and hence morally justified.[31]

Just as the U.S. Catholic press was almost universally supportive of the Sanctuary Movement, it was almost totally critical of the Kissinger Commission's report on Central America. An *NCR* article by Jesuit law professor Robert Drinan was typical of the position taken by the vast majority of Catholic periodicals. Drinan charged that the superficial nature of the commission's conclusions made it apparent that its members had neglected to concern themselves with the history of El Salvador before making their report. He next touched on specifics: They seemed to have no understanding of how *Matanza*, the brutal slaughter of thousands of Indians in 1932, colored later Salvadoran history. They knew nothing of the so-called Fourteen Families and how their confiscation of peasant lands had always been at the core of the country's problems. Such ignorance caused commission members to reduce the Salvadoran civil war to merely a chapter in the global struggle between East and West, to no more than a leftist attempt to impose Marxism on all of Central America, an attempt which must be stopped at all costs. Such, argued Drinan, was "a complete distortion of reality." The objective books of Thomas Walker and the "splendid" *Inevitable Revolutions* by Cornell professor Walter LaFeber should have been required reading for the commission, but its report gave no evidence that such scholarship was ever consulted.[32]

Whereas *Crisis*, the *Wanderer*, the *National Catholic Register*, and *Social Justice Review* cited the most conservative of the Salvadoran bishops in an attempt to undermine the position of the USCC on El Salvador, more progressive Catholic publications often quoted Archbishop Rivera Damas in support of the U.S. bishops. In an interview with Rivera, for example, *Our Sunday*

Visitor highlighted his remark that the Salvadoran people felt very close to the U. S. episcopacy since the latter was so supportive of their struggle for peace.[33]

Priest magazine, in an attempt to provide a wider U. S. forum for Rivera's views, reprinted his entire talk to an audience of seminarians in Florida. In it he criticized the United States for ignoring dialogue as a method for resolving Salvador's civil war while preferring instead to rely solely on a military solution. He informed his listeners that although there was reason for concern at the inroads being made by communism, there was nevertheless no doubt that the lack of basic social justice was at the heart of his country's problems. He further reminded North Americans that true peace must be premised on justice for the poor. If a peace was achieved that merely allowed the upper class to perpetuate the status quo, it was worthless and unacceptable.[34]

Especially interesting is the Catholic press's reaction to the 1984 presidential victory of José Napoleón Duarte and the triumph of his Christian Democratic Party (PDC) in the following year's National Assembly election. Although most in the secular media saw in the election results reason to hope that authentic democracy was just around the corner, Catholic periodicals were for the most part far less sanguine. Aside from the conservative journals covered in the previous chapter, *America* was perhaps the most optimistic. It actually commended Reagan officials for orchestrating a genuine election, adding that "the results . . . suggest that there is some hope at least that the Administration's strategy may yet prove successful."[35] It cautioned, however, that for true democracy to take root, Duarte would have to purge the armed forces of their repressive elements. Moreover, his success in this endeavor would depend wholly on whether the United States was willing to terminate all military aid should the Salvadoran power structure block his efforts.[36] *America*'s hopes soared even higher when the PDC won a majority in the National Assembly. In an April editorial it gloried in the belief that this election would give President Duarte the power needed to deal effectively with both the right wing and the rebels.[37]

Just four months later, however, the Jesuit magazine's hopes seem to have faded. The bestowal of an honorary doctorate on Duarte by the University of Notre Dame provided *America* author Kathleen Connolly with an opportunity to castigate the Salvadoran president. She pointed out bitterly that Duarte chose to reappoint Colonel Carlos Vides Casanova to the important post of Minister of Defense even though he was widely believed to have orchestrated a cover-up in the case of the four murdered U. S. churchwomen. In short, she contended that the Vides appointment showed Duarte to be no more than an opportunist who had sold out to the military.[38]

From the earliest announcement that democratic elections would be held in El Salvador, *Commonweal* proved to be more pessimistic than *America*. A piece by Jim Chapin and Jack Clark, written after the first round of the presidential contest, predicted that Duarte would defeat his ARENA rival Roberto d'Aubuisson in the final round. Yet the authors concluded that when all was said and done, the much-heralded election would prove to be no more than another in a long line of meaningless Salvadoran elections. Why? Because Duarte would be unable to govern effectively.[39]

Chapin seemed no more impressed with the PDC's legislative victory, although he conceded that it was unexpected and astonishing. The Christian Democrats won, he reasoned, because they promised to open negotiations with the Revolutionary Democratic Front–Farabundo Martí National Liberation Front (FDR-FMLN). Thus, there was no doubt that the tiny nation finally had a real chance to construct a workable peace, one in which the opposition was granted a role in government. Unfortunately it would not come to pass because the Reagan administration, clinging to its fantasy of total victory, would not permit a solution based on coalition building. Consequently, a great opportunity for meaningful peace would probably be wasted.[40]

Even less optimistic was *Our Sunday Visitor*'s Father Giese, who went to El Salvador as an observer of the presidential contest. Basing his analysis on unnamed "astute political observers," Giese conceded that the election was free of fraud, but only because the United States wanted it that way so it could justify increasing military aid. Thus, the real reason for the election was not to bring about democracy but to bolster the power of the Salvadoran military, and this represented "a deception of the people" who had voted in hope of peace.[41]

Matt Scheiber, also writing for *OSV*, was more evenhanded, citing both those who praised and those who criticized the Salvadoran president. He pointed out that Duarte in his first few months in office did manage to get some of the most notoriously violent military officers reassigned to overseas posts and that he did hold two rounds of peace talks with the FMLN. But on the other hand, while junta leader he had successfully engineered the reinstatement of U.S. military aid, which had been halted after the murders of Romero and the churchwomen, and had also failed to curtail the killing of about a thousand people a month by right-wing elements.[42]

One additional observation is in order concerning the 1985–86 elections. Although it is not within the scope of this study to methodically compare the election coverage of the U.S. Catholic press with that of its secular counterpart, the analysis and predictions of the former nonetheless seem to have been far more accurate than those of the latter.

The rout of the PDC by the ultra-right ARENA Party in the 1988 municipal and legislative elections proved that the pessimism of the U.S. Catholic press after the 1985–86 elections was well founded. As journalists throughout the United States penned opinion pieces ranging from shock to despair, *Commonweal* writer Jim Chapin, this time teamed up with Patrick Laiefield, once again published a commentary that was highly insightful. The two also articulated opinions with which few Catholic periodicals would disagree.

The authors began with a pithy quip on the Reagan administration's face-saving remark that the ARENA win was a victory for democracy: This "is like saying that the victory for the Nazis in the 1933 elections in Germany showed the strength of the Weimar Republic."[43] Contending that ARENA was no more democratic than the "Marxist-Leninist" FMLN, they further pointed out that the FDR allies of the FMLN, far from being Marxists, were social democrats. But most importantly, they argued that the Christian Democrats lost the election for two reasons: Duarte had promised to deliver peace and failed, and during his tenure in office the Salvadoran economy went from bad to terrible. The authors then got to the heart of the matter. Duarte was unable to end the civil war because the Reagan administration, intent on total victory, would not allow him to discuss power sharing with the FDR-FMLN. Moreover, as the Salvadoran economy deteriorated, the U.S. forced austerity measures on the Duarte administration that proved especially burdensome to the poor majority. Consequently, the Reagan administration's hard-line policies were actually counterproductive. They ironically destroyed the PDC's base of support among the country's poor majority, thereby virtually guaranteeing the party's defeat by ARENA in the 1988 elections.[44]

A 1988 article by Jesuit sociologist Joseph Fitzpatrick merits a closer look because it meticulously detailed the so-called "National Debate" launched by Archbishop Rivera. This "debate," little known in the United States, depicted another dimension of the important role the Salvadoran Catholic church played in the eventual creation of peace. It also illustrated just how adept the U.S. Catholic press was in informing its readers on even the most complex matters of the Central American church's option for the poor.

As Fitzpatrick related, since both the government and revolutionary opposition seemed unwilling to enter into serious dialogue, Rivera devised a plan whereby the Salvadoran people themselves would be able to take the initiative in creating their own version of a just peace. He had a questionnaire drawn up and presented to as many Salvadoran organizations as possible: business and professional associations, religious and political groups, and labor and peasant organizations. The groups were asked to articulate what they thought was most essential for the building of peace. Sixty-three groups responded. Church officials next collated the suggestions into a series of 180 propositions, which were then sent back to the various organizations. They were to be studied in preparation for a two-day church-sponsored meeting called the "National Debate." Representatives of sixty of the groups attended the debate, where they voted on and adopted all but sixteen of the propositions. Those that were passed can be summarized into the following: a call for an immediate cease-fire to be followed by a dialogue aimed at a peace settlement; requests for government-initiated legislation aimed at correcting long-standing injustices toward the poor; an end to U.S. military involvement in Salvadoran affairs; and the termination of guerrilla disruptions of transportation and public utility services.

Fitzpatrick pointed out that through the "National Debate" Rivera and the church had succeeded in creating a grassroots consensus demanding that the powers that be, both governmental and revolutionary, take peace negotiations seriously. He noted that many of the groups involved were collaborating with one another for the first time. Finally, he succinctly summed up for his readers the potential of the archbishop's initiative:

> Thus, the National Debate . . . has created a powerful grass-roots pressure that could be effective in moving the Government and the guerrillas towards a cease-fire and a negotiated peace. . . . [I]n their weariness and desperation, the people, under the leadership of the Archbishop, are making their voice heard as it has not been heard before. If this continues, in the long run it may be decisive.[45]

To help educate U.S. churchpeople on the "National Debate," *LADOC* translated the final document into English and published it in its March–April 1989 issue.[46]

One additional article from this time was based on statements made by Father Ignacio Martín Baró, Jesuit vice-rector of the Central American University (UCA), to members of a U.S. fact-finding group. The piece attempted to sum up the counterproductive effects of U.S. military aid on Salvadoran society. The vice rector contended that such aid had made the military officer class the most powerful force in the country. This in turn had created a situation whereby Duarte had been reduced to a military puppet and his PDC had been warped into a façade of democracy needed to keep the flow of U.S. dollars from drying up. Indeed, the country's predicament was such that neither the government nor the guerrillas could win the war. Because of its continuance, Duarte and the PDC had lost the support of the poor masses who voted for them thinking that they were voting for peace. After commenting that his residence had already been bombed six times by right-wing elements, Baró closed by telling his North American listeners: "Quote me, I have nothing to hide. My opinion is well known. The Government's file on me is large."[47] In hindsight these words are chilling, for a little over a year later Father Martín Baró was executed by a U.S.-trained and -equipped death squad.

Although filled with violence and tragedy, the year 1989 would ironically prove to be decisive in the eventual termination of the Salvadoran civil war. In March ARENA candidate Alfredo Cristiani was elected president, thereby consolidating his party's control of the national government. In September the government and the FMLN agreed to enter into a peace dialogue. However, little headway was made. Security forces continued to violate human rights with impunity. When in October a bomb blew up the headquarters of FENASTRAS (National Federation of Salvadoran Workers), killing ten labor leaders, FMLN officials broke off peace talks. Instead, they opted to begin a major offensive that had been in the planning stages for over two years. Launched on November 11, the insurrection lasted several days. Embarrassed by its inability to quickly terminate the offensive, the military made numerous raids on church agencies that it perceived to be pro-FMLN. On November 16 at about 1:00 a.m., thirty or so soldiers from the U.S.-created Atlacatl Brigade entered the Central American University. They dragged six Jesuits from their rooms and murdered them along with their housekeeper and her daughter. The cold-blooded execution of Ignacio Ellacuría, Ignacio Martín Baró, Segundo Montes, Juan Ramón Moreno, Amando López, Joaquin López y López, and Julia Elba Ramos and her daughter Celina ironically was the catalyst that would eventually bring peace to El Salvador. Facing international outrage and an embarrassed U.S. Congress which seemed finally ready to cut off Salvadoran military aid even if the Bush administration was not, the ARENA government had no real choice but to begin serious peace talks. In January 1990 the government and the FMLN entered into U.N.-mediated negotiations. In January 1992 a peace agreement was finally signed which allowed for the incorporation of a demobilized FMLN into the political life of the country, while drastically reducing the power and size of the military. It also called for the establishment of a United Nations "Truth Commission" to investigate human rights abuses committed during the war. The commission's final report would conclude that the Salvadoran military and security forces had been responsible for the vast majority of the 70,000 civilians murdered during the war and that the United States was not lacking in culpability. In other words, it validated what the Catholic press had been charging over the previous decade and a half.

The tone of *National Catholic Reporter* articles on El Salvador prior to the UCA murders typified that of most Catholic journals. Titles such as "Salvador's UCA Bombed Again,"[48] "Hooded Men Break into Salvadoran Church,"[49] "New Violence Wave Hits San Salvador,"[50] "Salvadoran Refugees Journey Home, Six Supporters Arrested,"[51] and "Death Squad Blamed for Salvadoran Blast"[52] all told a similar and well-worn story. Right-wing violence was as bad as ever, contrary to what the Bush administration reported to the American public. The *NCR*'s September 29 issue especially demonstrated this national weekly's indefatigability. It contained no fewer than six pieces on El Salvador. One highlighted the courageous efforts of Lutheran Bishop Medardo Gómez Soto, referring to him as the most prominent Salvadoran advocate for the poor and a champion of justice.[53] Another, announcing that ARENA and the FMLN had agreed to enter into dialogue, added that this meant there was hope, "though slight," for future peace.[54] A third report emphasized the prominent role of Archbishop Rivera in promoting the peace talks.[55] A fourth consisted of an interview with María Julia Hernández, director of Tutela Legal, who noted that bombings, torture, and disappearances had recently increased.[56] Still another told of a woman who had been forced to flee to Mexico after her husband was killed by police and she was jailed and gang-raped, all because her spouse had joined a labor union.[57] Finally, an editorial accused State Department officials of "telling us outright lies" and accused the ARENA government of repression.[58]

Six weeks later the *NCR* issued a front-page report revealing the claim of Caesar Joya Martínez, a former member of the Salvadoran army's First Infantry Brigade, that his unit had assassinated about seventy people and that he had personally participated in eight of these killings. Joya further asserted that two U. S. military advisers "were 'part and parcel' of death-squad operations" and that they provided his unit with $3,000 a month and civilian vehicles used to facilitate its violent activities. The piece did add, however, that a U. S. State Department spokesman denied the charges.[59]

An accompanying editorial noted that Joya's story was by no means the first account of such alleged U. S. involvement in El Salvador. After pointing out that the United States had by this time given $4.4 billion to this tiny country, the editorialist asked what we had gotten for our money. He then answered his own question: "[T]he return on our investment includes torture and murder with at least the implicit support of U. S. military personnel." He closed with a declaration that was certainly prophetic in that only six days later the six Jesuits and two women would be added to the long list of Salvadorans assassinated by the military: "It is way past time we stop supporting murderers and thugs."[60]

Whereas, as has been shown previously, conservative Catholic periodicals either ignored the murder of the Jesuits or tried to mitigate the U.S. and Salvadoran governments' culpability in the crime, this was certainly not the case for progressive Catholic journals. U.S. Jesuits were outraged by the executions of their co-religious in El Salvador, and over the next two months they made this evident in the pages of *America*. The earliest commentary, however, by associate editor Thomas Stahel, was surprisingly restrained. He attempted to place the tragic murders in the broader perspective of Jesuit service, remarking that the priests and brothers in his residence had received the news of the killings with anger and outrage but also with "sober exuberance" and "a sadness that was merry." Why? Because they knew that their slain fellow religious "had done the ultimate Jesuit thing." They had given their lives for those on whose behalf they had labored. He made his point more emphatic by noting that coincidentally the six were murdered on November 16, the same date that three other Iberian Jesuits were martyred in Paraguay in 1628 because of their work for the Indian poor.[61]

In an editorial the following week, the *America* staff was not so sedate. Four days after the assassinations, a woman at a Republican fund-raiser had shouted at President George Bush: "Why are we killing priests in El Salvador?" Bush brusquely retorted that we were not, adding: "Now you be quiet." Responding to the president's behavior with an editorial sarcastically dubbed "Now You Be Quiet, Oscar," the *America* staff noted the similarity between Bush's conduct and that of U.S. officials in 1980 who ignored Archbishop Romero's plea to stop sending military aid. Arguing that the more than $1 billion sent over the next decade had done nothing to mitigate military brutality, the editorial staff contended that Romero's words should have been taken seriously: "Military assistance should have stopped long ago."[62]

Former editor Joseph O'Hare took up the same theme a week later. After asserting that the six slain Jesuits had been men of peace who died because they chose to use their university to confront the crucial issues of the day, he turned to the question of U.S. military assistance. He argued that if the goal of U.S. aid was to foster democracy, then assistance to El Salvador had proven counterproductive, for it had actually impeded democratic progress. He tersely added that this was what Archbishop Romero had tried to tell the U.S. ten years earlier.[63] Included in the same December 16 issue was an open letter from Georgetown University President Leo O'Donovan to Salvadoran President Cristiani, a Georgetown alumnus. After expressing his outrage at the UCA killings and reminding the ARENA head of state of his Georgetown roots, O'Donovan called on him to follow the advice of the Salvadoran Catholic church by announcing a cease-fire and entering into serious peace negotiations with the opposition.[64] Lest the murdered women be forgotten, the final *America* issue of 1989 contained a poem "For Julia Elba Ramos."[65]

Several articles dealing with the Jesuit murders appeared in the various January 1990 issues of *America*. In one, Thomas Stahel commented that the rather belated admission by President Cristiani that the army was responsible for the executions was insufficient. It was essential that the higher-ups who ordered the assassinations be brought to justice.[66] This demand would be repeated many times in future articles in the U. S. Catholic press.

In a February article, Joseph Mulligan, a U. S. Jesuit who had visited the murder scene shortly after the crime was committed, related his disgust at what he encountered. Blood had been splattered everywhere. The priests' offices had been trashed, equipment destroyed, fires set, the community cars sprayed with bullets, the kitchen ransacked. He informed his readers that the military had brazenly announced beforehand over the radio what it intended to do to the UCA Jesuits and that soldiers who had surrounded the university campus did nothing to stop those who were committing the carnage, even though they obviously could hear what was taking place. In other words, the murders were not the work of a few rogue soldiers; they had to be part of a larger, well-coordinated plan. Mulligan was careful to interject that our tax dollars financed this horrible travesty of justice. But he concluded on a hopeful note: The blood of these martyrs had caused thousands in the United States to write to Washington, protest, fast, and so on. Perhaps this would finally bring about an end to U. S. military aid.[67]

In the month and a half following the UCA murders, *Commonweal* contained only two articles dealing with this crime. Both, however, cut directly to the heart of the matter, wasting few words on peripheral concerns. A lengthy December 1 editorial began by contrasting Berlin, where the wall was falling down, with El Salvador, which "is ruled by the gun and divided by walls of the mind."[68] It then posited that the UCA assassinations necessitated a reexamining of U. S. policy toward El Salvador. This led to a highly negative review of the U. S.-Salvadoran partnership over the last decade:

> After ten years of civil war; after a containment policy that included U. S. military advisers and $4.5 billion of U. S. economic and military assistance; after the murder of over 70,000 Salvadorans, mostly noncombatants, mostly the victims of right-wing death squads; after the displacement of one in ten Salvadorans and the exile of perhaps a fifth of the total population, we can only conclude that U. S. policy has been a massive failure. There is no peace, no victory, no democracy in El Salvador.[69]

The editorial next expanded on these last three points. First, there was no peace. Although it "is seldom reported in the U.S.," a vast chasm lay between the rich and the poor majority. All one had to do was spend a few hours outside the U.S. Embassy to see vast shantytowns where residents must walk for hours to fetch water and firewood. This reality contrasted sharply with the bunkered compounds and armored luxury cars of the elite. The cities and towns were filled with 57,000 soldiers intimidating and brutalizing residents—a law unto themselves. Second, there was no victory: Seventy thousand were dead, but there was a stalemate. In November the FMLN had launched its largest offensive of the war, but neither side had gained an advantage. There was no rush by the populace to join the guerrillas or to support the army. Finally, there was no democracy. "The six so-called democratic elections heralded by the U.S. in the last decade are largely cosmetic—a veneerocracy." A million Salvadorans, however, had voted with their feet; they had fled the country. Both sides murdered with impunity. Even on the heels of the Jesuit murders the Salvadoran Attorney General publicly threatened the bishops with violence. And he was in charge of investigating the Jesuit case![70] "The Bush administration should cut off military assistance now, and the U.S. Congress should begin by looking at the condition of the majority of Salvadorans and examining that people's desire for peace."[71] This was the message of the murdered Ignacio Ellacuría the day before his death. It was the same message delivered a decade earlier by Archbishop Romero. Finally, the poverty of the people must be addressed if society was to be saved.

The second *Commonweal* article was by Father Jon Sobrino, who had lived with the murdered Jesuits at the UCA but escaped death only because he was lecturing out of the country at the time of the killings. He pointed out that since before 1980 the Salvadoran Jesuits had continuously received death threats and the UCA had frequently been bombed. Why? Because they supported a peace dialogue and had transformed their university into a social force working for faith and justice. Sobrino was also careful to note that it was not only the Catholic church that was harassed by governmental forces. The Episcopalians, Lutherans, Mennonites and all other Christians who believed in justice were also oppressed.[72]

In keeping with the precedent it had set from the earliest days of its Central American coverage, the *National Catholic Reporter* dwarfed all other Catholic periodicals with the space it allotted to the Jesuit murders. Indeed, by December 8 alone it had devoted no fewer than twenty articles to the killings. Marked by an intensely assertive style at a time when many prestigious publications expressed caution in placing blame for the crime, the

NCR had by November 24 already declared its certainty that Salvadoran military or paramilitary forces were culpable and that the United States was their indirect accomplice.[73] Its aggressive approach was well articulated in the bold headline of its November 24 editorial: "U. S. Taxpayer Money Is Being Used to Kill Priests and It Must Stop Now." In the piece the editorialist not only contended that there was a definite link between U. S. aid and the more than 70,000 Salvadorans killed during the civil war, he also refused to allow U. S. citizens to wash their hands of the matter, asking, "How many more atrocities will it take before the American public rises up in outrage and demands an end to [U. S. involvement]?"[74]

NCR articles were especially vigilant in their attempts to connect the Bush administration with the Jesuit murders. Consequently, seldom did a negative report from a human rights or an academic group concerning this topic escape notice in the pages of this periodical. A December 8 piece informed its readers that the prestigious human rights organization Americas Watch had issued a report accusing U. S. officials from President Bush on down of attempting to create the "false impression" that leftists were responsible for the UCA murders. It cited the report's conclusion that the Bush administration had shamefully attempted "to disguise or to ignore the overwhelming evidence" that the Salvadoran armed forces had committed the crime. It pointed out that the report had also accused the U. S. Embassy in San Salvador of refusing to defend North American church workers who were being brutalized by Salvadoran authorities. Finally, it noted that the Americas Watch authors had chosen the word "dismal" to sum up its judgment of the overall conduct of the U. S. government in El Salvador.[75]

An article in the December 1 issue noted that despite the UCA assassinations Bush maintained that he would still not cut Salvadoran aid.[76] There followed a second piece revealing that a Washington-based human rights group, using the Freedom of Information Act, had uncovered the fact that for the past twelve years the State Department had maintained a file on the murdered Jesuits.[77] This report seemed to imply that the State Department's conduct in some way at least indirectly connected it to the Jesuit deaths.

Of all periodicals, both religious and secular, the *NCR* was most meticulous in citing military harassment of non-Jesuit churchpeople during and just after the FMLN offensive. A November piece reported the arrest of fourteen Lutheran church workers, including four from the United States.[78] Several December articles reported attempts by security forces to arrest Lutheran Bishop Medardo Gómez, who was eventually forced to flee the country.[79] A January piece detailed the detention, torture, and gang-rape of a pregnant housekeeper of the Lutheran World Federation. It added that seven

Episcopalian church workers who had been incarcerated were finally released due to the direct intervention of a Washington-based human rights organization.[80] The December 8 issue reported that Catholic, Episcopalian, and Lutheran church workers, as well as those from some other Protestant denominations, were being arrested throughout San Salvador and that many others had been forced to flee the country to avoid capture.[81] Another December piece told of the arrest of Scott Wright, a Catholic church worker, and how he had been blindfolded, handcuffed, and required to stand for hours at a time over a three-and-a-half-day period before being forced to leave the country.[82] Still another report related the arrest and eventual release of Jennifer Casolo, a U.S. worker for an ecumenical fact-finding group who was accused of hiding a large cache of guerrilla weapons in her yard. The report noted that several Bush administration officials publicly expressed doubts about her innocence.[83] Finally, a February article claimed that the Salvadoran military had successfully destroyed much of the infrastructure of church-linked community-help organizations by raiding their offices and "sometimes stripping them clean—right down to coffeepots," destroying their files, and arresting their members on suspicion of collaboration with the guerrillas.[84]

The *NCR* included several articles that focused on the outraged response of U.S. citizens, especially churchpeople, to the Jesuit murders. Most were careful to note that their anger was aimed not only at the Salvadoran military and government but also at U.S. officials who they felt shared complicity in the wrongdoing.[85] Some charged U.S. collusion in a cover-up and provided specific details to substantiate their claim. A late December article related that the FBI had used intimidation and blackmail tactics in an attempt to destroy the testimony of Lucia Barrera de Cerna, the only witness to the UCA murders.[86] According to a February 1990 piece, the head of U.S. military forces in El Salvador, Colonel Milton Menjivar, had informed the Salvadoran army high command that a Salvadoran Colonel Carlos Aviles had confidentially given the U.S. military the name of a high-ranking Salvadoran officer who he claimed was involved in the UCA killings. The *NCR* article pointed out that Menjivar's revelation clearly put the informant's life in jeopardy, to say nothing of destroying his career, thereby sending a message to any other Salvadoran military man who might have been willing to provide the United States with evidence concerning the Jesuit murder case.[87] A January article pointed out that the Atlacatl Battalion of the Salvadoran army had been implicated in several other civilian assassinations and had been trained in the United States.[88]

Following the UCA assassinations, the *NCR* sent reporter Tim McCarthy to El Salvador to investigate the crime firsthand. The result was a detailed point-by-point reenactment of the pertinent events leading up to the murders, evidence which overwhelmingly indicated that the Salvadoran military high command had planned and ordered the assassinations.[89]

But especially interesting was an entire page (page 9) accompanying the above article which contained three graphic photos of some of the murder victims, all in color. Particularly disturbing was the one of Julia Elba Ramos and her daughter Celina.[90] In their "Inside *NCR*" column the editors commented on the bloody depictions, concluding that "President George Bush may not have seen these photos. Readers may wish to send him page 9."[91] A statement of this nature is highly irregular. Its inclusion is illustrative of the bold style of the *NCR* staff, but it also can be said to represent its frustration, disgust, and outrage at the Bush administration, which it held in no small part responsible for the Jesuit murders. This December 29 issue of the *National Catholic Reporter* contained the boldest, most detailed, and most graphic coverage of the UCA murders to appear in the U. S. press.

NICARAGUA

Before examining U. S. Catholic coverage of Nicaragua in the mid- to latter 1980s, it should prove helpful to provide an overview of the contra war and how it affected church-state relations.

By 1985 the contras were well entrenched along the Honduran side of the Nicaraguan border. Aided by technical assistance from U. S. reconnaissance flights and radar-equipped ships operating off the Atlantic and Pacific coasts, they were able to launch forays into rural Nicaragua. There they terrorized peasants and wrought havoc on the country's infrastructure. Sandinista agricultural cooperatives and development projects were their primary targets, while local Sandinista government officials, teachers, and health care workers were especially marked for extermination. Along with supporting the contras, the United States also sent 50,000 of its own soldiers to southern Honduras, where they constructed the roads and airstrips that would be needed if a future invasion of Nicaragua were to take place. While there, they conducted joint military exercises with the Honduran army, exercises obviously meant to intimidate the Sandinistas by convincing them that a U. S. invasion was imminent.

To make matters worse from the Sandinista perspective, President Reagan declared a trade embargo against Nicaragua, and the U. S. Congress approved $27 million in contra aid, the first of several such appropriations. Moreover, White House officials blocked the Central American peace proposal of the so-called Contadora nations of Mexico, Colombia, Venezuela, and Panama. So severe was the U.S.-sponsored low-intensity war against the Sandinista government that the latter had been compelled by 1985 to spend approximately half its national budget on defense, thereby forcing a major reduction of governmental expenditures for the poor.

For their part, the Nicaraguan bishops, although constantly criticizing the Sandinistas (often with good reason), remained steadfast in their silence when it came to contra atrocities and economic hardship resulting from the embargo. But on Easter Sunday of 1984 the prelates became bolder when they indirectly attempted to legitimize the counterrevolutionary forces by issuing a pastoral letter calling for peace negotiations between the FSLN and opposition groups, including the contras. Both the Reagan administration and contra leaders quickly endorsed the bishops' proposal, but with the added recommendation that a bishop should serve as moderator. Understandably viewing these suggestions as an attempt by its enemies to stack the deck against them, FSLN leaders rejected the proposals, justifying their decision on the grounds that the contras were no more than U.S. surrogates and therefore not a legitimate Nicaraguan group. Claims by the bishops' critics that they were collaborators with the contras were bolstered when Obando, following his appointment as cardinal, went to Miami, where he celebrated mass with anti-Sandinistas, including prominent contra leaders.

Upon his return to Managua, Obando, armed with the prestige of being the first cardinal in Nicaraguan history, now took an even more aggressive anti-Sandinista stand. Traveling throughout the countryside, ostensibly for religious reasons, he attracted large crowds which applauded his attacks against the government. As Phillip Berryman noted, these pastoral visits were more like political rallies and were even advertised on contra radio stations operating from Honduras.[92] It was obvious to friend and foe alike that Obando had become the catalyst for the anti-Sandinista movement and was proving to be quite an effective adversary. For their part, the Sandinistas attempted to counter Obando's successful rural pilgrimage with one of their own. Father Miguel D'Escoto led a *Via Crucis* (Stations of the Cross) across the country, criticizing along the way the contras, the United States, and the Nicaraguan bishops and calling on them to change their hearts and work for peace.

As shown in the previous chapter, on the eve of a 1986 congressional vote for an additional $100 million in contra aid, Obando, Bishop Vega, and Father Carballo traveled to Washington, where they publicly accused the Sandinista government of persecuting the church and at least indirectly lobbied for the bill's passage. Thus, when the aid package was approved by

Congress, the Sandinistas, blaming church leaders for the affirmative vote, increased the intensity of their offensive against the church. Carballo was denied reentry into Nicaragua, and Vega and ten foreign priests were deported. Radio Católica was closed by the government along with the archdiocesan newspaper *Iglesia*. The church's Social Pastoral Office was occupied by state security forces, and large numbers of priests and church activists were harassed and a few were incarcerated for a few days.

Indeed, faced with the U. S. embargo, a spiraling inflation rate that would reach 36,000 percent by 1988, and a contra force strengthened by U. S. dollars and made more effective by thousands of peasant volunteers who blamed the Sandinistas for their economic hardship, the Sandinista government grew more authoritarian and repressive. Claiming a state of emergency, it curtailed civil liberties, initiated a compulsory military draft, and encouraged gangs of pro-Sandinista youths (*turbas*) to attack anti-FSLN groups and church congregations. Such actions only proved counterproductive and presented to friend and foe alike an image of a government desperate to keep power in the face of growing unpopularity. Taking advantage of their growing favor, the bishops became even bolder by calling on the populace to refuse to comply with the draft.

The momentum of the anti-Sandinista forces, however, was slowed somewhat when at the end of 1986 soldier of fortune and CIA operative Eugene Hasenfus was shot down and captured by Sandinista soldiers while attempting to deliver arms to the contras. This embarrassment to the Reagan administration, followed by the more serious revelation that White House officials had sold arms to Iran in order to finance the contras, made it clear that Reagan officials had been violating both U. S. and international law in their attempt to topple the Sandinistas from power. White House fortunes suffered another blow in 1987 when all of the Central American presidents, against Reagan's wishes, agreed to comply with Esquipulas II, the peace proposal of Costa Rican President Oscar Arias for the isthmus. Finally, the Nicaraguan bishops were embarrassed when Undersecretary of State Elliott Abrams, Reagan's key official for Central America, was forced to admit before a congressional hearing that the State Department had secretly channeled funds to elements in the Nicaraguan church, including Obando and Carballo.[93]

Taking advantage of these revelations, Sandinista President Daniel Ortega, acting in accordance with the Arias Peace Plan, proclaimed a cease-fire in the government's offensive against the contras and announced that national elections would be held in February 1990. It was too late, however. Reagan's low-intensity war and a disastrous economy, coupled with the effective onslaught of the Nicaraguan bishops and the Sandinistas' own counterproductive repressive policies, proved too much for the Nicaraguan people to bear. Presidential candidate Violeta Chamorro and her United National Opposition (UNO) soundly defeated Daniel Ortega and the FSLN. The decade-long Sandinista revolution was over.

Throughout the 1980s *America* remained a staunch foe of all U.S. interference in the internal affairs of Nicaragua, and in articulating its position it sometimes included articles that clearly contained a pro-Sandinista bias. Two such pieces should suffice in illustrating this point. A report by a Jesuit professor following a fact-finding trip to Nicaragua exhibited the usual indictment of contra atrocities and U.S. complicity in such conduct. It was, however, so overwhelmingly one-sided that its author's obvious lack of awareness of Sandinista shortcomings can only be attributed to his naiveté.[94] Another piece by a Methodist missionary who accompanied Nicaraguan Foreign Minister Miguel D'Escoto on his two-week *Via Crucis* journey across the country was similar in tone. Totally sympathetic to the Sandinistas and hostile to Cardinal Obando and his clerical supporters, the article implied that the D'Escoto-led pilgrimage was supported by virtually all of Nicaragua's poor. "[T]housands of campesinos . . . waited by the roadside with flowers and crude banners," joining the procession as it went by, the author tells us. Indeed, the enthusiasm of the peasants far exceeded the most optimistic expectations of the *Via Crucis* organizers.[95]

Articles such as the above, however, are the exception. By 1985 *America* was displaying an increasingly critical tone concerning the Sandinistas, and in this respect it typified most U.S. Catholic publications. Four *America* commentaries from 1985–86 illustrate this point. One emphatically stated that the magazine's "opposition to contra aid . . . should not be confused with support for the Sandinista regime."[96] A second implored Congress to hold firm in its opposition to contra aid in spite of the FSLN's undemocratic behavior and communist connection. The piece insisted, however, that the counterrevolutionaries were also far from satisfactory when it came to democratic behavior and that the Nicaraguan people should have the right to determine their own destiny without U.S. interference. It further pointed out that Nicaragua represented no immediate threat to its neighbors or to the United States and that the United States had learned to live with and influence governments far worse than that of the Sandinistas.[97]

The third commentary, while criticizing the U.S. imposition of a trade embargo on Nicaragua, admitted that the Sandinista regime "is clearly not an exemplary Government."[98] The fourth piece declared disingenuous President Ortega's claim that U.S. aggression had forced his government to curtail civil liberties. But it was careful to add that FSLN lies were matched only by those of the United States and that our Cold War conflict with the Soviets, rather than any concern for Nicaraguan liberties, was what really motivated our opposition to the FSLN.[99] It closed with the following advice:

> The United States would not be in such an embarrassing position if it had long ago adopted the policy outlined by U. S. bishops before Congress: opposition to military aid to either side in Nicaragua, repudiation, as illegal and immoral, of any attempts to overthrow the Nicaraguan Government, and encouragement of the Contadora negotiations.[100]

Other *America* editorials provided similar arguments. A March 1986 piece, for instance, made it clear that *America*'s opposition to funding the contras was premised not on a blindness to Sandinista faults but on the immorality of military intervention.[101] In the same vein, a July 1988 editorial entitled "How to Lose Friends" bluntly claimed that through its heavy-handed censorship the Sandinista government had embarrassed those in the United States who had defended the Nicaraguan right to self-determination and opposed the Reagan policy to overthrow the FSLN.[102]

Although increasingly more critical of the FSLN's harassment of the church, *America* nevertheless continued to show little empathy for the Nicaraguan bishops. One editorial called on them to "rein in their rhetorical excesses" and instead provide pastoral leadership by entering into dialogue with the Sandinistas and the popular church.[103] An article by a Jesuit political scientist accused Obando and the Nicaraguan hierarchy of actually welcoming contra attacks since they put pressure on the Sandinista government.[104] A third piece went so far as to chide the U. S. bishops for condemning the Sandinista deportation of Bishop Vega without first consulting with President Ortega as the latter requested. The editorialist remarked that Ortega's explanation—that Vega's support of contra aid just prior to the congressional vote was a seditious act justifying deportation—was not unreasonable. He then reminded the U. S. bishops that they had repeatedly called on Ortega to open a dialogue with dissident Nicaraguan factions, yet when he asked to speak to them they denied his request.[105]

Concerning the Hasenfus case, *America* reminded its readers that fundamental culpability lay not with the downed pilot but with the Reagan administration, which had promoted such activities, and with Congress, which had voted to fund them.[106] Another editorial charged that the Iran-contra affair proved Reagan to be a rigid ideologue dominated by a few dangerous ideas.[107] In a later commentary the Jesuit magazine stated that the sordid revelations coming from the scandal should at least have the positive effect of convincing Congress to finally end contra aid.[108] But when U. S. lawmakers refused to do so, *America* termed their action astonishing and sleazy.[109]

America of course reported favorably on the signing of the Arias peace plan by the five Central American presidents. More interesting, however, is the fact that the magazine equated the White House's request for additional congressional aid for the contras with an attempt to derail Esquipulas II. "The Reagan Administration gives the impression of being sorry the peace process is still alive," stated a 1988 editorial. "Congress should vote 'no' on more contra aid. Let the Arias peace plan be."[110] Another commentary on the Esquipulas proposal pointed out that "one does not have to be a fan of the Sandinistas to oppose contra aid and the Administration's contra policy."[111] Indeed, this declaration succinctly encapsulated the thrust of the U. S. Catholic press's position on Nicaragua throughout the latter half of the 1980s.

Commonweal in the second half of the 1980s was even more critical in its treatment of the FSLN than *America.* But like the latter journal it remained adamant in its opposition to the Reagan administration's Nicaraguan policy in general and to contra aid in particular. As early as 1985 it states that "the Sandinistas are undeniably pro-Soviet; however much U. S. policy has cemented this orientation, it was evidently their own choice from the start."[112] Another editorial from the same year called Reagan's Nicaraguan embargo an unwise move while commending Congress for rejecting a proposal for $14 million in contra aid. But it nevertheless admitted that the Sandinistas were guilty of "serious human rights abuses" and had "curtailed civic freedoms."[113]

A 1986 article by Philip McManus of the Fellowship of Reconciliation and Witness for Peace noted that, contrary to what some affirmed, "the Sandinistas are definitely less than the popular heroes who can do no wrong," but that they were likewise not the totalitarians that others claimed.[114] Following a visit to war-torn Nueva Guinea, he concluded that many there dreaded the military, which forced them to fight a war they wished to avoid and imprisoned those it suspected of collaborating with the enemy. But they also feared the contras, since the latter regularly kidnapped villagers and killed health care workers, teachers, and members of farm cooperatives. In general the Sandinistas seemed to be a mixed bag, but one whose positive features probably outweighed the negative:

> The Nicaraguan revolution is clearly imperfect. The impressive social gains it had achieved before the war curtailed such efforts show it also to be, on the whole, an earnest attempt to serve the poor majority. While it

has been less vigilant in defense of political liberties, it nonetheless compares favorably with other Central American countries in that regard. . . . Eastern Bloc influence is significant. But the charge that Nicaragua, after decades of struggle to throw off U. S. domination, will trade that for Soviet or Cuban domination reveals a lack of familiarity or concern for the needs, aspirations, and determination of the Nicaraguan people.[115]

Edward Sheehan, writing a month earlier, was less sanguine. He began by stating that after a five-week stay in Nicaragua he continued to oppose contra aid and Reagan's Central American policy. On the other hand, his views on the FSLN had undergone a drastic reversal: "I found the Sandinista government an ugly, repressive military regime, run at the top by incompetent comandantes who have alienated most of their people, ruined the economy, and are growing more despotic."[116]

After visits to numerous places where he talked to countless Nicaraguans, including the leading church figures of both the anti- and pro-Sandinista factions, he concluded that the Sandinistas were typical communists bent on controlling every aspect of Nicaraguan life, including the church. As for the popular church, it was totally politicized and at the service of the state. Moreover, it had virtually no appeal in the eyes of the people. Although he felt that liberation theology had many merits, he had come to believe that "most of the poor either don't understand it, don't want it, or have never heard of it."[117] And of Cardinal Obando:

I do not suggest that the cardinal's methods in this crisis are above reproach. Though he speaks constantly of national dialogue and reconciliation of all Nicaraguans, there may be at least a grain of truth in the standard Sandinista charge that he sympathizes with the contras and hopes for their eventual victory. . . .

My own feeling is that, however imperfect his tactics, Cardinal Obando essentially has no choice but to battle the Sandinistas with every weapon at his command, not least his own immense popularity among Nicaraguans. (I have no doubt that he and John Paul II are the most popular men in Nicaragua.)[118]

A 1987 *Commonweal* commentary following the exposé of the Reagan administration's Iran-contra scandal was similar in tone. At first it lambasted the CIA for providing the contras with detailed diagrams for destroying Nicaraguan dams, bridges, and communications systems: "There is a stench in this terrorist plan, as there is in the entire conduct of the Reagan-contra

war."[119] It then took on the contras, accusing them of drug smuggling, kidnappings, forced recruitments, indiscriminate killings of civilians, including the "slitting of babies' throats," attacks on cooperatives, and the mining
of roads.[120] But the Sandinistas were not immune from *Commonweal*'s
wrath. They were guilty of

> the suppression . . . of *La Prensa, La Iglesia,* and *Radio Católica;* the ex-
> pulsion . . . of two Catholic churchmen without due process; a system
> of political courts which return verdicts of guilty-as-charged 99 per-
> cent of the time; the harassment of non-Sandinista labor unions; the
> recent arrest of protesters on International Women's Day; the 200,000
> Nicaraguan citizens who have fled to Honduras and Costa Rica, a cho-
> rus in exile; and the postponement of promised local elections.[121]

The piece ended with an impassioned plea for U.S. support for the Arias
peace plan.[122]

Our Sunday Visitor was likewise more inclined to criticize the FSLN in
the second half of the 1980s. Interspersed with the pro-Sandinista reports of
Father Giese and the more even-handed articles of Robert Holton were
pieces harshly critical of the Sandinistas and those clerics who supported
them. An article by Desmond O'Grady, *OSV*'s Vatican correspondent,
should suffice to illustrate this point. It was unusually sympathetic to the
exiled Bishop Vega. Indeed, the author warned that his expulsion would
probably be followed by that of another "troublesome priest," Cardinal
Obando. O'Grady next delivered an attack on the renowned Belgian sociologist Father François Houtart, who had defended Sandinista rule, writing
him off as a longtime "apologist for communist regimes."[123]

More than any other U.S. Catholic periodical, the *National Catholic Reporter* took it upon itself to champion the cause of the Latin American progressive church. Following Vatican attacks on liberation theology, for instance, it included a lengthy article by Maryknoll Father David Kelly that
attempted to address the theological criticisms coming from conservative
churchmen and Vatican officials. The piece was restrained, dignified, and devoid of name-calling and unsubstantiated charges.[124] A second article by
Mary Beth Moore, a U.S. Sister of Charity working in Peru, aspired to defend liberation theology from the perspective of the pastoral worker rather
than the theologian. Again, the piece refrained from attacks on opponents,
choosing instead to limit itself to an explanation of how this controversial
theology was applied and lived out in a pastoral context.[125]

The *NCR* does not always desist from questioning the integrity of the critics of liberation theology. Its attacks, however, usually remained within the bounds of responsible journalism. A 1984 editorial illustrates this point. It argued that liberation theology had to be judged on its own merits and if so treated it would easily pass scrutiny. To prove its contention, it noted that Gustavo Gutiérrez's latest book, *We Drink from Our Own Wells,* contained almost four hundred scriptural references and relied on such figures as John of the Cross, Francis of Assisi, Ignatius Loyola, Teresa of Avila, and even John Paul II, while containing not a single reference to Karl Marx. Nevertheless, Cardinal Joseph Ratzinger, head of the Vatican's Congregation for the Doctrine of the Faith, insisted that Gutiérrez made a Marxist option and reduced faith to politics. While conceding that in a few of his writings Gutiérrez did employ some tools of Marxist analysis, particularly the notion of class struggle, the *NCR* asked how a responsible modern thinker could fail to do so. Not to notice that a class struggle was taking place in Latin America would certainly be myopic, argued the editorialist. Thus, Gutiérrez was merely stating the obvious. The thrust of the rest of the editorial was summed up in the following paragraph:

> It is dismaying and disheartening to see people such as Gutiérrez treated so shabbily. This kind of treatment does not belong in the church. It is particularly sad to see theologians, as a result of service to the Gospel and God's people, allowed to become open targets of the politically powerful and their ecclesiastical allies.[126]

Although this piece did not shy from imputing the motivations of the critics of liberation theology, it backed up its charges with facts and reasoned argumentation. Thus, along with the two aforementioned articles, it contributed in a positive manner to the debate on liberation theology.

Needless to say, the *NCR* was quite critical of the Nicaraguan bishops. It asked why the prelates, so vigilant in denouncing the FSLN, never once condemned contra violence or U. S. covert operations in Nicaragua.[127] It also wondered why the U. S. government, which prior to Nicaraguan elections had continuously quoted Cardinal Obando's claims of Sandinista persecution of the Nicaraguan church, never raised the question of governmental church persecution as a factor in Salvadoran elections. This was especially curious, it sarcastically noted, since "in Nicaragua, not a single priest has been killed or imprisoned," while in El Salvador twenty-seven priests, including an archbishop, had been murdered by government-sponsored death squads.[128] It further questioned the propriety of the bishops' acceptance of funds from agencies with ties to the CIA.[129]

On the other hand, the *NCR* could be quite critical of the FSLN and the pro-Sandinista clergy and CEBs. A 1984 editorial, after accusing the Reagan administration of attempting to exacerbate conflict between the Sandinistas and the Nicaraguan church, turned its wrath on the FSLN:

> The recent expulsion by the Sandinistas of 10 foreign priests charged with planning "to provoke a confrontation between church and state" is a wrongful and inexcusably harsh action. It is a political blunder and ironically does much to provoke an even more serious church and state confrontation. . . . To the degree the Sandinistas carry out acts of repression, they lose credibility at home and in the eyes of their supporters worldwide. To the degree they so act, they also fulfill the hopes of Reagan and his supporters.[130]

A second piece in the same issue by Michael Garvey was strongly critical of Ernesto Cardenal for his advocacy of violence: "What divides Ernesto Cardenal and Jerry Falwell is political preference and not much else. Neither man has said much about the gospel that doesn't sound, well, phony."[131]

But a 1984 article by Chris Hedges merits special attention. He stated that the Sandinistas had successfully purged the labor unions, schools, youth groups, and other social organizations of opposition people and replaced them with cadres loyal to the FSLN. Since the church was the only institution still powerful enough to challenge them, the Sandinistas, assisted by their clerical and CEB supporters, had attempted to co-opt it. Nineteen priests and nuns who had criticized the popular church had been deported, while pro-FSLN clergy had replaced saint figures in their churches with Sandinista heroes. Hedges added, however, that elements within the traditional church had been just as blatantly political as their counterparts in the popular church.[132] When several letters to the editor in a later issue of the *NCR* castigated Hedges for criticizing the Sandinistas, he defended his position with journalistic eloquence:

> I do not abandon my motives for writing or my outrage at injustice to accommodate particular governments or ideologies. If conservative priests are being marginalized, harassed and expelled by Caesar's government in Nicaragua, then I believe it is my job to give them a voice. The theology espoused by Monsignor (Miguel) Obando y Bravo is not

my theology, but this does not justify the stoning of his car or the censoring of his homilies. It does not justify "reeducation," as distasteful
and misleading a phrase as any turned out by our [own] government.[133]

Hedges went on to state that he was in accord with the letter writers who
pointed out that the situation in Nicaragua was complex, but he added
forcefully that complexity could not be a euphemism and rationalization to
explain away gangs and government censors.

How different this article was from those that appeared in *Crisis,* the
Wanderer, Social Justice Review, and the *National Catholic Register.* Whereas
the latter accentuated Sandinista atrocities while ignoring virtually all violence perpetrated by the Salvadoran, Guatemalan, and U.S. governments,
the *National Catholic Reporter,* like *America, Commonweal,* and *Our Sunday
Visitor,* for the most part proved capable of criticizing both sides when their
conduct merited such criticism. This explains why such publications carried more weight with U.S. Catholic leaders concerned with Central American affairs than did their right-wing counterparts.

Before closing this chapter, the reaction of the U.S. Catholic press to
the stunning Sandinista defeat in the February 1990 elections still needs to
be discussed. The response of conservative Catholic journals has already
been covered. It was well summed up in the euphoric front-page headline
of the *National Catholic Register:* "Adios, Danny: Violeta Wins, and Penance
May Be in Order for Some U.S. Christians."[134] To these publications the
meaning of the elections could not be clearer. The UNO victory meant that
the much-maligned Reagan-Bush Central American policy had been vin-
dicated. Moreover, it had exposed the naiveté of those North American
churchpeople who, deluded by the spell of "Marxist" liberation theology,
had erroneously convinced themselves that the FSLN was the party of the
people and therefore had supported the Sandinistas throughout the previous decade.

Not surprisingly, progressive Catholic periodicals interpreted the election outcome differently. The *National Catholic Reporter* took a position
which was most in accord with that of Christian activists who had consistently supported the Sandinistas. A bitter March editorial succinctly summarized its view. Its scenario was as follows: Nicaragua had refused to accept dependency on U.S. economic interests and had declared a nonaligned foreign
policy. Consequently, Washington had destroyed her. While the *NCR* admitted that "the Sandinistas have shown unexcusable intolerance," it argued that
this must be interpreted within the context of a brutal U.S.-sponsored war.

In summary, the United States sent a message that rang loud and clear not only to Nicaragua but to other Latin American nations as well: "Choose our ways, our economic policies—or bleed."[135]

An *NCR* opinion piece by Holly Sklar invoked the same theme:

> Most people crack under torture. Nicaragua has been militarily, economically and psychologically tortured by Washington, D.C. in a decade-long effort to overthrow the Sandinista revolution. Bush administration actions indicated that the torture would not stop if the Sandinistas were reelected. Many Nicaraguans took the out offered by the ballot and voted for the U.S.-backed United National Opposition. [Thus,] Washington showed again . . . that procedurally democratic elections can provide the coup de grace in a destabilization campaign.[136]

A third piece by *NCR* publisher Bill McSweeney at least conceded that Sandinista failures might have played a role, albeit a minor one, in the party's defeat. McSweeney felt that several factors had contributed to the UNO victory. First, Nicaraguans realized that the fall of communism in Eastern Europe meant that the Sandinistas could no longer expect aid from the Soviet bloc. Thus, many concluded that an FSLN election victory would mean even more belt-tightening for the already hard-pressed masses; this would not be the case, however, if the opposition coalition won. Second, the U.S. invasion of Panama caused some Nicaraguans to fear that if the Sandinistas were victorious, Nicaragua too would probably be invaded. Third, many voted against the FSLN because it supported the compulsory draft and for UNO because it promised to do away with it. Fourth, some were victims of Sandinista injustice—"real or imagined"—and therefore voted against the FSLN. But, argued McSweeney, the U.S.-sponsored contra war far outweighed the other reasons for the victory of the opposition coalition. Nicaraguans believed that if the FSLN won, the war would continue perpetually; but if UNO was victorious there was a good chance it might end. Simply put, the Nicaraguan people voted for peace.[137]

In contrast to the conservative Catholic journals covered in this study, the *National Catholic Reporter* deserves credit for allowing an opinion different from its own to appear in its pages, a piece by Paul Berman, Nicaraguan correspondent for *Mother Jones* and *The Village Voice*. In his analysis published under the headline "Another View," Berman strongly disagreed with the *NCR*'s analysis. While conceding that the Sandinistas were initially popular with the Nicaraguan people, he argued that they had destroyed themselves with their ideological extremism. Deep down the FSLN had always been Cuban-style Marxist-Leninists, and, like all communists, they believed that anyone who disagreed with them was a potential counterrevolutionary and therefore could not be tolerated. Consequently, they attempted to eliminate all views contrary to their own. Berman next provided examples:

> They set up the notorious block committees to pry into people's private opinions and to threaten nonconformists with loss of food rations. They worked an element of political coercion into trade unions, the artisan cooperatives, the campesino agencies, the schools. They organized mobs to roam the streets anytime anti-Sandinistas seemed to be getting popular. And though tyranny in Nicaragua never reached a totalitarian level, it nevertheless succeeded in angering the Nicaraguan people.[138]

But before closing, Berman made an important point that differentiated his analysis from that of the conservative Catholic periodicals. He insisted that the Sandinista defeat did not mean that the Nicaraguan people had rejected the revolution. Rather, they had made it clear that what they wanted was revolution with democracy.[139]

Most major progressive Catholic journals took a position that was more centrist than that of the *NCR* in analyzing the UNO victory. They were more willing to emphasize Sandinista intolerance and ineptitude as major factors in the election results, but, like the *NCR*, they continued to view the Nicaraguan policy of the Reagan-Bush administrations with nothing but disdain and to consider it the major factor in the Sandinistas' demise. A March 24 *America* editorial typified this outlook. It noted that in retrospect no one should have been surprised at the victory of Violeta Chamorro's UNO. Pre-election polls had shown that 61 percent of the Nicaraguan people thought that the quality of life in their country had deteriorated under Sandinista rule. Moreover, 55 percent blamed the FSLN, not the contra war, for their nation's economic problems. But, the editorial continued, hardship inflicted on the masses by the United States certainly contributed to the FSLN's defeat:

> Whether Sandinista central planning on its own would have put one-third of the labor force out of work and produced thousand-digit inflation, we will never know. What we do know is that the Nicaraguan people, exhausted by war and U. S. economic sanctions, cried uncle—enough![140]

Indeed, if any hero had emerged from the Nicaraguan elections, *America* contended that it was President Arias of Costa Rica:

> That there was an election at all in Nicaragua owes no thanks to the White House's fixation that force, and force alone, speaks to revolutionary vanguards. The credit belongs first to Oscar Arias . . . whose peace plan for the region called for free, closely supervised elections in exchange for disbanding the contras. And second, credit belongs to Sandinista hubris.[141]

The piece concluded by praising the FSLN for promising to accept the will of the voters and to act as a legitimate opposition party.

A second *America* article, by Jeff Gillenkirk, former speechwriter for Mario Cuomo, pointed to the important role played by Cardinal Obando in the election outcome. In contrast to the 1984 elections when he was silent, the prelate this time urged Nicaraguans to vote, and although he denied it, he made it clear whom he wanted them to vote for. "The Cardinal's heart clearly belonged to UNO." Why? Because the Sandinistas planned "to muscle out the traditional church hierarchy while creating their own parallel community-based church permanently aligned with the Sandinista revolution rather than with Rome." This was obviously unacceptable to the institutional church both in Nicaragua and in Rome.

But Gillenkirk was no fan of the bishops. "Two largely authoritarian institutions," the FSLN and the Nicaraguan hierarchy, "set out to consolidate their own power—and painfully stepped on everyone's toes in the process." Therefore, "it is impossible to put complete blame on either side" for the tragic blunders that had caused ten years of war and misery in Nicaragua.[142] Thus, like the U. S. Catholic press in general, Gillenkirk found few heroes in the Nicaragua of the 1980s.

Commonweal, which since 1984 had been the harshest of the progressive Catholic periodicals when it came to criticizing the Sandinistas, nevertheless credited them with establishing the democratic base that ironically resulted in their ouster from power. In a March editorial it remarked that even with their economic ineptitude the Sandinistas' early reforms—a literacy campaign, universal education, redistribution of land and resources—enabled the people to transform themselves into a democracy. Unfortunately for the FSLN, however, the people chose to use their newly acquired power to vote the Sandinistas out of office. The piece concluded by expressing hope that the Bush administration would refrain from trying to inflict a U. S. agenda on post-Sandinista Nicaragua. "We cannot impose democracy in Nicaragua," warned the editorialist. " It is something they must achieve for themselves."[143]

A second *Commonweal* article, by Fr. J. Bryan Hehir of the USCC, repeated *America*'s claim that the Arias Peace Plan was the main ingredient in bringing about free elections in Nicaragua. He took it a step further, however, proposing that the United States now rethink its Central American strategy and allow the Arias plan to be used for the creation of a cease-fire and meaningful elections in El Salvador.[144]

In closing, it seems that Hehir's suggestion typified the thrust of the U. S. Catholic press throughout the 1980s and into the 1990s. Most Catholic periodicals refused to be discouraged by a setback or satisfied by a success in one Central American country or another. Instead, the Catholic press remained determined to continue its quest for peace with justice throughout the isthmus. If fighting ended in one nation and fair elections took place, it was not satisfied. It demanded no less for the other Central American countries. Moreover, it insisted that peace and elections be linked with justice for the poor masses. As part of its effort, it continually called upon the United States to turn from what it considered its outdated Cold War mind-set, moving instead to a policy that placed a priority on the well-being of the poor majority. Indeed, while others turned their attention away from Central America in the 1990s, the U. S. Catholic press refused to follow suit. When one peruses the pages of the *National Catholic Reporter, America, Commonweal,* and other Catholic journals today, one still finds articles informing readers on current events in the isthmus from the perspective of the poor. Every year there are editorials calling for the closing of the School of the Americas at Fort Benning, Georgia, and reports on the annual protests held there in March. The 1998 murder of Bishop Juan Gerardi in Guatemala, after he released his report on government human rights abuses during the prior two decades, received extensive coverage, as did news on the investigation of that crime. Articles and editorials informed readers of the suffering and destruction resulting from Hurricane Mitch and the Salvadoran earthquakes. U. S. Jesuits still regularly visit El Salvador and Nicaragua and report their impressions in *America,* and the *National Catholic Reporter* still leads all Catholic periodicals in the coverage it allots to isthmian affairs. In so doing, the U. S. Catholic press continues to bring credit to itself and to the church it serves.

Conclusion

To fully understand the implications of U.S. Catholic press coverage of Central America, one must place it within the broader context of U.S. Catholic history. U.S. culture is grounded in the seventeenth-century arrival of English Anglicans and Puritans. Raised during the religious wars and rivalries that followed the Reformation, these Protestants equated Catholic "popery" with ultimate evil. Indeed, in his study of U.S. anti-Semitism, historian Leonard Dinnerstein notes that "until the twentieth century Catholics were more intensely abhorred than Jews were"[1] and that "the anti-Papist strain in the American mind was strong and violent" until relatively recent years.[2]

From the 1620s on, New England Calvinists saw themselves as God's new chosen people and their colony as the "New Jerusalem," the city on a hill that God had preordained to serve as a model for others who wanted to create a righteous state. This Puritan way of thinking soon came to permeate the psyche of American culture. In the 1830s and 1840s it would intertwine with "Manifest Destiny," the notion that Divine Providence had preordained that the United States would come to rule a continent and export its enlightened ideas to other lands.

Following the American Revolution the Puritan mind-set was linked to secular concepts from the European Enlightenment. An official policy of separation of church and state and toleration of all religions but government support of none became part of the American way, as did representative government and liberal democracy.

All of these concepts were anathema to the Vatican. For this reason, John Carroll, the first U. S. Catholic bishop, not only was forced to expend much energy defending Catholicism in the face of Protestant mistrust but also had to justify American beliefs against Vatican charges of modernism, secularism, and radicalism.[3]

The fact that Catholics composed such a minuscule percentage of the overall U. S. population made it easier for them to blend into American life without too much notice. This changed dramatically, however, after 1830. From that year until the end of the century, millions of mostly poor and uneducated Catholic immigrants from Ireland, Germany, Italy, and Eastern Europe migrated to America. By 1850 Catholicism had become the largest single religious denomination in the United States.[4] Protestants feared that if their country became "Catholicized" it would mean the end of their American way of life. Many responded in a bigoted fashion, and at times Catholics were victimized by violence. Books and pamphlets were written warning those of Anglo-Saxon stock of the consequences of the "mongrelizing" of their country. Lurid tales of lechery and outlandish conduct supposedly committed by nuns and priests in schools and convents were widely circulated. Xenophobia and anti-Catholicism coalesced, resulting in the 1840s in the formation of the nativist American Party, popularly known as the Know Nothings, and in the 1880s in the American Protective Association, both of which were dedicated to excluding Catholics from public office and from the nation.

But Protestant uneasiness with the rapid growth of Catholicism in their country was not totally rooted in bigotry. Catholic European leaders had long expressed disdain for notions of church and state that were sacred to Americans. This is perhaps best illustrated by the promulgation of the so-called Syllabus of Errors in 1864 by Pope Pius IX, in which the pontiff anathematized the ideology of modern secular liberalism—in other words, the ideology of the United States. Included in his condemnation were capitalism, religious toleration of non-Catholics, Protestantism, separation of church and state, public schools free from ecclesiastical authority, the belief that it was no longer expedient that the Catholic religion should be the only religion of the state to the exclusion of other forms of worship, and the notion that the pope should reconcile himself to progress, liberalism, and modern civilization.[5]

The declaration in 1870 of the dogma of papal infallibility, which bound all Catholics to accept the belief that the pope could not err in matters of faith and morals, was also troubling to Protestants who saw "popery" growing at an alarming rate in their country. Indeed, U. S. Protestantism, rooted in the democracy of the Puritan town meeting, the religious pluralism and toleration of Roger Williams' Rhode Island, and a repulsion for monarchs who interfered in religious matters, was understandably apprehensive of a Roman pontiff who claimed infallible powers and demanded unquestioned obedience from Catholics worldwide.

Protestant mistrust was further compounded by a new breed of Catholic bishops and urban political bosses. The former, ruling over their flocks in monarch-like fashion, built a vast network of Catholic institutions that reinforced Catholic separateness by attempting to protect the laity from the "cancer" of Protestant and modernist thought. The latter built political machines, ousting U. S.-born Protestants from city hall while blatantly dispensing political jobs and favors on their foreign-born co-religious, who in turn blindly voted for them.

Faced with Protestant animus and bigotry, the immigrant church began to withdraw into itself, creating its own "Catholic ghetto." Following the humiliating defeat in 1928 of Governor Alfred E. Smith, the first Catholic presidential candidate of a major political party, this segregation process was completed. By the 1930s the immigrant church had created a whole system of institutions and societies that paralleled those of the larger American society. These included a separate parochial school system staffed by Catholic nuns and brothers, Catholic hospitals, Catholic lawyers' guilds and medical societies, Catholic youth groups with Catholic sports leagues, Catholic war veterans', police, and businessmen's associations, Catholic fraternal organizations, and even Catholic life insurance companies.[6] Perched atop the hierarchical social structure of this ghetto was the bishop, followed by the parish priest, both of whom seemed to work harmoniously with political bosses who were frequent speakers at Sunday communion breakfasts. In short, U. S. Catholics had finalized the creation of a remarkably successful Catholic ministate within a state.

But their hostile Protestant neighbors who viewed them, by dint of their antidemocratic faith and their separateness, as incapable of blending into American society, need not have worried. The new immigrant underclass gloried in the American way of life as much as in their Catholicism. Catholic immigrants and their offspring attributed their ever-growing economic and political success to opportunities open to them because of freedoms rooted in U. S. democratic values and traditions. If the tenets of their religion ran contrary to those of the United States, most either were ignorant of the fact or did not care. Indeed, so Americanized had most U. S. Catholics become that the Vatican felt the need to condemn the so-called heresy of Americanism in 1899, a movement supposedly aimed at adapting the external life of the church to modernist cultural ideals.

By the latter decades of the nineteenth century, U.S. Catholics faced a paradoxical situation. They had segregated themselves from an American culture of which they desperately wanted to be a part. Furthermore, they were bitterly indignant at the suggestion that they were less American than their neighbors and consequently became obsessed with proving their patriotism. Thus, in 1898, for instance, when the United States involved itself in a war with Catholic Spain, U.S. Catholic leaders not only refused to question the highly suspect motives of U.S. policy but actually encouraged Catholics to volunteer for military service, which they did in large numbers. Indeed, until the late 1960s, the U.S. Catholic institutional church and nearly all of its members uncritically championed almost every aspect of U.S. foreign policy, including all U.S. wars. Cultural historian Mark Massa explains such thinking by placing it in its proper historical perspective:

> Much of American Catholic life in both the nineteenth and twentieth centuries had been consumed with "fitting in" and striving after bourgeoisie "normalcy." In answer to the charge of being outsiders in an overwhelmingly Protestant culture, Catholic intellectual and ecclesial leaders had sought to prove how thoroughly *American* their religious tradition was. Thus, the heroes of American Catholic culture had been, generally speaking, "Americanist" accommodationist leaders who sought a church adapted to a democratic, pluralist culture.[7]

But try as they may, by the end of World War II Catholics had failed to chill the hostility of the majority of their fellow countrymen and women. Protestant misgivings were perhaps best articulated by the publication in 1949 of Paul Blanshard's *American Freedom and Catholic Power,* which Massa calls "arguably the classic twentieth-century American statement of 'progressive' fears of Catholic authoritarianism."[8]

Protestant misgivings would begin to dissipate, however, in the 1950s, largely due to changes brought about by the Cold War. The passage of the Servicemen's Readjustment Act of 1944, popularly known as the G.I. Bill, enabled large numbers of Catholic war veterans to attend college, something few U.S. Catholics had previously been able to do. This would alter the nature of American Catholicism by producing in the 1950s a sizable class who would move from the Catholic ghetto to suburbia—in other words, from the margins of U.S. culture into the mainstream.

The end of World War II also brought about a new enemy, international communism centered in the Soviet Union. Catholics had been warned of the evils of communism as early as 1864 in the papal encyclical *Quanto Cura.*

But Catholic fear of Marxist-Leninism reached new heights in the late 1940s following the brutal Russian takeover of the Catholic countries of Eastern Europe. Religion was viciously suppressed by Stalinist communists, and prelates like Poland's Cardinal Joseph Mindszenty and Archbishop Aloysius Stepinac of Hungary became Catholic heroes as a result of the suffering they courageously endured at the hand of "godless" communists.[9] Thus, when liberal and evangelical Protestants began to debate the merits of an emerging U.S. Cold War policy, Catholics had already united in their demand for a hard-line approach to Stalinist Russia. Communism had to be contained and rolled back regardless of the cost, they reasoned, and the United States must take the lead if Western Christian culture was to survive. The tragic persecution of Catholics in Eastern Europe made this crystal clear. There was no need for debate.

As Republicans and southern Democrats on the House Committee of Un-American Activities began to question the anticommunist credentials of the Truman administration, first- and second-generation Catholic Americans were already emerging from their ghetto as superpatriots who saw Catholic and American values as the two sides of the only force capable of saving the world from communism. They soon found their champion in an Irish-Catholic senator from Wisconsin who had emerged from obscurity to take leadership of the anticommunist hysteria that was beginning to sweep the nation. From his famous speech in Wheeling, West Virginia, in February 1950, in which he claimed to have a list of 205 known communists working in Truman's State Department, until his fall from grace in 1954, Senator Joseph McCarthy received the enthusiastic support of some of the most prominent members of the American Catholic establishment. Prestigious Catholic journals like *Our Sunday Visitor, Catholic World, Ave Maria,* the *Brooklyn Tablet,* and the *Wanderer* defended his cause, as did Cardinal Francis Spellman, most other bishops, and leaders of many of the most prominent Catholic universities. Scholars have long debated whether McCarthyism can be called a "Catholic crusade," but it cannot be doubted that the Wisconsin demagogue played on the bitterness that Catholics had long felt as a result of Protestant animosity toward them. Massa is correct when he states:

"Tail Gunner Joe" had had a remarkably successful career in selling his methods and rhetoric to millions of fellow Catholics in America in far higher numbers than to Protestants. . . . It was surely no accident that the major players in the "conspiracy so immense" adumbrated by McCarthy were all "WASPs with three goddam last names" (as [top

McCarthy aide] Roy Cohn so colorfully put it). Arrayed against . . . Protestant "insiders" who had purportedly betrayed the nation at the very highest levels . . . McCarthy enlisted the aid of the American descendants of Oliver Cromwell's Catholic "victims." . . . Therefore, on at least one level of symbolic discourse, it would appear problematic to imply that McCarthy's was *not* a "Catholic crusade."[10]

Or as Daniel Patrick Moynihan so aptly put it, at the height of the Cold War "it was Fordham men who checked the anticommunist and patriotic credentials of Harvard men."[11] But if that gave some Catholics satisfaction, the truth of the matter was that McCarthy overreacted and was destroyed. Far from raising Catholics to respectability in the eyes of their fellow Americans, he had accentuated the uneasiness that Protestants felt toward them. In short, if Catholics hoped to reach respectability in the eyes of other Americans and play a leading role in the Cold War against communism, they would have to produce more respectable leaders. They successfully did so with a clerical television evangelist and two unlikely lay heroes.

Bishop Fulton J. Sheen's weekly television series, *Life Is Worth Living,* ran from 1952 to 1957.[12] It was the most widely viewed religious series in the medium's history, reaching an audience of thirty million at its peak in 1955. Handsome, witty, and a spellbinding speaker, Sheen presented a thoroughly Catholic image to his audience even to the point of wearing his full episcopal garb on every show. Yet Protestants made up a sizable minority of his viewers.

Sheen's appeal to non-Catholics can be attributed in part to his skillful ability to mix religion with anticommunism. Yet although his TV program aired during the high-water years of McCarthyism, he always maintained a discreet silence concerning the controversial Republican senator. This is an important point, for unlike McCarthy, whose anticommunism was steeped in unsubstantiated charges aimed at Ivy League–educated members of the Protestant establishment, Sheen's anticommunism, although virulent, was grounded in the intellectual realm of Catholic neo-Thomist philosophy. Far from repelling most Protestants, it intrigued them. This is why Donald Crosby, author of *God, Church, and Flag: Senator Joseph McCarthy and the Catholic Church,* calls Sheen and not the Wisconsin senator "the prophet and philosopher of American Catholic anti-Communism."[13]

But Bishop Sheen was a clergyman. U.S. Catholics also needed lay leaders who appealed to Protestant as well as Catholic tastes. They found the right man in Thomas A. Dooley, a medical doctor who so adroitly balanced fact and fiction, public life and private, that he became the All-American poster boy not only for U. S. Catholicism but for the CIA as it made ready for the transfer of the war against communism from Korea to Vietnam.

Dooley, following medical school, enlisted in the U. S. Navy Medical Corps. Assigned to Vietnam, he played a major role in relocating nearly a million Catholic Vietnamese from the communist North to the noncommunist South. Seeing potential for anticommunist propaganda in his refugee work, some U. S. intelligence operatives urged Dooley to draw up a patriotic account of what he witnessed. The result was the best-selling *Deliver Us from Evil.* In it he painted a picture of North Vietnamese officials cruelly murdering and torturing their courageous Catholic countrymen and women because the latter had opted to relocate in the "democratic" South, where they would be free to practice their religion. *Deliver Us from Evil* catapulted Dooley into national prominence overnight. With the help of his U. S. intelligence sponsors, he soon embarked on an immensely successful lecture tour in which he convinced countless Americans who had never heard of Vietnam that Southeast Asia would fall to the communists unless the U. S. committed itself wholeheartedly to the South Vietnamese regime of Ngo Dinh Diem. But Dooley was a valuable asset not only for American Cold War ideologues. To U. S. Catholic leaders in search of an anticommunist hero to replace the discredited Joe McCarthy, he was a godsend. Unfortunately, however, he was soon forced by the Navy to resign his commission due to charges of homosexual behavior. The reason for his resignation was kept confidential so as not to embarrass high-ranking naval officers who had championed his anticommunist crusade.

With the collaboration of the CIA, which evidently decided that he was too valuable a propaganda asset to lose, it was announced that Dooley had left the Navy to begin a humanitarian medical mission in Laos. As his biographer, James T. Fisher, notes, after the publication of his second best-seller, *Edge of Tomorrow,* an account of his service at his new post, he had arguably become the most popular Catholic in America. Indeed, a 1959 Gallup Poll listed him as the seventh most admired man in the world.[14] In 1961 the young doctor died of cancer, following the publication of his third best-seller, *The Night They Burned the Mountain,* an account of MEDICO, an organization he helped found to provide doctors for Third World areas.

Like Bishop Sheen, Dooley found a place in the hearts of the American public by combining anticommunism with Catholic and American values. But Fisher points out a more important contribution of Dooley's to the annals of U. S. Catholic history:

Dooley helped pave the way for the election of Kennedy as president of the United States by demonstrating that a devout Catholic could serve effectively as the head of a nonsectarian, international program designed to bring medical aid and Americanism to the Third World.[15]

John F. Kennedy, of course, would play the final and most crucial role in solidifying a place for U. S. Catholicism in mainstream American culture. Yet if Dr. Tom Dooley was an unlikely poster boy for U. S. Catholicism, the same can be said for Kennedy. The son of a pious mother and a millionaire father who was determined to make his son president, John had little serious interest in religion. Unlike most Catholics of the day, Kennedy did not attend Catholic schools. Instead, his father enrolled him in the most prestigious secular institutions of learning, reasoning that these schools would give him the pedigree needed for entrance into the highest echelon of American society. Consequently, Kennedy always felt more comfortable with secular Ivy Leaguers than with those who had found success after emerging from the Catholic ghetto. Indeed, he was quite taken aback when the media and some Protestant clergymen made an issue of his Catholicism during his 1960 run for the presidency. As Massa remarks:

> On one level, the very issue of Kennedy's religion in the campaign could easily be seen as ironic, as Jack Kennedy had never been accused of being overly pious at any point in his life. His wife, Jacqueline, had reportedly told journalist Arthur Krock that she was mystified over the religious issue, as "Jack is such a poor Catholic."[16]

Thus, through no fault of his own, Kennedy's Catholicism was a key issue and one that the Massachusetts senator had to face head on if he were to have any chance of winning the presidency. He did so by insisting that his religion was a private matter that would have no bearing on how he would conduct policy as president, since he was an advocate of total separation of church and state. Skillfully taking the offense, he scolded the media for neglecting truly important issues like the expansion of communism into the Western Hemisphere while choosing instead to focus on the irrelevant question of his religion.

Ironically, Kennedy's "secularization" of politics and "privatization" of religion caused much discomfort among the Catholic hierarchy. Nevertheless, it seemed to ease the minds of enough Protestants, for he won the presidency, albeit in one of the closest election in U. S. history.

True to his word, the thirty-fifth president of the United States conducted his thousand days in the White House in a totally secular fashion,
thereby convincing most of his fellow countrymen and women that it made
no difference whether the president was Protestant or Catholic. Moreover,
his tragic assassination created a myth of Kennedy greatness that indirectly
eroded most of whatever anti-Catholic prejudice still remained. His un-
timely death in 1963 also coincided with the first year of the Second Vatican
Council, which, by its conclusion, had reshaped the church in ways much
more compatible with U. S. culture. Thus, by the mid-1960s Catholics had
finally achieved their long-sought dream of being accepted as equals by
their fellow Americans.

It was precisely during these years, when U. S. Catholics were making the
transformation into mainstream American culture, that the Catholic church
and its press first took an interest in Central America. Positioning itself in the
vanguard of the Cold War struggle against communism, almost all Catholic
periodicals called on the United States to rid the Western Hemisphere of the
"communist" government of Guatemala. This Cold War mind-set also motivated those North American Catholic missionaries who flocked to Central
America in the late 1950s and early 1960s. They reasoned that by spreading
U. S. values along with those of Catholicism they would nip the threat of
communism before it spread throughout Latin America. But by the end of
Vatican II, these same missionaries, as well as the Catholic press that followed their progress, were beginning to reassess their blueprint for the isthmus and for Latin America in general. After establishing countless U. S.-style
Catholic parishes and schools and pouring large sums of money into development projects that mostly failed, they began to conclude that their efforts
were making little difference to the Latin American majority, which continued to live in misery. They wondered if unjust structures that enhanced the
wealth of the elite class at the expense of the poor might not be the primary
cause of Latin suffering. Following the Medellín Bishops' Conference, the
publication of Ivan Illich's "Seamy Side of Charity," and the failed revolutionary movement of the Melvilles, these missionaries now began to publicly
express their doubts concerning the Catholic Cold War way of thinking and
how it had been applied to Central and South America.

Let us stop here for a moment and review another aspect of North
American Catholicism—its concern for social justice. Most historians of the
U. S. Catholic church would agree with Dorothy Dohen, who, in her book
Nationalism and American Catholicism, published in 1968, concluded that
throughout its history the U. S. Catholic church had basically supported the

status quo.[17] Consumed with the needs of millions of immigrants and faced with a hostile U.S. population that questioned their patriotism and ability to be good citizens, U.S. Catholics retreated into their ghetto and limited themselves to their own parochial concerns. Craving acceptance from the Protestant-dominated majority, they elected to play virtually no part prior to the 1960s in the antislavery, antiwar, or anti-imperialism movements. They contributed little to the black civil rights cause, and, rather than condemn the virulent anti-Semitism of Protestant America, they too often took part in Jew bashing of their own. When Mexican officials in the early part of the twentieth century began persecuting Catholic opponents, the Knights of Columbus, a few bishops, and the U.S. Catholic press called on the White House to intervene against the "Bolshevik" government of Mexico. Nevertheless, when it was obvious that such a demand had become an irritant to U.S. officials, the National Catholic War Council—the major U.S. bishops' organization at that time—attempted to reel in its malcontents and make peace with Washington.[18] Indeed, U.S. Catholics and their leaders proved to be enthusiastic supporters of every U.S. war and of virtually every aspect of U.S. foreign policy prior to the 1970s.

One would have to look to the Catholic Worker movement to find the first U.S. Catholic social justice organization to transcend the narrow parameters of the Catholic ghetto; it showed an interest in issues that were not purely sectarian but involved broader ethical questions affecting American society as a whole. Indeed, one would also have to look to this small group founded by Dorothy Day and Peter Maurin, to find a Catholic organization that broke from the accommodationist mentality of its co-religious by publicly questioning the morality of certain facets of U.S. social policy.

From its inception in 1933, the group's newspaper, the *Catholic Worker*, addressed social concerns avoided by virtually all other U.S. Catholic periodicals—issues such as racism, the suffering of the urban and rural poor, and inequalities resulting from the American capitalist system. It was also an advocate of pacifism, holding firm to this unpopular position even during World War II. As the Cold War commenced, the Catholic Worker movement expanded its social justice agenda to include opposition to the nuclear arms race. Beginning in 1955, it publicized its position through demonstrations against a law that required all people to stay off the streets during government-mandated air-raid drills. For their efforts, Day and some of her associates were sentenced to short jail terms. The Workers and their cause, however, received little sympathy from the American Catholic clergy and laity. Of all Catholic periodicals, only *Commonweal* attempted to explain to its readers the rationale behind the lawbreakers' conduct. Nevertheless, the Catholic Workers had set a precedent. By being the first Catholic group to publicly protest U. S. Cold War policy, they served as role models for those Catholics who, following the call of the Second Vatican Council, searched to commit themselves to social justice causes.

Since Vatican II and the civil rights movement of Dr. Martin Luther King, Jr., coincided, and since King's movement was grounded in Gospel values and nonviolence, progressive Catholics gravitated toward this cause. Indeed, the 1965 Selma march probably marks the first time that American Catholics experienced the sight of large numbers of priests and nuns in full religious dress demonstrating against U. S. law (in this case, state law upholding segregation).

But by the end of 1965 the civil rights movement was turning away from the nonviolent philosophy of King and toward the more militant concepts of the "Black Power" movement. Feeling uncomfortable with this change, white Catholics moved away from active participation in the black civil rights cause and toward the newly emerging antiwar movement.

Beginning in 1963, some Catholic Workers in New York City began a small daily protest against the Vietnam War. In 1964 they joined with such other Catholics as the Berrigan brothers and Thomas Merton to form the Catholic Peace Fellowship and began to protest more vigorously. In 1965 Catholic Workers pioneered a new method of protest—publicly burning their draft cards.

But the Catholic bishops, some of whom had at least come to accept the participation of clergy in the civil rights movement, were unable to go so far as to accept clerical participation in actions critical of U. S. Cold War policy. In 1966 they issued a joint encyclical, "Peace and Vietnam," which declared that U. S. actions in Vietnam were morally justified. When the Berrigan brothers and others began to destroy draft records, most bishops became thoroughly alarmed. Led by Cardinal Spellman, they condemned the tactics of what had by now become known as the "Catholic Left."[19] Meanwhile, some Catholic missionaries who had returned from Latin America became involved in the antiwar movement, which they viewed as another dimension of the same U. S. foreign policy that they felt had contributed to injustice in the countries of their missionary activities. In other words, they linked U. S. policy in Vietnam with U. S. policy in Latin America.

The Catholic antiwar movement gradually declined in the early 1970s. After the war ended in 1975, many of its veterans gravitated toward the cause of social justice in Central America. This time they found little opposition for their cause from a North American hierarchy that by now had faced much criticism for its "uncritical" support of U. S. violence in Vietnam.

Following the 1980 murders of Archbishop Oscar Romero and the four
U. S. churchwomen, the U. S. bishops, by now thoroughly informed of the
Central American situation by the enormous numbers of U. S. missionaries
returning from Latin America, as well as by the leadership of religious orders and the Catholic press, added their important collective voice to the
criticism of U. S. policy in Central America. Thus, the U. S. Catholic institutional church—that is, its bishops, clergy and religious, its press, and many
of its social and grassroots organizations—spoke out for the first time in
American history as a unified force in protest of U. S. foreign policy. Such a
stunning development would have been impossible prior to the emergence
of the American Catholic church from its ghetto in the late 1950s and early
1960s and the acceptance of American Catholics by their fellow citizens as a
respected patriotic part of U. S. society. Such a change would likewise not
have occurred had it not been for the *aggiornamento* of Vatican II. John
Tracy Ellis, the dean of American Catholic historians, puts the influence of
the Second Vatican Council on the U. S. Catholic church in perspective
when he comments that "American Catholics have known no comparable
experience to what broke over them about 1966, nor, indeed, has there been
anything of a like character within universal Catholicism since the French
Revolution shook the Church to its foundations."[20]

Thus, by the mid-1960s the U. S. Catholic church had become thoroughly integrated into mainstream U. S. society. It had moved from the immigrant phase of its history into a new "mainline American" phase. As an
acceptable part of the "establishment," it was now more willing to speak out
forcefully concerning the ethical nature of U. S. policy, and it chose to do so
on Central America.

So what did it say? One finds the U. S. Catholic church's position clearly
laid out in meticulous detail in the hundreds of articles on the isthmus
published in national Catholic periodicals. Most essential was the conviction that U. S. Central American policy, premised on an outmoded anticommunist Cold War hypothesis, was not only flawed but also immoral
and counterproductive. Although communism was a dangerous reality in
Central America, it was not the root cause of the region's problems. It was,
on the other hand, an inevitable outgrowth of a society in which a small but
powerful minority was enhancing its own wealth by perpetuating unjust
structures that relegated the majority to poverty and misery. Instead of
showering oppressive governments and their militaries with aid merely because they declared themselves anticommunist, the United States should
use its influence and resources in a way that would ameliorate the condition

of the poverty-stricken masses. In other words, the United States should, like the bishops at Medellín, make an option for the poor.

The Catholic press further argued that a U. S.-dictated military solution to civil war in the isthmus was not only unrealistic but undesirable. Even though the oligarchic-military governments of El Salvador and Guatemala and the Nicaraguan contras received billions of dollars in overt and covert aid from the United States in the 1980s, they were able to achieve no better than a stalemate in their civil wars. And even if they could attain victory, the result would be a prolongation of an unjust status quo that, in the long run, would make future violent revolution inevitable. Instead, the United States should support peace talks aimed at incorporating not only the guerrilla forces but the popular organizations into the political and economic structures of the region. This is what Archbishops Romero and Rivera Damas called for. It is what the U. S., Guatemalan, and Nicaraguan bishops called for. It is also what the Contadora and Arias peace plans called for. By refusing to support such a peace dialogue, the United States was degrading itself in the eyes of the world.

Since the progressive Catholic press called for peaceful change in Central America, it was consistent in condemning violence from the right and the left. One would look in vain to find support in Catholic journals for the Farabundo Martí National Liberation Front or the various Guatemalan guerrilla movements. And although many Catholic periodicals initially attempted to mitigate some Sandinista abuses by labeling them "mistakes" resulting from an immoral U. S. policy, by the mid-1980s virtually all were highly critical of FSLN abuses.

More specifically, the U. S. Catholic press refused to allow Guatemala to be consigned to obscurity. It chided the secular media for ignoring the violence inflicted by Guatemalan security forces on Indian communities, labor union members, church workers, students, and university faculty and staff. Yet it took care to note that the indigenous communities, like church personnel who worked with them, were caught between a murderous army and a violent guerrilla movement, neither of which they supported. When the Reagan administration attempted to renew overt aid to the Guatemalan government and military, the Catholic press loudly protested, strengthening its objection by providing numerous specific examples of army or paramilitary massacres of Indians and murders and kidnappings of church workers.

When Reagan officials decided to prosecute those involved in the Sanctuary Movement and claimed that Guatemalans and Salvadorans who entered the country illegally did so for economic reasons, the Catholic press challenged them. It portrayed Sanctuary workers as selfless seekers of justice whose actions were grounded in their religious commitment. It likewise presented copious examples of Central Americans who were forced to flee government-connected death squads in their home countries. It also asked why the U.S. government denied the requests of virtually all Guatemalans and Salvadorans who applied for asylum when similar petitions from those fleeing communist countries were routinely granted.

Although the Vatican was uneasy with the conduct of the outspoken bishops Oscar Romero and Arturo Rivera Damas in El Salvador, the progressive Catholic press showed no such reservations. It publicized their sermons and their peace initiatives and castigated those Salvadoran bishops who opposed them. When the Carter administration attempted to exonerate the Salvadoran government and military from the assassination of Romero and accused the left of initiating the violence at his funeral, the progressive Catholic press destroyed the White House's claims by presenting evidence from U.S. bishops, priests, and religious who either were eyewitnesses at the scene of the crimes or were in El Salvador when they occurred. Indeed, citing religious personnel on hand in Central America to refute claims by the U.S. government became standard in the repertoire of the North American Catholic media. Catholic progressive journals likewise strongly challenged the claim of both the Carter and Reagan administrations that the Duarte-led government was moderate, reformist, and the only reasonable alternative to violence-prone extremists of the Salvadoran right and left. Instead, they presented his government as no more than a powerless façade, which the Salvadoran oligarchy and military allowed to exist because by doing so they could continue to receive U.S. aid.

But more significant, the progressive Catholic press, faced with a Reagan administration which it saw as disingenuous and adversarial, broke new ground by calling on its readers to take an activist approach to the Central American crisis. People of faith were implored to participate in protest marches and hunger strikes, to sign petitions and write letters to their congresspersons and newspapers, to organize and take part in ecumenical religious services for Romero and the four U.S. churchwomen, to hold educational workshops on the isthmus and speak before church groups and at religious services, and to make fact-finding trips to Central America and tell others what they found. In short, the Catholic press asked its readers to use whatever peaceful means were necessary to change U.S. policy toward El Salvador and Nicaragua.

The complex nature of the Nicaraguan situation made this country the toughest challenge for the U. S. Catholic media. Even though the FSLN espoused a Marxist-oriented philosophy and was anathema to the Vatican, most U. S. Catholic periodicals initially supported the Sandinista government with great enthusiasm. They had little sympathy for the Nicaraguan bishops and somewhat cavalierly wrote off their claims of persecution at the hands of the Sandinistas as a typical reaction by a pre–Vatican II–oriented hierarchy that had no sympathy for the plight of the poor and craved influence with the wealthy. No progressive Catholic publication seemed to be overly concerned with the conflict between the bishops and the so-called popular church and its radical clergy.

Although at times quite critical of Sandinista misdeeds, most Catholic journals too often made excuses for revolutionary excesses, especially in the first half of the 1980s. By 1984 or 1985, however, virtually every U. S. Catholic periodical that concerned itself with events in Nicaragua had become critical of the Sandinista government. FSLN "mistakes" were now referred to as "abuses," and the Sandinistas were soundly castigated for undemocratic behavior, although their rule was still seen as preferable to all available alternatives.

Throughout the decade the vast majority of Catholic publications opposed U. S. aid to the contras and vigorously condemned the Nicaraguan policy of the Reagan and Bush administrations. With the exception of a few conservative journals, the Catholic press consistently declared U. S. conduct in Nicaragua immoral and partly responsible for pushing the Sandinistas toward authoritarianism. Indeed, a 1987 *America* editorial succinctly encapsulated the thinking of the Catholic press when it remarked that "one does not have to be a fan of the Sandinistas to oppose contra aid and the Administration's contra policy."[21]

Although liberation theology was under constant attack from Vatican officials, U. S. politicians, many Latin American prelates, and the conservative faction of the U. S. Catholic press, progressive Catholic periodicals throughout the latter quarter of the twentieth century defended it and patiently attempted to explain its message to readers. Finally, although a small number of conservative Catholic publications expended much energy defending U. S. policy in Central America, they lost a valuable opportunity to influence the Catholic debate on this issue. By impugning the integrity of those who disagreed with them rather than debating the merits of their opponents' arguments, and by accentuating Sandinista misdeeds while ignoring those of the Salvadoran, Guatemalan, and Honduran governments, these conservative Catholic periodicals proved to be their own worst enemy.

Before closing this study, a few additional remarks are in order. First, the views on Central America found in the progressive Catholic press are for the most part the same as those of the USCC, the leadership of U.S. Catholic religious orders and congregations, the vast majority of U.S. Catholic missionaries serving in Latin America, and the scores of grassroots ecumenical groups dedicated to changing U.S. policy in the isthmus. Few prominent U.S. Catholic churchpeople publicly dissented from these views, and those that did seem to have had little impact on overall U.S. Catholic opinion and even less on that of U.S. Catholic religious leaders. Thus, one is correct in identifying the Central American position articulated in the progressive Catholic press as that of the U.S. Catholic church as a whole.

Second, this position evolved over several decades. Whereas in the 1950s the U.S. church's focus on Central America was based on secondhand information garnered for the most part from U.S. government sources, the secular press, and Archbishop Rossell of Guatemala, this was not the case by the late 1970s. U.S. missionaries who had entered Central America in large numbers in the late 1950s and especially in the 1960s and 1970s now played a major role in the formulation of the North American church's views on the isthmus. These missionaries had worked with the poor in urban shantytowns and isolated rural villages. Consequently, unlike most U.S. governmental officials and secular newspaper reporters, they experienced firsthand on a daily basis the oppression of the Central American poor. When they returned to the United States they informed their religious superiors and congregations, as well as their parishioners, of the violent realities of Central America. The positions articulated by Latin American bishops, clergy, and religious—grounded in the resolutions emanating from the 1968 Bishops' Conference at Medellín and supported by the convictions of Vatican II—also greatly influenced their counterparts in the United States. Thousands of U.S. people of faith, both lay and religious, Catholic and Protestant, who throughout the 1980s made fact-finding trips to the isthmus and returned to tell what they had found to church and civic groups— in short, to anyone who would listen—also influenced Catholic leaders.

Third, from the late 1970s on, the U.S. Catholic church's response to U.S. policy in Central America represents something new in the annals of American Catholicism. Never before had the U.S. Catholic church taken such a critical position on a question of American foreign policy.

Fourth, U.S. governmental officials would have been better served had they heeded U.S. Catholic (and mainline Protestant) leaders concerning the isthmus. On this point the advice of a 1985 *America* editorial quoted earlier in this study bears repeating:

> The United States would not be in such an embarrassing position if it had long ago adopted the policy outlined by U.S. bishops before Congress: opposition to military aid to either side in Nicaragua, repudiation, as illegal and immoral, of any attempts to overthrow the Nicaraguan Government, and encouragement of the Contadora negotiations.[22]

Although the message of this editorial is limited to Nicaragua, it rings equally true for all of the isthmus. Let us hope that in the new millennium the U.S. government will take more seriously the insights of the North American Catholic church concerning not only Central America but all of Latin America. Had it done so in the latter quarter of the twentieth century, much suffering and death could have been avoided.

Notes

INTRODUCTION

1. In the late 1950s and early 1960s, Cardinal Richard Cushing provided U. S. missioners to Latin America with J. Edgar Hoover's *Masters of Deceit* and his own *Questions and Answers on Communism.* Prior to the mid-1970s U. S. Catholic missionaries often cooperated with U. S. intelligence operatives in Central America, providing them with information on local leaders and organizations. A few even became involved with the CIA in covert projects, receiving salaries, bonuses, or expenses for their efforts. See Gerald M. Costello, *Mission to Latin America: The Successes and Failures of a Twentieth-Century Crusade* (Maryknoll, N.Y.: Orbis Books, 1979), 38, 192–194.

2. From the late 1950s to his death in 1970 Cardinal Cushing was the most effective U. S. prelate in creating North American Catholic consciousness of Latin America. He recruited U. S. missionary personnel for the region and channeled millions of dollars into their projects. He was also responsible for the creation of the important Latin American Bureau of the National Catholic Welfare Council (NCWC), the U. S. bishops' council of that time, and the selection of the able John Considine, M. M., as its director. In 1962 the Bureau together with the U. S. Bishops' Subcommittee for Inter-American Cooperation established the Catholic Inter-American Cooperative Project (CICOP) for the purpose of creating dialogue between the North and Latin American churches. Bishop William Quinn of the NCWC laid the groundwork for CICOP by setting up informal luncheon meetings for U. S. and Latin American bishops who were in Rome participating in Vatican II. For most of the prelates involved, this was their first opportunity for such intercommunication. From 1964 to 1972 CICOP organized five important conferences in which Latin American church leaders explained the realities of their continent to U. S. Catholics. Influenced by the new Latin American theology of liberation, these

conferences provided many U. S. church leaders with their first unsanitized reports on the role of the United States south of the border.

In 1972 the National Conference of Catholic Bishops issued a pastoral letter on the missions in which they urged U. S. Catholics to take a personal interest in the needs of their less fortunate neighbors. In 1979 Archbishop John Quinn of San Francisco, then president of the National Conference of Catholic Bishops, attended the Latin American Bishops' Conference at Puebla, Mexico. In his report to his North American episcopal colleagues he called on them to participate more fully in the public debate concerning U. S. policies on Latin America. He further suggested that the Latin American prelates' "preferential but not exclusive love for the poor" be used as a model for the U. S. church. See John Quinn, "Invitation to Assess the U. S. Church," *Origins* (May 10, 1979), 741–745. See also Angelyn Dries, *The Missionary Movement in American Catholic History* (Maryknoll, N.Y.: Orbis Books, 1998), 179–214, and Robert S. Pelton, *From Power to Communion: Towards a New Way of Being Church Based on the Latin American Experience* (Notre Dame, Ind.: University of Notre Dame Press, 1994), 27.

3. Edward T. Brett, "The Attempts of Grassroots Religious Groups to Change U. S. Policy towards Central America: Their Methods, Successes, and Failures," *Journal of Church and State* (Autumn 1994), 773–794, and Christian Smith, *Resisting Reagan: The U.S. Central America Peace Movement* (Chicago: University of Chicago Press, 1996).

4. James Hennesey, *American Catholics: A History of the Roman Catholic Community in the United States* (New York: Oxford University Press, 1983), 272–273.

5. John Cogley, *Catholic America* (New York: Image Books, 1973), 142.

6. Editors, *Catholicism in Crisis: A Journal of Lay Catholic Opinion* (November 1982), 1.

7. See Michael Glazier and Thomas Shelley, eds., *The Encyclopedia of American Catholic History* (Collegeville, Minn.: Liturgical Press, 1997), for individual entries on the more significant Catholic periodicals, as well as for collective articles on the Catholic press and Catholic periodicals.

ONE. GUATEMALA TO THE OVERTHROW OF JACOBO ARBENZ

1. D. Manousos, "Nicaraguan Interlude," *Catholic Digest* (August 1944), 36–37.

2. Agnes Rothery, "In the Church of Santo Tomas," *Commonweal* (June 15, 1934), 182.

3. For background on this relationship, see Hubert J. Miller, "Catholic Leaders and Spiritual Socialism during the Arévalo Administration in Guatemala, 1945–1951," in Ralph Lee Woodward, Jr., ed., *Central America: Historical Perspectives on the Contemporary Crises* (New York: Greenwood Press, 1988), 86–87, and Bruce J. Calder, *Crecimiento y cambio de la iglesia católica guatemalteca, 1944–1966* (Guatemala City: Editorial José de Pineda Ibarra, 1970), 170–190.

4. Richard Pattee, "Portrait of a Dictator: General Jorge Ubico," *Sign* (April 1945), 463–464.

5. Ibid., 465. For Ubico, see Kenneth J. Grieb, *Guatemalan Caudillo: The Regime of Jorge Ubico* (Athens: Ohio University Press, 1979).

6. Gerard Sloyan, "Archbishops Wear Red, Too," *Sign* (September 1946), 18.

7. Ibid., 18–21. For Sanabria, see Ricardo Blanco Segura, *Monseñor Sanabria: Apuntes biográficos* (San José: Editorial Costa Rica, 1962); Santiago Arrieta Quesada, *El pensamiento político social de Monseñor Sanabria* (San José, Costa Rica: EDUCA, 1977); and Eugene D. Miller, *A Holy Alliance? The Church and the Left in Costa Rica, 1932–1948* (Armonk, N.Y.: M. E. Sharpe, 1996).

8. From 1945 through June 1950 I found fourteen articles on Guatemala and three on Costa Rica. From July 1950 through December 1954 I found twenty-seven on Guatemala and one each on Costa Rica, Honduras, and Nicaragua.

9. Piero Gleijeses, *Shattered Hope: The Guatemalan Revolution and the United States, 1944–1954* (Princeton, N.J.: Princeton University Press, 1991), 36–37, and Stephen Schlesinger and Stephen Kinzer, *Bitter Fruit: The Untold Story of the American Coup in Guatemala* (Garden City, N.Y.: Anchor Books, 1983), 50.

10. Jim Handy, *Gift of the Devil: A History of Guatemala* (Boston: South End Press, 1984), 107–110.

11. Harry Sylvester, "Graustark and the Indians: Report on Guatemala," *Commonweal* (August 23, 1946), 448.

12. Ibid., 447.

13. Ibid., 448.

14. "Press Freedom in Guatemala," *America* (May 17, 1947), 172.

15. Miller, "Catholic Leaders and Spiritual Socialism," 90–97.

16. Miller writes: "Arévalo made every effort to maintain good relations with the church." Ibid., 101. Holleran agrees, pointing out that throughout the Liberal period Guatemalan government officials insisted they did not oppose Catholicism but only "political Catholicism" and adding that "North American Catholics seldom understand this situation—they quickly raise the cry of persecution, and reacting emotionally, they want the United States government to intervene." Mary Holleran, *Church and State in Guatemala* (New York: Columbia University Press, 1949), 242–243. It should be noted that North American academic scholarship on Central America prior to the late 1960s is very limited. Aside from Holleran's study and Frederick Pike's "The Catholic Church in Central America," *Review of Politics* (January 1959), 83–113, there is virtually nothing in English on the Central American church. Such ignorance on isthmian history and culture perhaps explains at least in part why U. S. analysis of Central American events in the 1940s and 1950s was so skewed.

17. "Guatemala Goes Red," *Ave Maria* (March 27, 1948), 389.

18. Ibid.

19. Gleijeses maintains that Arévalo "was an anti-communist who believed that individual communists should not be persecuted unless they violated the law," and in the McCarthy era this was enough for the United States to view him as a

communist or a communist sympathizer. Piero Gleijeses, "Juan José Arévalo and the Caribbean Legion," *Journal of Latin American Studies* (February 1989), 133.

20. "Report on Guatemala," *America* (July 8, 1950), 366.

21. Ibid.

22. Ibid.

23. Ibid.

24. Handy, *Gift of the Devil*, 127–129; Gleijeses, *Shattered Hope*, 149–164. Aybar de Soto states: "The transformation of Guatemala from an underdeveloped country with a predominantly feudal economy into a modern capitalist [economy] was one of the developmental objectives set by the Arbenz government." José Aybar de Soto, *Dependency and Intervention: The Case of Guatemala in 1954* (Boulder, Colo.: Westview Press, 1978), 168.

25. "Harassed United Fruit," *Commonweal* (November 9, 1951), 108.

26. Ibid.

27. "Pro-Communism in Guatemala," *America* (July 28, 1951), 409–410.

28. "The Faith in Latin America," *America* (February 23, 1952), 549.

29. Ibid.

30. Secret NIE-84 (May 19,1953), in *Foreign Relations of the United States: 1952–1954*, vol. 4, *American Republics* (Washington, D.C.: United States Government Printing Office, 1954), 1065–1066.

31. S/P-NSC Files, lot 61D167 (August 19,1953), in *Foreign Relations*, 1080.

32. José Luis Chea, *Guatemala: La cruz fragmentada* (San José, Costa Rica: Flaso, 1988), 78–80.

33. Although *America* was far from being the most extreme, it was the most prolific among U.S. Catholic periodicals in attacking the Arbenz administration as communist. Of thirty-two articles on Guatemala in the U.S. Catholic press between July 1951 and July 1955, seventeen are in *America* and one is in *The Catholic World*, a Jesuit subsidiary of *America*.

34. "Reds at Work in Guatemala," *America* (March 7, 1953), 610.

35. H.C. McGinnis, "Commies on Our Doorstep," *St. Joseph Magazine* (August 1953), 33.

36. Ibid., 4.

37. Ibid., 4–5.

38. Ibid., 4.

39. Ibid., 4–5.

40. Ibid., 34.

41. "Guatemala, Good Neighbor?" *Ave Maria* (July 10, 1954), 5.

42. Jim Bishop, "Reds Run Guatemala," *Catholic Digest* (May 1954), 7.

43. Ibid., 6–7.

44. Ibid., 9.

45. Ibid., 10.

46. Ibid., 8.

47. Ibid., 9.

48. Ibid., 8.

49. Ibid., 9.
50. Ibid., 8.
51. Ibid., 9.
52. Ibid., 8.
53. "Strikes in Honduras," *America* (June 12, 1954), 289–290. For the Honduran strike, see Robert MacCameron, *Bananas, Labor, and Politics in Honduras: 1954–1963* (Syracuse, N.Y.: Maxwell School of Citizenship and Public Affairs, Syracuse University, 1963), and Victor Meza, *Historia del movimiento obrero hondureño* (Tegucigalpa, Honduras: Guaymuras, 1981), 75–91. For the strike's effect on the Honduran church, see Edward T. Brett and Donna W. Brett, "Facing the Challenge: The Catholic Church and Social Change in Honduras," in Woodward, *Central America*, 109–111.
54. Charles Lucey, "Catholic Resistance in Guatemala," *America* (June 26, 1954), 337.
55. Ibid., 337–338.
56. Blake D. Pattridge, "The Catholic Church in Revolutionary Guatemala, 1944–1954: A House Divided," *Journal of Church and State* (Summer 1994), 527–528.
57. Ibid., 530–532.
58. Gleijeses, *Shattered Hope*, 212, 288.
59. Hunt writes: "A senior Guatemalan churchman had come to our notice through his anti-Communist pronouncements. Cardinal Spellman arranged clandestine contact between him and one of our agents so that we could coordinate our parallel efforts. Anti-Arbenz and anti-Communist pastoral letters were given wide publicity in the Latin American press, and we air-dropped many thousands of leaflets carrying the pastoral message into remote areas of Guatemala where they otherwise might have escaped notice." E. Howard Hunt, *Undercover: Memoirs of an American Secret Agent* (New York: Berkley, 1974), 98–99.
60. Schlesinger and Kinzer, *Bitter Fruit*, 155; Anita Frankel, "Political Development in Guatemala, 1944–1954: The Impact of Foreign, Military and Religious Elites" (Ph.D. diss., University of Connecticut, 1969), 235; Gleijeses, *Shattered Hope*, 288; Richard H. Immerman, *The CIA in Guatemala: The Foreign Policy of Intervention* (Austin: University of Texas Press, 1982), 164.
61. "The Need for Understanding," *Commonweal* (October 23, 1953), 51.
62. "Danger in Latin America," *Commonweal* (October 30, 1953), 77.
63. "Caracas," *Commonweal* (March 12, 1954), 568–569.
64. "Guatemala," *Commonweal* (June 11, 1954), 236–237.
65. "The Popes and Guatemala: Land for the Landless," *Catholic Worker* (April 1954), 3.
66. Ibid.
67. Ibid.
68. John C. O'Brien, "North Dakota's First Diplomat," *Extension* (June 1954), 22.
69. Ibid., 57.
70. Ibid., 23.
71. Ibid., 22.
72. Ibid., 57.

TWO. CARLOS CASTILLO ARMAS AND THE CATHOLIC CHURCH

1. Gleijeses, *Shattered Hope,* 383; Susanne Jonas, *The Battle for Guatemala: Rebels, Death Squads, and U.S. Power* (Boulder, Colo.: Westview Press, 1991), 41; Thomas Melville and Marjorie Melville, *Guatemala: The Politics of Land Ownership* (New York: Free Press, 1971), 103.

2. Jonas, *Battle for Guatemala,* 42; Melville and Melville, *Guatemala,* 86, 100–101.

3. Jonas, *Battle for Guatemala,* 41–42; Melville and Melville, *Guatemala,* 91–103.

4. Jonas, *Battle for Guatemala,* 41–42. See Pike, "Catholic Church in Central America," 83–113, for an interesting contemporary analysis of Guatemalan church-state relations up through the 1950s.

5. Mariano Rossell Arellano, *Carta pastoral sobre la paz, fruto de la justicia y del amor* (Guatemala City: Tipografía Sanchez y De Guise, 1954), 1. Gleijeses states that after the overthrow of Arbenz, the bodies of many who were executed by Castillo Armas's forces were displayed to foreign reporters as people murdered by the Arbenz government. Gleijeses, *Shattered Hope,* 317 n. 180, 333–334.

6. Mariano Rossell Arellano, *Oración funebre pronunciada en los funerales celebrados en la Catedral Metropolitana por el eterno descanso de las almas de todas las víctimas asesinadas en Guatemala durante el terror comunista y de los muertos en los campos de batalla* (Guatemala City: Tipografía Sanchez y De Guise, 1954), 2.

7. For the conflict of the church and *la Reforma,* see Hubert J. Miller, *La iglesia y el estado en tiempo de Justo Rufino Barrios* (Guatemala City: Universidad de San Carlos de Guatemala, 1976); Holleran, 151–209.

8. Hubert J. Miller, "Las relaciones entre la Iglesia Católica y el Estado in Guatemala, 1927–1944: La disminución del Anticlericalismo," *Anales de Geografía e Historia de Guatemala* (1996), 123–124.

9. Richard N. Adams, *Crucifixion by Power* (Austin: University of Texas Press, 1970), 280.

10. Frankel, "Political Development in Guatemala," 183; Handy, *Gift of the Devil,* 132; Miller, "Catholic Leaders and Spiritual Socialism," 87.

11. Calder, *Crecimiento y cambio,* 51–52; Holleran, *Church and State in Guatemala,* 212–218; Adams, *Crucifixion by Power,* 280; Miller, "Catholic Leaders and Spiritual Socialism," 86; Chea, *Guatemala,* 68–71.

12. Agustín Estrada Monroy, *Datos para la historia de la iglesia en Guatemala,* vol. 3 (Guatemala City: Tipografía Nacional, 1979), 505–507, 518.

13. Miller, "Catholic Leaders and Spiritual Socialism," 86.

14. Virginia Garrard Burnett, *Protestantism in Guatemala: Living in the New Jerusalem* (Austin: University of Texas Press, 1998), 71–72.

15. Miller, "Catholic Leaders and Spiritual Socialism," 89.

16. Frederick C. Turner, *Catholicism and Political Development in Latin America* (Chapel Hill: University of North Carolina Press, 1971), 135.

17. K. H. Silvert, *A Study of Government: Guatemala* (New Orleans: Middle American Research Institute, Tulane University, no. 21, 1954), 209–211, 218, 221, 226, 228, 232, 234.

18. Holleran, *Church and State in Guatemala,* 252.

19. Virginia Garrard Burnett, "Protestantism in Rural Guatemala, 1872–1954," *Latin American Research Review* (1989), 135.

20. Ibid., 134.

21. Mariano Rossell Arellano and the Guatemalan Bishops, *Carta pastoral colectiva sobre la amenaza comunista en nuestra patria* (Guatemala City: Tipografía Sánchez y De Guise, 1945), 6.

22. Mariano Rossell Arellano, *Instrucción pastoral al pueblo católico de Guatemala sobre el deber y condiciones del sufragio* (Guatemala City: Imprenta Sansur, 1948), 7–8.

23. Mariano Rossell Arellano, *Aclaraciones sobre la recta y firme postura de la iglesia de Guatemala con relación al presente momento político, y protesta por las insidiosas calumnias de partidos políticos contra el clero de nuestra patria* (Guatemala City: Tipografía Sánchez y De Guise, 1950), 2–6.

24. Mariano Rossell Arellano, *Exhortación pastoral para pedir oraciones por la "iglesia del silencio"* (Guatemala City: Unión Tipografía, 1953), 1. These pastoral letters are cited by Turner, *Catholicism and Political Development,* 131–132.

25. J. Lloyd Mecham, *Church and State in Latin America* (Chapel Hill: University of North Carolina Press, 1966), 320.

26. Turner, *Catholicism and Political Development,* 136.

27. Adams, *Crucifixion by Power,* 284.

28. Ibid., 321.

29. Ibid.

30. Ibid., 311.

31. "Dust Settles in Guatemala," *America* (July 10, 1954), 369.

32. Ibid.

33. "Our Friends Abroad on Guatemala," *America* (September 11, 1954), 558.

34. "Social Justice in Guatemala," *America* (July 24, 1954), 411.

35. Charles Lucey [no title], *America* (July 16, 1955), 384.

36. "Social Justice in Guatemala," 411.

37. Lucey [no title], 384.

38. Mariano Rossell Arellano, "Aftermath of Revolution," *Catholic Mind* (October 1954), 637–640.

39. "Our Friends Abroad on Guatemala," 558–559.

40. "Social Justice in Guatemala," 491.

41. Charles Lucey, "Washington Front," *America* (August 14, 1954), 472.

42. "U. S. White Paper on Reds in America," *America* (August 21, 1954), 489.

43. "In the Shadow of the Volcano," *Commonweal* (July 2, 1954), 308.

44. Ibid., 309.

45. "After Guatemala," *Commonweal* (July 9, 1954), 331.

46. Ibid.
47. "Masonry in Guatemala," *Ave Maria* (March 5, 1955), 4.
48. "Guatemala Recovering," *Ave Maria* (February 19, 1955), 4.
49. Ibid.
50. Ibid.
51. Ibid.
52. Edwin Lahey, "Guatemala's Year of Freedom," *Catholic Digest* (October 1955), 51–52.
53. Jim Bishop, "Two Who Died in Guatemala," *Catholic Digest* (February 1955), 109.
54. Cited in Melville and Melville, *Guatemala*, 123.
55. Edwin A. Lahey, "Guatemala: Experiment in Democracy," *Extension* (November 1957), 15.
56. Ibid., 14.
57. Ibid.
58. Ibid., 15.
59. Ibid., 56.
60. Ibid.
61. "Carlos Castillo Armas," *America* (August 10, 1957), 478.
62. Ibid.
63. Ibid.
64. Handy, *Gift of the Devil*, 152–153.
65. Oona Sullivan, "The Case of Guatemala," *Jubilee* (December 1961), 29.
66. Joseph B. Judge, "Report from Guatemala," *Jubilee* (July 1961), 4.
67. "Guatemalans to the Polls," *America* (January 25, 1958), 472.
68. Eugene K. Culhane, "Guatemala through American Eyes," *America* (February 8, 1958), 529.
69. C. J. McNaspy, "Good Gringos in Guatemala," *America* (July 23, 1966), 97.
70. Nino Marilano, "Before It's Too Late," *Commonweal* (February 9, 1962), 514–515.
71. Ibid., 515.
72. Ibid., 516.
73. "Democracy in Latin America," *Commonweal* (April 12, 1963), 59.

THREE. THE TRANSFORMATION OF THE LATIN AMERICAN CATHOLIC CHURCH

1. David C. Kelly, "Maryknoll in Central America, 1943–1978," unpublished regional history (Guatemala City: Maryknoll Missioners, 1980), 2–14; Penny Lernoux, *Hearts on Fire: The Story of the Maryknoll Sisters* (Maryknoll, N.Y.: Orbis Books, 1993), 154; Edward T. Brett, "Maryknoll Order," in Barbara A. Tenenbaum, ed., *Encyclopedia of Latin American History and Culture* (New York: Charles Scribner's Sons, 1996), vol. 3, 540–541; Sullivan, "The Case of Guatemala," 33.

2. Leo J. Sommer, "Jacaltenango: The Wonder Valley," *Maryknoll* (March 1948), 4.

3. "Tough Work in Fairyland," *Maryknoll* (March 1949), 7.

4. "Meet the Mayas," *Maryknoll* (March 1948), 16–19.

5. Alfred E. Smith, "Juan Carries On," *Maryknoll* (September 1947), 5.

6. Arthur F. Allie, "Indian Leaders for Guatemala," *Maryknoll* (October 1949), 21.

7. Ibid., 20.

8. Hugo M. Gerbermann, "Cracking the Shell," *Maryknoll* (June 1950), 22.

9. George L. Krock, "Report from the Mountains," *Maryknoll* (August 1950), 16.

10. Ibid.

11. J. Edmund McClear, "Soloma Trails: A Busy Day in the Saddle," *Maryknoll* (September 1949), 17.

12. Poverty in Guatemala was first mentioned in a 1950 article: "Poverty is never very far away from the Guatemalan Indian." Leo Sommer and Felix Fournier, "Guatemala Day," *Maryknoll* (May 1950), 36.

13. Felix Fournier and Carl Puls, "Guatemala's Farming Revolution," *Maryknoll* (May 1963), 3–5.

14. Donald J. Casey, "The Lime Workers of Cabrican," *Maryknoll* (April 1964), 3–4. The Maryknoll priest was Thomas Melville.

15. Donald J. Casey, "Mission Today," *Maryknoll* (October 1967), 13–17.

16. Donald Thorman, "What's Needed to Survive," *Maryknoll* (August 1968), 3.

17. Ibid., 2–7.

18. George A. Mueller, "To Free Men for Life," *Maryknoll* (July 1968), 10–11.

19. Ibid., 12.

20. Ibid.

21. Ibid., 13.

22. George A. Roberts, "All Saints Write Home," *Maryknoll* (December 1969), 14–15.

23. Patricia O'Mera, "Salvation and Liberation Are Synonymous," *Maryknoll* (October 1970), 59.

24. Ibid.

25. Ibid.

26. Ibid.

27. William J. Price, "The Bitter Tree," *Maryknoll* (August 1969), 11.

28. Ibid.

29. Ibid., 14.

30. Ibid.

31. Ibid., 11.

32. Darryl Hunt and Joel Alegria, "The Anxious Demand for Liberation," *Maryknoll* (August 1970), 12.

33. Ibid., 13.

34. Ibid.

35. Ibid.

36. Ibid.

37. Mecham, *Church and State*, 321.

38. Sullivan, "Case for Guatemala," 33; Kelly, "Maryknoll in Central America," 8–13.

39. Robert A. White, "Structural Factors in Rural Development: The Church and the Peasant in Honduras" (Ph. D. diss., Cornell University, 1977), 196–200; Brett and Brett, "Facing the Challenge," 107–109; Mecham, *Church and State*, 328; John J. Considine, *New Horizons in Latin America* (New York, 1958), 337ff, quoted in Leonard Bacigalupo, *The American Franciscan Missions in Central America: Three Decades of Christian Service* (Andover, Mass.: Charisma Press, 1980), 99.

40. Kelly, "Maryknoll in Central America," 10; Mecham, *Church and State*, 325; Bacigalupo, *American Franciscan Missions*, 99.

41. Mecham, *Church and State*, 331, 335; Bacigalupo, *American Franciscan Missions*, 99–100. I have included bishops in the number of priests in 1960 in the Central American countries.

42. Costello, *Mission to Latin America*, 44.

43. *Commonweal* and *America*, from 1961 through 1963, contained numerous articles lauding the Alliance and Peace Corps.

44. Edward Cleary, *Crisis and Change: The Church in Latin America Today* (Maryknoll, N.Y.: Orbis Books, 1985), 60–61.

45. Archbishop Marcos McGrath, *Cómo vi y vivé: El Concilio y el Postconcilio* (Bogota, Colombia: Ediciones Paulinas con CELAM, 2000), especially chap. 2.

46. Cleary, *Crisis and Change*, 42.

47. Daniel Levine points out that contrary to what we have been led to believe by many authors, the radical CEB model is not typical of all CEBs. In truth there are many different models, ranging from the pietistic conservative type to the "radical ideal" form, to use Levine's term. It is my own opinion that the radical, social justice oriented form was more prevalent in conflictive countries like Guatemala, El Salvador, and Nicaragua. See Daniel Levine, *Popular Voices in Latin American Catholicism* (Princeton, N. J.: Princeton University Press, 1992), 45–48.

48. Cleary, *Crisis and Change*, 11.

49. Phillip Berryman, *Liberation Theology: The Essential Facts about the Revolutionary Movement in Latin America and Beyond* (New York: Pantheon, 1987), 5–6.

50. Ibid., 8.

51. Costello, *Mission to Latin America*, 65, 106–108; Mary M. McGlone, *Sharing Faith across the Hemisphere* (Washington, D. C.: United States Catholic Conference, 1997), 107–108, 126 n. 41; Joseph P. Fitzpatrick, "Training Center at Cuernavaca," *America* (February 24, 1962), 678–680.

52. Costello, *Mission to Latin America*, 124–125.

53. Ibid., 122.

54. McGlone, *Sharing Faith across the Hemisphere*, 114.

55. Ivan Illich, "The Seamy Side of Charity," *America* (January 21, 1967), 88–89.

56. Ibid., 89.

57. Ibid.

58. Ibid., 89–90.

59. Ibid., 91. McGlone compares the intemperate message of Illich to the "more profound," moderate critique delivered at a 1966 Latin American Episcopal Conference (CELAM) meeting by Archbishop Helder Cámara. See McGlone, *Sharing Faith across the Hemisphere*, 114–117.

60. Costello, *Mission to Latin America*, 125. Joseph P. Fitzpatrick attempts to defend Illich's thesis by defusing the intemperance of his argumentation. See his "What Is He Getting At?" *America* (March 25, 1967), 444–449.

61. Thomas Melville and Marjorie Melville, *Whose Heaven, Whose Earth?* (New York: Alfred A. Knopf, 1971); Blase Bonpane, *Guerrillas of Peace: Liberation Theology and the Central American Revolution* (Boston: South End Press, 1985); Arthur Melville, *With Eyes to See: A Journey from Religion to Spirituality* (Walpole, N.H.: Stillpoint Publishing, 1992); Lernoux, *Hearts on Fire*, 154–160; Kelly, "Maryknoll in Central America," 18–20; Francis X. Gannon, "Catholicism, Revolution and Violence in Latin America: Lessons of the Guatemala Maryknoll Episode," *Orbis* (1969), 1204–1225.

62. Personal correspondence from Thomas Melville to the author, August 26, 1993.

63. Lernoux, *Hearts on Fire*, 155–156. For an interesting analysis of the Melville affair and the conflictive approaches to priestly ministry of the native and foreign clergy, see Paul Tortolani, "Political Participation of Native and Foreign Catholic Clergy in Guatemala," *Journal of Church and State* (1973), 407–418.

64. Kelly, "Maryknoll in Central America," 19–20.

65. Costello, *Mission to Latin America*, 163. There were 3,391 U.S. Catholic missionaries in Latin America in 1968.

66. "Yankees v. Latins," *Commonweal* (May 28, 1965), 310.

67. "The Real Enemy: Millions of the Dispossessed," *Commonweal* (June 18, 1965), 400.

68. "Latin America Reacts," *Commonweal* (September 3, 1965), 614–615.

69. "Latin America to Date," *Commonweal* (March 4, 1966), 628.

70. "Arms Race in Latin America," *Commonweal* (December 16, 1966), 313.

71. "On Latin American Radicalism," *America* (May 28, 1966), 763.

72. Cogley, *Catholic America*, 143.

73. Norman Gall, "Guatemala Guerrillas Slaughtered," *National Catholic Reporter* (June 7, 1967), 1.

74. Ibid., 10.

75. Ibid.

76. "Two U.S. Maryknollers Join Guerrilla Forces," *National Catholic Reporter* (January 24, 1968), 1, 10.

77. "Missioners Back Guerrillas," *National Catholic Reporter* (January 24, 1968), 1, 7.

78. "Guatemala: 2% Wealth, 98% Misery," *National Catholic Reporter* (January 31, 1968), 7.

79. Thomas R. Melville, "Revolution Is Guatemala's Only Solution," *National Catholic Reporter* (January 31, 1968), 5.

80. Ibid.

81. Ibid.

82. Ibid.

83. Ibid.

84. Francis X. Gannon, "Catholicism, Revolution and Violence in Latin America: Lessons of the 1968 Guatemala Maryknoll Episode," *Orbis* (1969), 1204–1225.

85. "Rebels and Religious," *Commonweal* (February 2, 1968), 521.

86. Ibid.

87. Ralph Clark Chandler, "Guerrilla Priests: A Few Kind Words," *Commonweal* (August 9, 1968), 526.

88. Ibid.

89. Ibid., 527.

90. Ibid., 528.

91. "Turning a Page of History," *America* (February 10, 1968), 174.

92. Ibid.

93. Sidney Lens, "Keeping the Latins Poor," *National Catholic Reporter* (April 2, 1969), 7.

94. Warren Sloat, "Guatemala 1970: Flashpoint for Terror," *Commonweal* (October 10, 1969), 38.

95. Ibid.

96. Harry Sylvester, "Graustark and the Indians: Report on Guatemala," *Commonweal* (August 23, 1946), 447–448.

97. Sloat, "Guatemala 1970," 38.

98. Marcio Moreira Alvez, "Kidnapped Diplomats: Greek Tragedy on a Latin Stage," *Commonweal* (June 26, 1970), 313.

99. Ibid., 312.

100. Ibid.

101. Ibid.

102. Ibid.

103. Rick Casey, "Guatemala Missioners Claim Fraud in Elections," *National Catholic Reporter* (May 24, 1974), 2.

104. Gordon L. Bowen, "How Things Are Getting Better in Guatemala," *Commonweal* (October 18,1985), 555.

105. Gordon L. Bowen, "News, Too, Disappears: Facts Unreported or Minimized," *Commonweal* (October 18, 1985), 556.

106. See, for instance, Robert F. Drinan, "American Guns, Guatemalan Justice," *America* (June 13, 1981), 478–480; Gordon L. Bowen, "No Roadblocks to Death: Guatemala's War against the Church," *Commonweal* (June 15, 1984), 361–364.

107. See, for example, Edward Brett and Donna W. Brett, "A Teacher and a Martyr in Guatemala," *America* (October 30, 1982), 253–255, an article on the murder of U.S. Christian Brother James Miller, which was condensed and published by *Catholic Digest* as "An American Martyr, 1982," *Catholic Digest* (March 1983), 31–34.

FOUR. THE CATHOLIC PRESS ON EL SALVADOR

1. Rodolfo Cardenal, "The Church in Central America," in Enrique Dussel, ed., *The Church in Latin America* (Maryknoll, N.Y.: Orbis Books, 1992), 255, 262–265; for a more detailed analysis of the relationship of the Salvadoran church and the Liberals, see Rodolfo Cardenal, *El poder eclesiástico en El Salvador (1871–1931)* (San Salvador: UCA/Editores, 1980). For more on Chávez y González, see Phillip Berryman, *The Religious Roots of Rebellion: Christians in Central American Revolutions* (Maryknoll, N.Y.: Orbis Books, 1984), 97–107, 115–122; Rosa Carmelita Samos, *Sobre el magisterio de Mons. Luis Chávez y González: Estudio teologico de sus cartas pastorales* (Guatemala City: Universidad Francisco Marroquín, 1986); Andrew J. Stein, "El Salvador," in Paul E. Sigmund, ed., *Religious Freedom and Evangelization in Latin America: The Challenges of Religious Pluralism* (Maryknoll, N.Y.: Orbis Books, 1999), 116.

2. Cited in James R. Brockman, *Romero: A Life* (Maryknoll, N.Y.: Orbis Books, 1989), 177.

3. The best study of Romero in English is Brockman, *Romero*. Jesús Delgado, *Oscar A. Romero, biografia* (San Salvador: UCA Editores, 1995), is also valuable and contains some information not found in Brockman. For Rivera Damas, see Edward T. Brett, "Arturo Rivera Damas: Another Salvadoran Hero," *America* (March 11, 1995), 13–16, and Jeffrey Klaiber, *The Church, Dictatorships, and Democracy in Latin America* (Maryknoll, N.Y.: Orbis Books, 1998), 168–192. A brief but good overview of the post-Medellín Salvadoran church is Jorge Cáceres Prendes, "Political Radicalization and Popular Pastoral Practices in El Salvador, 1969–1985," in Scott Mainwaring and Alexander Wilde, eds., *The Progressive Church in Latin America* (Notre Dame, Ind.: University of Notre Dame Press, 1989), 103–148. See also Tommie Sue Montgomery, "The Church in the Salvadoran Revolution," *Latin American Perspectives* (1982), 62–87; Tommie Sue Montgomery, "Cross and Rifle: Revolution and the Church in El Salvador and Nicaragua," *Journal of International Affairs* (1982), 209–221; Tommie Sue Montgomery, *Revolution in El Salvador: From Civil Strife to Civil Peace* (Boulder, Colo.: Westview Press, 1995), 81–99; and Stein, "El Salvador," 113–128.

4. John J. O'Connor, "The Church in El Salvador," *Magnificat* (May 1959), 46–48.

5. Thomas Anderson, "The Great *Fútbol* War," *Commonweal* (August 8, 1969), 479–480.

6. *Newsweek* was especially flippant, as the following illustrate: "The two-week war between El Salvador and Honduras has unreeled like a vintage Peter Sellers film—complete with rococo communiqués, blustering generals, and powder-puff battles" (August 11, 1969), 34; "Salvadoran and Honduran officers worked out the conditions for a local cease-fire with the help of slices of watermelon provided by OAS observers" (August 4, 1969), 51. *Time,* although less sarcastic, gave more emphasis to the soccer games than to the immigration problem (July 25, 1969), 29–30.

U.S. News and World Report called the conflict a "banana war" dubbed the "soccer war" (July 28, 1969), 6.

7. Thomas Anderson, "The Revolutionary Matrix," *Continuum* (Fall 1969), 387–391. For the "soccer war," see Thomas P. Anderson, *The War of the Dispossessed: Honduras and El Salvador, 1969* (Lincoln: University of Nebraska Press, 1981); for the 1932 conflict, see Thomas P. Anderson, *Matanza: El Salvador's Communist Revolt of 1932* (Lincoln: University of Nebraska Press, 1971).

8. June Carolyn Erlick, "El Salvador's Romero Risks Life Living Gospel Call," *National Catholic Reporter* (October 12, 1979), 12.

9. J. C. Erlick, "Archbishop to U. S.: Cut Off All Aid," *National Catholic Reporter* (June 1, 1979), 6.

10. J. C. Erlick, "New Junta, Old Violence?" *National Catholic Reporter* (December 28, 1979), 21.

11. Erlick, "El Salvador's Romero Risks Life Living Gospel Call," 13.

12. J. C. Erlick, "Credibility Crisis Hits El Salvador Junta," *National Catholic Reporter* (December 28, 1979), 9.

13. J. C. Erlick, "Right Wing Bombs El Salvador Catholic Radio Center, Library," *National Catholic Reporter* (February 29, 1980), 1.

14. Erlick, "El Salvador's Romero Risks Life," 12.

15. C. Shreiner, "Archbishop Romero Called Saint by Poor," *Our Sunday Visitor* (April 15, 1979), 1.

16. Charles Savitskas, "Central America's Grim Situation Looks Bleaker Daily," *Our Sunday Visitor* (January 6, 1980), 6.

17. "Salvadoran Archbishop Asks Carter to End Military Aid," *Origins* (March 13, 1980), 634–635.

18. Ed Moran [pseud.], "El Salvador's Climate of Terror," *America* (February 18, 1978), 117–118; Ed Moran, "Human Rights for Peasants: The Roots of Violence in El Salvador," *Commonweal* (October 13, 1978), 659–662.

19. "Land of Massacres," *America* (June 16, 1979), 485.

20. Ibid.

21. "A Ray of Hope for El Salvador," *America* (November 3,1979), 246.

22. "Hoping Past Hope," *America* (March 22, 1980), 238.

23. Philip Land, "Military Aid to El Salvador," *America* (March 22, 1980), 245–246.

24. Ibid., 245.

25. "Something Vile in This Land," *Time* (April 14, 1980), 61. See also *Time* (April 7, 1980); *Newsweek* (April 7 and 14, 1980); *U.S. News and World Report* (April 7, 1980); *Washington Post* (March 31, 1980); *New York Times* (March 31 and April 7, 1980); Brockman, *Romero*, 249; Raymond Bonner, *Weakness and Deceit: U.S. Policy and El Salvador* (New York: Times Books, 1984), 184–185. It should be noted that by 1981 reports and opinion columns in the *New York Times* by Raymond Bonner, Christopher Dickey, Sydney Schanberg, Anthony Lewis, and Flora Lewis and in the *Washington Post* by Alma Guillermoprieto and others had become highly critical of U. S. Salvadoran policy. This was so much so that a front-page *Wall Street Journal*

editorial from February 10, 1982, charged Bonner and Guillermoprieto and to a lesser degree the above-named others with biased reporting, implying that they were willing dupes of the communists. This editorial set off a heated dispute carried out in editorial pages throughout the United States and on television talk shows. Feeling the pressure, in August the editors of the *Times* recalled Bonner from his Central American post, whereupon he resigned from the paper. Commenting on this imbroglio, Bonner later writes: "It is widely believed that the *Journal*'s editorial had a significant impact on the reporting from El Salvador, in favor of the administration. The editorial 'turned the press around,' General [Wallace] Nutting [senior U.S. military commander for all of Latin America] told a reporter some months later. The foreign editor of one major newspaper sent copies of the editorial to his correspondents in Central America. 'Let's not let this happen to us' was the message, according to one of the paper's reporters." Bonner, *Weakness and Deceit*, 341. Also see Mark Danner, *The Massacre at El Mozote: A Parable of the Cold War* (New York: Vintage Books, 1993), especially 228–233.

26. Stephanie Russell, "Millions Mourn Slain Romero," *National Catholic Reporter* (April 4, 1980), 4.

27. James L. Connor, "El Salvador's Agony and U.S. Policies," *America* (April 26, 1980), 361.

28. Ibid., 360.

29. Ibid., 362.

30. Ibid.

31. Ibid., 363.

32. "Romero: A Pastoral Message," *Catholic Mind* (September 1980), 34–43.

33. Charles Savitskas, "March Goes out in Storm of Gunfire in El Salvador," *Our Sunday Visitor* (April 13, 1980), 6.

34. Moises Sandoval, "The Death of Romero," *St. Anthony Messenger* (July 1980), 18–24.

35. Jon Sobrino, "Death and the Hope for Life," *Catholic Worker* (September 1980), 1, 3, 8.

36. "Hooked on Juntas," *Commonweal* (November 7, 1980), 612.

37. Ibid.

38. Ibid.

39. Richard Alan White, "El Salvador between Two Fires," *America* (November 1, 1980), 262.

40. Ibid., 265–266.

41. "Tragedy and Truth in El Salvador," *America* (December 13, 1980), 380.

42. June Carolyn Erlick, "Persecution Hits Church," *National Catholic Reporter* (November 7, 1980), 6; Max Echegaray, "Oppressed Church, People Gird for War," *National Catholic Reporter* (September 5, 1980), 28.

43. June Carolyn Erlick, "Salvadoran Troops Responsible for Deaths," *National Catholic Reporter* (November 14, 1980), 6.

44. June Carolyn Erlick, "San José: A Village Becomes a 'Ghost Town,'" *National Catholic Reporter* (September 19, 1980), 8.

45. June Carolyn Erlick, "Left Drives Refugees from El Salvador," *National Catholic Reporter* (September 19, 1980), 7–8.

46. June Carolyn Erlick, "Cleveland Team: We'll Stay," *National Catholic Reporter* (September 5, 1980), 1, 4, 28.

47. For the churchwomen, see Donna Whitson Brett and Edward T. Brett, *Murdered in Central America: The Stories of Eleven U.S. Missionaries* (Maryknoll, N.Y.: Orbis Books, 1988), 187–320; Ana Carrigan, *Salvador Witness: The Life and Calling of Jean Donovan* (New York: Simon and Schuster, 1984); and Judith Noone, *The Same Fate as the Poor* (Maryknoll, N.Y.: Maryknoll Sisters, 1984).

48. For more extensive coverage of these organizations, see Brett, "Attempts of Grassroots Religious Groups," 773–794.

49. Janice McLaughlin, Moises Sandoval, and Stephanie Russell, "Four Heroic Lives End in Martyrdom," *National Catholic Reporter* (December 19, 1980), 1, 27–29; "Four Modern Martyrs," *Catholic Digest* (April 1981), 52–60.

50. June Carolyn Erlick, "Four U.S. Women Slain," *National Catholic Reporter* (December 12, 1980), 3–4.

51. June Carolyn Erlick, "Whither Salvadoran Relations with U.S.?" *National Catholic Reporter* (December 19, 1980), 3.

52. June Carolyn Erlick, "U.S. Report Indicates El Salvador Cover-up," *National Catholic Reporter* (December 26, 1980), 7, 11; James W. Michaels, "El Salvador Aid Renewed," *National Catholic Reporter* (December 26, 1980), 11.

53. "The Martyrs of El Salvador," *America* (December 20, 1980), 401.

54. "Change in El Salvador?" *America* (December 27, 1980), 421.

55. Ibid.

56. Four additional U.S. citizens were killed by Salvadoran security forces in the month following the murders of the churchwomen. On December 17, Thomas N. Bracken was "accidentally" shot to death by Salvadoran soldiers after claiming to have information on the churchwomen's murders. On December 28, reporter John Sullivan was kidnapped and executed, presumably by security forces. On January 4, 1981, Michael Hammer and Mark Pearlman of the American Institute for Free Labor Development were gunned down by Salvadoran soldiers. All four murders were reported by the *National Catholic Reporter*. See James Michaels, "El Salvador Clash Grows," *National Catholic Reporter* (January 16, 1981), 3, 19, and Pat Williams, "Did Salvador Killing Stifle Evidence on Slain Women?" *National Catholic Reporter* (April 22, 1983), 1, 40. For more extensive coverage, see Brett and Brett, *Murdered in Central America*, 303–308.

57. "The Salvadoran Tragedy," *America* (January 31, 1981), 74.

58. Richard Alan White, "Green Light for Terror," *Commonweal* (January 16, 1981), 14.

59. Ibid., 16.

60. Ibid.

61. "Holy Wars in El Salvador," *America* (February 21, 1981), 152.

62. "Realpolitik in El Salvador," *America* (March 14, 1981), 192.

63. Arthur Jones, "U.S. 'Alone in El Salvador,'" *National Catholic Reporter* (February 13, 1981), 1.

64. Jane Sammon, "El Salvador and the U.S.," *Catholic Worker* (March 1981), 1–2.

65. "Into El Quagmire," *Commonweal* (March 13, 1981), 133.

66. Brett and Brett, *Murdered in Central America*, 193–195.

67. Stephanie Russell, "Nuns Hide Machine Guns?" *National Catholic Reporter* (March 13, 1981), 2.

68. Peggy Scherer, "A Country in Crisis," *Catholic Worker* (January/February 1981), 3.

69. "El Salvador—Stop the Repression!" *Catholic Worker* (March 1982), 5.

70. Stephanie Russell, "Catholics Protest Salvadoran Arms," *National Catholic Reporter* (March 6, 1981), 1.

71. Ibid., 1, 4.

72. "Longshore Union Spurns Arms for El Salvador," *National Catholic Reporter* (January 16, 1981), 19.

73. "New Anti-War Movement Born at D.C. Rally," *National Catholic Reporter* (January 23, 1981), 4; "Murders, Disappearance Mark Salvador," *National Catholic Reporter* (February 20, 1981), 5; June Carolyn Erlick, "U.S. Guns Kill U.S. Nuns—Embassy Rally," *National Catholic Reporter* (January 30, 1981), 20.

74. Robert J, McClory, "Fasters End Protesting in Chicago," *National Catholic Reporter* (January 9, 1981), 4.

75. "Salvadoran Catholics Support Revolt," *National Catholic Reporter* (January 30, 1981), 20.

76. June Carolyn Erlick, "Negotiate El Salvador Peace," *National Catholic Reporter* (April 10, 1981), 24.

77. "El Salvador: Pressure Kept on U.S. Officials," *National Catholic Reporter* (September 11, 1981), 8.

78. Christopher P. Winner, "Congress View of El Salvador Shifting," *National Catholic Reporter* (May 15, 1981), 21.

79. Judy Ball, "Orchestrated News from El Salvador Slightly Off Key," *Our Sunday Visitor* (March 22, 1981), 5.

80. Vincent J. Giese, "Beans, Bullets, Poverty and Terror the Way of Life in Central America," *Our Sunday Visitor* (March 22, 1981), 8.

81. Vincent J. Giese, "El Salvador: Refugees from Terror on Edge of Darkness," *Our Sunday Visitor* (March 29, 1981), 8–10.

82. Vincent J. Giese, "Perspective," *Our Sunday Visitor* magazine section (March 29, 1981), 2.

83. Robert E. Burns, "Red or Not, Bogeymen Are Just That," *U.S. Catholic* (May 1981), 2.

84. Carlos Cabarrus, "El Salvador: The Church under Militarization," *New Catholic World* (September/October 1981), 205–209; in the same issue, Cynthia Arnson, "El Salvador," 221–224, and Melinda Roper, "Seeds of Liberty," 225–228.

85. Sister Regis Flannery, "Reflections on the Paschal Death of a Missionary," *Sisters* (January 1981), 297–301; Donald B. Sharp, "El Salvador and the Prophetic Tradition," *Sisters* (February 1981), 344–347; Melinda Roper, "Reflections at a Mass," *Sisters* (April 1981), 468–470.

86. Maura Clarke, "Christian Witness," *Sign* (February 1981), 28–29; James Brockman, "Death of an Archbishop," *Sign* (May 1982), 30–32.

87. Mary Frohlich, "The Year of the Martyr: The Prayer to Join the Two Americas," *Liturgy: The Journal of the Liturgical Conference* (1982), 65–68.

FIVE. NICARAGUA TO 1980

1. An enormous amount has been written about the Nicaraguan church between 1979, when the Sandinistas came to power, and 1992, two years after their election defeat. As one would expect, virtually all authors have strong feelings—either pro-Sandinista or anti-Sandinista—that greatly color their interpretations of events. Those who are sympathetic to the FSLN and the "popular church" far outnumber those who are not. Some of the most cited of the former are Michael Dodson and Tommie Sue Montgomery, "The Churches in the Nicaraguan Revolution," in Thomas Walker, ed., *Nicaragua in Revolution* (New York: Praeger, 1981), 161–180; Michael Dodson and Laura Nuzzi O'Shaughnessy, *Nicaragua's Other Revolution: Religious Faith and Political Struggle* (Chapel Hill: University of North Carolina Press, 1990); Laura Nuzzi O'Shaughnessy and Luis H. Serra, *The Church and Revolution in Nicaragua* (Athens: Ohio University Center for International Studies, 1986); Margaret Randall, *Christians in the Nicaraguan Revolution* (Vancouver, B.C.: New Star Books, 1983); Teófilo Cabestrero, *Ministers of God, Ministers of the People* (Maryknoll, N.Y.: Orbis Books, 1983); Berryman, *Religious Roots of Rebellion;* Phillip Berryman, *Stubborn Hope: Religion, Politics, and Revolution in Central America* (Maryknoll, N.Y.: Orbis Books, 1994); César Jérez, *The Church and the Nicaraguan Revolution* (London: CIIR [Catholic Institute for International Relations, Justice Papers No. 5], 1984); Philip J. Williams, *The Catholic Church and Politics in Nicaragua and Costa Rica* (Pittsburgh, Pa.: University of Pittsburgh Press, 1989); Philip J. Williams, "The Limits of Religious Influence: The Progressive Church in Nicaragua," in Edward Cleary and Hannah Stewart-Gambino, eds., *Conflict and Competition: The Latin American Church in a Changing Environment* (Boulder, Colo.: Lynne Rienner, 1992), 129–146; Oscar González Gary, *Iglesia Católica y revolución en Nicaragua* (Mexico City: Claves Latinoamericanas, 1986); Roger Lancaster, *Thanks to God and the Revolution: Popular Religion and Class Consciousness in the New Nicaragua* (New York: Columbia University Press, 1988); Manzar Foroohar, *The Catholic Church and Social Change in Nicaragua* (Albany: State University of New York Press, 1989); Joseph E. Mulligan, *The Nicaraguan Church and the Revolution* (Kansas City, Mo.: Sheed and Ward, 1991); John M. Kirk, *Politics and the Catholic Church in Nicaragua* (Gainesville: University of Florida Press, 1992); and Andrew Bradstock, *Saints and Sandinistas: The Catholic Church in Nicaragua and Its Response to the Revolution* (London: Ep-

worth Press, 1987). Those opposed to the Sandinistas and sympathetic to the bishops are Humberto Belli, *Christians under Fire* (Garden City, Mich.: Puebla Institute, n.d.); Humberto Belli, *Breaking Faith: The Sandinista Revolution and Its Impact on Freedom and Christian Faith in Nicaragua* (Garden City, Mich.: Puebla Institute, 1985); and Domingo Urtasun, *Miguel Obando Bravo, Cardenal por la paz* (Managua: Editorial Hispamer, 1994). The information that follows in the historical overview is compiled from the above publications of Williams, Berryman, Kirk, and Dodson and O'Shaughnessy, which are the best of these studies. Although overly biased, the works of Mulligan, Foroohar, and Belli have also been used because they contain some valuable details not found elsewhere.

Although publications treating the Nicaraguan church have dropped off considerably in the 1990s, recent studies by Andrew J. Stein merit mention in that he is one of the few scholars who has been reevaluating church-state relations from the perspective of the post-Sandinista era. Consequently, his works are more balanced and in some ways more insightful than earlier studies, partly due to the advantage of hindsight. See his "The Prophetic Mission, the Catholic Church and Politics: Nicaragua in the Context of Central America," (Ph.D. diss., University of Pittsburgh, 1995); "The Church," in Thomas W. Walker, ed., *Nicaragua without Illusions: Regime Transition and Structural Adjustment in the 1990s* (Wilmington, Del.: SR Books, 1997), 235–247; and "Nicaragua," in Sigmund, *Religious Freedom and Evangelization*, 175–186. Margaret E. Crahan, "Religion and Politics in Revolutionary Nicaragua," in Mainwaring and Wilde, *Progressive Church in Latin America*, 41–63, is also noteworthy for its evenhanded analysis.

2. Kirk, *Politics and the Catholic Church*, 36. For more on the Somoza regime, see Richard Millett, *The Guardians of Dynasty: A History of the U.S.-Created Guardia Nacional de Nicaragua and the Somoza Family* (Maryknoll, N.Y.: Orbis Books, 1977), and Knut Walter, *The Regime of Anastasio Somoza García, 1936–1956* (Chapel Hill: University of North Carolina Press, 1994).

3. Mulligan, *Nicaraguan Church*, 74.

4. Quoted in Williams, *Catholic Church and Politics*, 19.

5. Jorge Eduardo Arellano, *Breve historia de la Iglesia en Nicaragua, 1523–1979* (Managua: n.p., 1980), 85.

6. Kirk, *Politics and the Catholic Church*, 48–51.

7. Sister Maura Clarke, prior to going to El Salvador, worked with the CEBs in San Pablo.

8. See Ernesto Cardenal, *The Gospel in Solentiname*, 4 vols. (Maryknoll, N.Y.: Orbis Books, 1976–1982).

9. Foroohar, *Catholic Church and Social Change*, 97–98.

10. The most thorough treatment of the hunger strike and protest letters is found in Mulligan, *Nicaraguan Church*, 117–119.

11. Pablo Vega, "El socialismo, la iglesia, y Cardenal," *La Prensa* (July 18, 1971).

12. Mulligan, *Nicaraguan Church*, 120.

13. Dodson and Montgomery, "Churches in the Nicaraguan Revolution," 168.

14. Cited in Mulligan, *Nicaraguan Church*, 99.

15. Cited in Mulligan, *Nicaraguan Church,* 128.

16. "Mensaje al Pueblo Nicaragüense," quoted in Mulligan, *Nicaraguan Church,* 130.

17. Berryman, *Religious Roots of Rebellion,* 250.

18. Dodson and Montgomery, "Churches in the Nicaraguan Revolution," 177.

19. Kirk, *Politics and the Catholic Church,* 107.

20. Douglas J. Roche, "Nicaragua: Sunny Land of Rot," *Sign* (July 1962), 30.

21. Ibid., 70.

22. Roderick Brenan, O. F. M. Cap., "Sacred Heart and Nicaragua," *Worldmission* (Summer 1958), 110–112.

23. Reyna De Kinloch, "Vines, Monkeys, Magic: Our Jungle Home," *Sign* (March 1964), 46–48.

24. "A Groundswell Grows," *America* (June 27, 1959), 462–463.

25. James R. Brockman, "The End of Fear in Nicaragua," *America* (August 19, 1978), 84–86.

26. James R. Brockman, "Nicaragua in January," *America* (February 24, 1979), 138.

27. "A Long and Consistent Disaster," *America* (October 7, 1978), 216. The Somoza lobby is also mentioned in James R. Brockman, "Our Man in Managua," *America* (March 26, 1977), 268–269, and Wayne H. Cowan, " The Chances for Nicaragua," *Commonweal* (June 6, 1980), 332, as well as in other Catholic publications.

28. "Letting Go," *America* (July 14, 1979), 5.

29. "Nicaragua, a New Hope," *America* (October 6, 1979), 164.

30. Ibid., 164–165.

31. "Aid to Nicaragua," *America* (September 20, 1980), 133.

32. Ibid.

33. "Nicaragua, a New Hope," 165.

34. "Nicaragua on the Brink," *America* (December 9, 1978), 421.

35. Chris N. Gjoring, "Nicaragua's Unfinished Revolution," *America* (October 6, 1979), 170.

36. Ibid., 171.

37. Tennant C. Wright, "Ernesto Cardenal and the Humane Revolution in Nicaragua," *America* (December 15, 1979), 387–388.

38. Robert F. Drinan, "Nicaragua after Somoza," *America* (February 9, 1980), 101–102.

39. Thomas E. Quigley, "The Bishop's Tale: Who Was That Mitered Man?" *Commonweal* (April 25, 1980), 229–231.

40. Wayne H. Cowan, "The Chances for Nicaragua," *Commonweal* (June 6, 1980), 331–333.

41. Archbishop John Quinn, "Ruthless Terror in Nicaragua," *Origins* (June 28, 1979), 96.

42. "The Church and the Revolution," *Origins* (March 13, 1980), 626–631.

43. June Carolyn Erlick, "Blood in Managua, Protest in N.Y.," *National Catholic Reporter* (September 22, 1978), 5.

44. Ibid.

45. June Carolyn Erlick, "Religious Fiestas Can't Disguise Repression," *National Catholic Reporter* (August 18, 1978), 15.

46. June Carolyn Erlick, "Nicaragua's *Los Doce:* They Might Try to Kill One of Us," *National Catholic Reporter* (August 18, 1978), 13–14.

47. June Carolyn Erlick, "In Nicaragua, You Can't Be in the Middle," *National Catholic Reporter* (August 18, 1978), 16.

48. June Carolyn Erlick, "Provisional Government Hope of Nicaraguans," *National Catholic Reporter* (June 29, 1979), 3.

49. June Carolyn Erlick, "Hopes, Not Bricks, Dreams, Not Dollars as Country Builds," *National Catholic Reporter* (September 7, 1979), 7, 30–31.

50. June Carolyn Erlick, "Nicaragua Today Is 'Laboratory for All of Latin America,'" *National Catholic Reporter* (February 22, 1980), 26–27.

51. Bill Kenkelen, "Cubans Criticizing Religion," *National Catholic Reporter* (February 22, 1980), 26.

52. Erlick, "Nicaragua Today Is 'Laboratory for All of Latin America,'" 27.

53. June Carolyn Erlick, "Volunteers from Cuba Aid Nicaragua," *National Catholic Reporter* (January 8, 1980), 5.

54. Peter Hebblethwaite, "Cardenal in Rome: The War Is Not Yet Over," *National Catholic Reporter* (May 2, 1980), 6.

55. Ibid.

56. June Carolyn Erlick, "Not All Priests to Quit Politics," *National Catholic Reporter* (May 16, 1980), 19.

57. June Carolyn Erlick, "Deadline Nears; Priests' Fate Still Unclear," *National Catholic Reporter* (December 12, 1980), 20.

58. Charles Savitskas, "Nicaragua's Bishops Emphasize Church Stand in Straightforward Message to New Regime," *Our Sunday Visitor* (August 26, 1979), 2.

59. "Nicaraguan Bishops Get Papal Lesson," *Our Sunday Visitor* (May 4, 1980), 2.

60. D. P. Noonan, "Nicaragua Today: After Somoza Is the Country Doomed to Marxism?" *Our Sunday Visitor* (May 25, 1980), 6.

61. Joseph McKenna, "Nicaragua's Image Distorted by 'Bad Press' Jesuit Says," *Our Sunday Visitor* (August 17, 1980), 8.

62. Charles Savitskas, "Splintered Church May Pinpoint Nicaragua's Direction," *Our Sunday Visitor* (December 28, 1980), 3.

SIX. NICARAGUA IN THE 1980S

1. Quoted in Mulligan, *Nicaraguan Church,* 176.

2. Penny Lernoux, *People of God: The Struggle for World Catholicism* (New York: Viking Press, 1989), 370.

3. Quoted in Berryman, *Stubborn Hope,* 33.

4. Ibid., 34.

5. Some examples are Robert F. Drinan, "Nicaragua: Reagan's New Target?" *National Catholic Reporter* (November 4, 1983), 20; "Betrayal," *America* (April 9, 1983), 272; "Chronology of U.S.-Nicaragua Relations under Reagan: A Study in Provocation," *National Catholic Reporter* (June 3, 1983), 9–10; "Nicaragua and Neutrality," *America* (September 29, 1984), 157; "Sacrificial Pawns," *Commonweal* (March 26, 1982), 164–165; Peggy Scherer, "Nicaragua," *Catholic Worker* (April 1982), 1, 5, 7; "U.S.-Nicaraguan Actions Immoral," *National Catholic Reporter* (November 19, 1982), 17.

6. See, for instance Steve Askin and Gene Palumbo, "U.S. Religious Oppose Intervention," *National Catholic Reporter* (August 12, 1983), 28; Vincent F. A. Golphin, "O'Connor, Law Buck USCC on Contras," *National Catholic Reporter* (March 28, 1986), 11; Steve Askin, "Reagan Liaison to U.S. Catholics Talks to Officials," *National Catholic Reporter* (December 30, 1983), 1, 6.

7. Some examples are John M. Swomley, Jr., "U.S. Double Standard Nicaragua's Chief Foe," *National Catholic Reporter* (June 3, 1983), 18; Daniel Berrigan, S.J., "One Thing We Could Do: Go to Nicaragua . . . El Salvador with Our Shame, Concern," *National Catholic Reporter* (September 14, 1984), 16–17; Tim Brennan, "Fighting 'the Good Fight' from Spain to Nicaragua," *National Catholic Reporter* (May 11, 1984), 11; Howard V. O'Shea, O.F.M., "Truth in Nicaragua," *America* (May 19, 1984), 372; Vincent Giese, "Nicaragua: Rays of Light on the Edge of Darkness," *Our Sunday Visitor* magazine section (March 22, 1981), 7–10; "U.S. Nicaraguan Actions Immoral," *National Catholic Reporter* (November 19, 1982), 17.

8. A few examples are June Carolyn Erlick, "Sandinista Supporters' Attacks Threaten 'Fragile' Pluralism Plan," *National Catholic Reporter* (March 27, 1981), 3; Mary Ann Lambert, "Nicaraguan Pendulum Moves to Extreme Left, Limits Basic Freedoms," *National Catholic Reporter* (November 11, 1983), 11; "The Making of a Second Cuba," *America* (November 24, 1984), 334; J. H. Evans and Jack Epstein, "Nicaragua's Miskito Move Based on False Allegations," *National Catholic Reporter* (December 24, 1982), 3, 22.

9. James Brockman, "Revolution 'Sharply Divides' Nicaraguan Church," *National Catholic Reporter* (March 19, 1982), 5; Tennant C. Wright, "Mixing Church, Politics in Nicaragua," *National Catholic Reporter* (October 30, 1981), 16; Margaret D. Wilde, "Nicaragua: Human Rights and the Miskito Indians," *America* (April 17, 1982), 295–297.

10. Vincent J. Giese, "Perspective," *Our Sunday Visitor* magazine section (March 29, 1981), 2.

11. V. J. Giese, "Sandinistas Deny Mistreating Miskito Indians," *Our Sunday Visitor* (August 8, 1982), 4–5.

12. Ibid., 5.

13. V. J. Giese, "Looking at Nicaragua Today: The Third Anniversary of the Sandinista Revolution," *Our Sunday Visitor* (July 18, 1982), 5.

14. Giese, "Sandinistas Deny Mistreating Miskito Indians," 4.

15. Ibid.

16. Jim Castelli, "Sandinistas Treat Miskito Humanely, Priest Says," *Our Sunday Visitor* (August 22, 1982), 8.

17. V. J. Giese, "Miskito Indians in Flight from Nicaragua, Unhappy in Honduras," *Our Sunday Visitor* (August 8, 1982), 6.

18. Giese, "Looking at Nicaragua Today," 4–5.

19. Ibid.

20. "Delegation Says Nicaraguans Fear Invasion from North," *Our Sunday Visitor* (November 14, 1982), 8.

21. V. J. Giese, "White Paper on Nicaragua," *Our Sunday Visitor* (November 7, 1982), 1, 3–5.

22. V. J. Giese, "Pope John Paul: A Tense Day in Nicaragua," *Our Sunday Visitor* (April 17, 1983), 8–10.

23. "Pope Opposed 'Popular Churches,' Priests in Politics," *Our Sunday Visitor* (August 22, 1982), 8.

24. "Vatican Hits 'Increasing' Tension in Nicaragua," *Our Sunday Visitor* (September 5, 1982), 3.

25. "U. S. Bishop Protests Nicaragua's Attacks on Church," *Our Sunday Visitor* (September 26, 1982), 8.

26. "The Honduran Card," *Commonweal* (November 5, 1982), 581.

27. Ibid., 580.

28. "Sacrificial Pawns," *Commonweal* (March 26, 1982), 164–165.

29. Ibid., 165.

30. Thomas Quigley, "When Research Masquerades," *Commonweal* (April 5, 1985), 208–210.

31. John C. Cort, "Raised Voices in Nicaragua," *Commonweal* (November 21, 1986), 629.

32. Ibid., 631.

33. Peggy Scherer, "Nicaragua," *Catholic Worker* (April 1982), 1, 5, 7.

34. "The Moscow Connection," *America* (November 19, 1983), 301.

35. Arthur F. McGovern, "Nicaragua's Revolution: A Progress Report," *America* (December 12, 1981), 378.

36. Van Pulley, "The Reagan Plan for Nicaragua," *America* (March 10, 1983), 208–210.

37. James R. Brockman, "A Visit to Nicaragua," *America* (March 9, 1985), 187–188.

38. Margaret D. Wilde, "Nicaragua: Human Rights and the Miskito Indians," *America* (April 17, 1982), 295–297.

39. McGovern, "Nicaragua's Revolution," 380.

40. Stephen T. De Mott, "Nicaragua: Press Freedom and Family Feuds," *America* (April 17, 1982), 298.

41. Gary MacEoin, "Nicaragua: A Church Divided," *America* (November 10, 1984), 294–299.

42. Humberto Belli, "Nicaragua's Bishops: A Response to Gary Mac Eoin," *America* (February 23, 1985), 145–148.

43. "Trouble in Nicaragua," *America* (November 14, 1981), 293.

44. "Nicaragua's Army," *America* (January 23, 1982), 44.

45. "Nicaragua's Peace Plan," *America* (November 5, 1983), 264.

46. "Church and State in Nicaragua," *America* (July 28, 1984), 21–22.

47. "The Making of a Second Cuba," *America* (November 24, 1984), 334.

48. "U. S. Nicaraguan Actions Immoral," *National Catholic Reporter* (November 19, 1982), 17.

49. Arthur Jones and Vincent F. A. Golphin, "Analysts Contend Reagan's Trade Embargo Shoves Nicaragua Closer to Soviet Embrace," *National Catholic Reporter* (May 10, 1985), 1.

50. Bill Kenkelen, "Critics Ask Why Most Media Missed Bombing Story," *National Catholic Reporter* (July 18, 1986), 23.

51. Daniel Charles, "U. S. Will Fund Anti-Sandinista Newspaper," *National Catholic Reporter* (May 24, 1985), 5.

52. Mark Lester, "Exiled Bishop Seen as Useful Ally in Contra War," *National Catholic Reporter* (August 15, 1986), 5.

53. Penny Lernoux, "Polarization, Confusion Ravage Nicaragua," *National Catholic Reporter* (May 16, 1986), 26–28.

54. "On Homefront, U. S. 'War' Rages in Congress, Media, White House and Church Network," *National Catholic Reporter* (April 26, 1985), 5.

55. Arthur Jones, "Anti-Contra Campaign Gains Strength in U. S.," *National Catholic Reporter* (February 14, 1986), 56.

56. Michael J. Farrell, "The Evil That Men Do Lives in Nicaragua," *National Catholic Reporter* (February 14, 1986), 56.

57. Anne Manuel, "Former Contra Honcho Claims No Peace If Rebels Supported," *National Catholic Reporter* (June 21, 1985), 6.

58. Dick Ryan, "Citizen Is Fed up with Reagan's Bull; Grabs It by Horns," *National Catholic Reporter* (May 10, 1985), 20.

59. Peter Hebblethwaite, "Nicaragua after the Revolution: Bitter War Fought Not with Weapons, but with Media," *National Catholic Reporter* (May 24, 1981), 1, 40.

60. Jones, "Anti-Contra Campaign Gains Strength in U. S.," 7.

61. J. C. Erlick, "Pope's 'Watershed' Nicaraguan Visit," *National Catholic Reporter* (March 18, 1983), 4.

62. Mark R. Day, "Interruption during Homily 'Unplanned,' Observers Say," *National Catholic Reporter* (March 25, 1983), 7.

63. William R. Callahan and Dolores C. Pomerleau, "'Irresponsible' Words Polarize Nicaraguans," *National Catholic Reporter* (March 25, 1983), 7.

64. Andrew Reding, "If Borge Is a Marxist, What Is a Christian?" *National Catholic Reporter* (March 29, 1985), 22.

65. Ibid., 23.

66. Cort, "Raised Voices in Nicaragua," 631.

67. J. C. Erlick, "Priests Told to Quit Politics," *National Catholic Reporter* (June 19, 1981), 2, 6.

68. J. C. Erlick, "Nicaraguan Bishops Say Priests May Keep Posts," *National Catholic Reporter* (July 31, 1981), 3, 4.

69. Michael Garvey, "Caesar in Nicaragua," *National Catholic Reporter* (July 17, 1981), 2.

70. Tennant C. Wright, "Mixing Church, Politics in Nicaragua," *National Catholic Reporter* (October 30, 1981), 9, 16.

71. James Brockman, "Revolution 'Sharply Divides Nicaraguan Church,'" *National Catholic Reporter* (March 19, 1982), 5.

72. J. H. Evans and Jack Epstein, "Miskito Indians Talk of Nicaragua," *National Catholic Reporter* (November 12, 1982), 26.

73. J. H. Evans and J. Epstein, "Nicaragua's Miskito Move Based on False Allegations," *National Catholic Reporter* (November 12, 1982), 26.

74. Penny Lernoux, "Play It Again, Uncle Sam," *National Catholic Reporter* (April 25, 1986), 7.

75. Peter Hebblethwaite, "Contras for Peace and Justice," *National Catholic Reporter* (April 26, 1986), 8, 45.

76. J. C. Erlick, "Nicaragua: Tomorrow," *National Catholic Reporter* (August 13, 1982), 1, 25.

77. Stephen T. De Mott, "Nicaragua Today," *National Catholic Reporter* (August 13, 1982),24.

78. Robert White, "Do U.S., Nicaragua Mean What They Say?" *National Catholic Reporter* (October 8, 1982), 21.

79. Mary Ann Lambert, "Nicaraguan Pendulum Moves to Extreme Left, Limits Basic Freedoms," *National Catholic Reporter* (November 11, 1983), 11.

80. Chris Hedges, "Strife within Church 'Really War of Western Socialist Mores,'" *National Catholic Reporter* (September 7, 1984), 1.

81. Ibid., 25.

82. Ibid.

83. Alan Gottlieb, "Nicaraguan Martyrs Inspire Faith Celebrations," *National Catholic Reporter* (January 16, 1987), 5.

SEVEN. THE CONSERVATIVE CATHOLIC PRESS ON CENTRAL AMERICA

1. *Catholicism in Crisis* (November 1982), 1.

2. Ralph McInerny, "Multa Obstant," *Catholicism in Crisis* (September 1983), 1.

3. Ibid., 2.

4. Ibid. Beginning in 1977 and continuing throughout the 1980s, bishops and other spokespersons for the USCC testified before congressional committees concerning U. S. policy toward Central America. Their message was consistent. They recommended diplomatic rather than military solutions to regional crises. In particular they condemned military aid to the contras while calling for economic and humanitarian aid to the Nicaraguan people. They called for peaceful dialogue between the government and guerrilla forces in El Salvador and a reduction in military aid. They spoke out against too large a military buildup in Honduras and rejected aid in any form whatsoever for the Guatemalan government or military. They also advocated more lenient policies for Central American refugees. See Pelton, *From Power to Communion,* 28, and Mark Falcoff and Robert Royal, eds., *The Continuing*

Crisis: U.S. Policy in Central America and the Caribbean (Lanham, Md.: Ethics and Public Policy Center, 1987), 79–90.

5. Philip Lawler, "The Bishops at the White House," *Catholicism in Crisis* (June 1984), 53.

6. Terry Hall, "Sandinophilia," *Catholicism in Crisis* (May 1986), 61.

7. Ibid.

8. Michael Schwartz, "U.S. Bishops, Nicaraguan Bishops, Do They Speak with One Voice?" *Crisis* (October 1986), 20–23.

9. Philip Lawler, "Saboteur at the USCC?" *Catholicism in Crisis* (October 1984), 58.

10. Philip Lawler, "USCC Watch," *Catholicism in Crisis* (January 1985), 49–50.

11. Philip Lawler, "USCC Watch," *Catholicism in Crisis* (April 1985), 43.

12. Dinesh D'Souza, "Cry of the People," *Crisis* (April 1990), 16.

13. Dinesh D'Souza, "Viva la Democracia," *Crisis* (June 1989), 14.

14. Charlotte Low, "Message from Rome: Maryknoll Seminary to Close This Fall," *Crisis* (April 1988), 11.

15. Ibid., 12.

16. Ibid., 13.

17. Charlotte Hayes, "Lost Horizons at Maryknoll," *Crisis* (April 1987), 9.

18. Ibid., 14.

19. Berryman, *Stubborn Hope*, 36.

20. Hayes, "Lost Horizons," 13.

21. Geraldine O'Leary De Macias, "The Popular Church as Foreign Intervention," *Catholicism in Crisis* (September 1983), 33.

22. See "Sandinistas' Efforts Divide Nicaraguan Church, Speakers Say," in the *St. Louis Review* (November 4, 1983), reprinted in *Social Justice Review* (May–June 1984), no page number.

23. Robert Royal, "Maryknoll's Failed Revolution," *Catholicism in Crisis* (March 1985), 21.

24. Ibid., 20.

25. Ibid., 21.

26. William R. Burleigh, "Jesuits, Come Home," *Catholicism in Crisis* (July 1985), 31–33.

27. Kimberly J. Gustin, "Letter from a Jesuit Prep School," *Crisis* (September 1989), 47.

28. Ibid.

29. Humberto Belli, "The Sandinistas and the Pope, Will Eyes Open?" *Catholicism in Crisis* (May 1983), 8–9.

30. Michael Novak, "On Nicaragua," *Catholicism in Crisis* (July 1983), 1.

31. Ibid., 3.

32. Tom Bethell, "Collapse from Within," *Catholicism in Crisis* (July 1984), 51.

33. Ibid.

34. Ibid.

35. Ibid., 52.

36. Tom Bethell, "Their Sunday Visitor," *Catholicism in Crisis* (September 1983), 50.

37. Tom Bethell, "Feminism and the Failure of Authority," *Catholicism in Crisis* (January 1985), 50.

38. Ibid., 50–51.

39. Ibid., 51. Bethell would later work as a journalist for the conservative *American Spectator*, the journal responsible for unleashing the Clinton sex scandals.

40. M. Holt Ruffin, "The Sanctuary Scam: The Politics of Selective Compassion," *Catholicism in Crisis* (May 1986), 37.

41. Ibid., 32.

42. Pablo Antonio Cuadra, "Responsibilities of the Church in Central America," *Crisis* (September 1986), 10.

43. Ibid., 9–14.

44. Kenneth R. Craycraft, Jr., "False Promises," *Crisis* (April 1990), 48–50.

45. David B. Hartman, Jr., "Religion without History," *Crisis* (May 1990), 33.

46. Ibid., 35.

47. Henry J. Hyde, "Liberation Theology and American Foreign Policy," *Crisis* (January 1987), 15–19.

48. For J. Guadalupe Carney, see Brett and Brett, *Murdered in Central America*, 38–66; and J. Guadalupe Carney, *To Be a Revolutionary: An Autobiography* (San Francisco: Harper and Row, 1985).

49. Scott Walter, "How Not to Debate Liberation Theology," *Crisis* (June 1987), 31.

50. Colin Garvey, "The Philosophy of Liberation," *Catholicism in Crisis* (April 1985), 34–39.

51. Paul E. Sigmund, "Whither Liberation Theology? A Historical Evaluation," *Crisis* (January 1987), 5–14.

52. Ernesto Rivas-Gallont, "Peace without Freedom Is Hollow," *Catholicism in Crisis* (May 1984), 46–48.

53. Philip Lawler, "Bishop Revelo Speaks for Himself," *Catholicism in Crisis* (May 1984), 53.

54. Ibid.

55. Brockman, *Romero*, 177.

56. McInerny, "Multa Obstant," 2.

57. Joan Frawley, "The Idea of El Salvador in the United States," *Catholicism in Crisis* (June 1984), 57.

58. See Tommie Sue Montgomery, *Revolution in El Salvador: From Civil Strife to Civil Peace* (Boulder, Colo.: Westview Press, 1995), 78–79; and Bonner, *Weakness and Deceit*, 145–167.

59. Frawley, "The Idea of El Salvador in the United States," 31.

60. Joan Frawley Desmond, "Liberation through Reconciliation," *Crisis* (July–August 1987), 14.

61. Dinesh D'Souza, "Viva la Democracia," *Crisis* (June 1989), 14.

62. Richard Rodriguez, "Losing Ground," *Crisis* (November 1989), 40–42.

63. Richard Alleva, "Killing Romero Twice," *Crisis* (November 1989), 49–53.

64. "Salvadoran Blues," *Crisis* (September 1990), 3–4.

65. See Teresa Whitfield, *Paying the Price: Ignacio Ellacuría and the Murdered Jesuits of El Salvador* (Philadelphia: Temple University Press, 1995), 86–90, 93–97, 166–167, 175, 186–187, 263–265, 274–277, 391; and Berryman, *Stubborn Hope*, 98–100.

66. Quidam, "Christmas in Nicaragua," *Catholicism in Crisis* (February 1983), 5–6.

67. Humberto Belli, "Persecution of Protestants in Nicaragua," *Catholicism in Crisis* (June 1980), 18–20. See Berryman, *Stubborn Hope*, 33–34.

68. John J. Metzler, "Congress to Pay Bills for Nicaragua's Marxist Junta," *Wanderer* (May 29, 1980), 7.

69. Paul Scott, "Dark Shadow over Caribbean," *Wanderer* (February 1980), 5.

70. "El Salvador's Archbishop Murdered," *Wanderer* (April 3, 1980), 3.

71. John Metzler, "International Brigade Supports Nicaragua's Sandinistas," *Wanderer* (February 2, 1984), 5.

72. Paul A. Fisher, "White House Briefing Exposes Catholic Bias for Latin Marxists," *Wanderer* (March 29, 1984), 5.

73. "Those Peaceful Sandinistas," *Wanderer* (January 9, 1986), 4.

74. John Boland, "Nicaraguan Bishops Wrong; No Religious Persecution Says 'Center of Concern,'" *Wanderer* (February 23, 1984), 3.

75. Ibid.

76. Joseph T. Gill, "Giving Political Advice Is Not Properly the Cardinal's Job," *Wanderer* (February 9, 1984), 4.

77. Paul A. Fisher, "Guerrilla Links Jesuits with Revolutionists' Weapons," *Wanderer* (December 25, 1980), 3, 6.

78. Ibid., 6.

79. Paul A. Fisher, "*The Wanderer* Asks Orlando de Sola about Death and Marxism in El Salvador," *Wanderer* (December 25, 1980), 1, 6. For Ellacuría's early career, see Whitfield, *Paying the Price*, 21–45, and Jon Sobrino, Ignacio Ellacuría, and Others, *Companions of Jesus: The Jesuit Martyrs of El Salvador* (Maryknoll, N.Y.: Orbis Books, 1990), 59–63. For a more revealing, in-depth view of the de Sola faction of the coffee oligarchy, see Jeffery M. Paige, "Coffee and Power in El Salvador," *Latin American Research Review* (1993), 7–40. In interviews conducted by Paige with de Sola members, the latter called for another 1932–style *Matanza* to rid the country of "Communist stooges;" they ridiculed the U.S. low-intensity warfare strategy for El Salvador as too little, too late; and they justified the army's making lists of priests to be assassinated (33).

80. Paul A. Fisher, "*The Wanderer* Asks Members of the ARENA Party of El Salvador about Death Squads, the Assassination of Archbishop Oscar Romero, the Agrarian Reform Program," *Wanderer* (March 22, 1984), 6.

81. Gary Potter, "Inter Urbem Extraque," *Wanderer* (December 7, 1989), 8.

82. Ibid.

83. Violeta de Chamorro, "Freedom of the Press Does Not Exist in Nicaragua," *Social Justice Review* (May–June 1983), 83, 96.

84. Bernard Nietschmann, "The Miskito Indians of Nicaragua," *Social Justice Review* (January–February 1984), 9–12.

85. J. B. A. Kessler, "Nicaraguan Indians Have Good Cause to Mistrust Sandinistas," *Social Justice Review* (January–February 1984), 13–14.

86. William C. Doherty, "A Revolution Betrayed: Free Labor Persecuted," *Social Justice Review* (July–August 1984), 113–116.

87. Oscar Rodríguez, "The Church and Refugees in Central America," *Social Justice Review* (May–June 1986), 94.

88. Ibid., 91.

89. Ibid., 92.

90. "Chronology of Events: The Church in Nicaragua," *Social Justice Review* (July–August 1986), 138–141.

91. Dick Goldkamp, "Papal Invasion of a Hornet's Nest," *Social Justice Review* (September–October 1985), 130, 157–158. Cardinal Ratzinger's "Instruction on Certain Aspects of the Theology of Liberation" (Vatican City: Vatican Polyglot Press, 1984), which was extremely harsh in its appraisal of liberation theology, caused much consternation among the Latin American and U.S. bishops. Consequently, the cardinal issued a second report, "Instruction on Christian Freedom and Liberation," *National Catholic Reporter,* pullout section (April 25, 1986), which was more nuanced and even-handed. In 1986 also, Pope John Paul II further defused the debate over this controversial theology when he told the Brazilian bishops that it had a "useful and necessary" role in ministry.

92. Oliver Starr, "Sandinistas' Record Makes Clergy Support a Mystery," *Social Justice Review* (May–June 1984), 96.

93. "Activities of Religious Elements in Central America," *Social Justice Review* (May–June 1984), 76.

94. "Marxist Influences in U.S. Including the Religious Field," *Social Justice Review* (May–June 1984), 77.

95. Linda Westrom and Jane Otten, "Report on Travel Seminar: Mexico, El Salvador and Nicaragua—Women in Mission: A View from Latin America," *Social Justice Review* (June–August 1985), 115–121.

96. Ibid., 117.

97. Ibid., 119.

98. Ibid., 120.

99. Robert G. Breene, "Central America Trip Findings," *Social Justice Review* (September–October 1984), 138.

100. "El Salvador, U.S. Observer to 1985 Election," *Social Justice Review* (March–April 1985), 58.

101. Ibid., 59.

102. "Bernardin Raps U.S.," *National Catholic Register* (December 18, 1983), 2.

103. Joan Frawley, "Nicaraguan Church Official Says USCC Staffer Hindered Bishops," *National Catholic Register* (September 9, 1984), 1, 8.

104. Joan Frawley, "Nicaragua's Revolution: A House Divided," *National Catholic Register* (April 7, 1983), 8.

105. Joan Frawley, "Melba Is More Than Just a Pretty Face," *National Catholic Register* (April 7, 1983), 1.

106. Terry Mulgannon, "Witnesses Describe the Two Nicaraguas," *National Catholic Register* (July 17, 1983), 8.

107. Richard Bodurtha, "Dialogue," *National Catholic Register* (October 9, 1983), 6.

108. Joan Frawley, "Former Medic Visits Miskitos, Rips Conditions," *National Catholic Register* (January 8, 1984), 1.

109. Ibid., 8.

110. Joan Frawley, "The Sandinistas' Death Cult," *National Catholic Register* (September 11, 1983), 1.

111. Joan Frawley, "Sandinistas Publish Stolen Memo in Attempt to Discredit Archbishop," *National Catholic Register* (August 19, 1984), 1, 9.

112. Joan Frawley, "Nicaragua's One Party System," *National Catholic Register* (April 22, 1984), 1, 8.

113. E. Michael Jones, "Reagan Aide Greeted by Notre Dame Hecklers," *National Catholic Register* (May 6, 1984), 1, 10.

114. Frawley, "Nicaragua's Revolution: A House Divided," 8.

115. Joan Frawley, "Religious Activists Tour Nicaragua," *National Catholic Register* (July 24, 1983), 1, 9.

116. Paul Hollander, "Sojourners in Nicaragua: A Political Pilgrimage," *National Catholic Register* (May 29, 1983), 1, 7, 9.

117. "Salvadorean Strife Engulfs Church," *National Catholic Register* (December 21, 1980), 3.

118. Richard Araujo, "Violence Escalates in El Salvador," *National Catholic Register* (December 14, 1980), 1, 9.

119. "Economy Cited as Why Salvadorans Come to U. S.," *National Catholic Register* (September 28, 1986), 3.

120. Michael Novak, "Salvador: What to Do?" *National Catholic Register* (April 3, 1983), 1.

121. Ibid.

122. Joop Koopman, "Bishop Warns U. S. Troops May Be Needed," *National Catholic Register* (February 5, 1984), 9.

123. See Brockman, *Romero*, 128, 177, 182.

EIGHT. THE PROGRESSIVE U. S. CATHOLIC PRESS ON CENTRAL AMERICA IN THE 1980S

1. Gordon L. Bowen, "Guatemala's War Against the Church: No Roadblocks to Death," *Commonweal* (June 15, 1984), 361.

2. A plethora of articles on priests and religious murdered in Guatemala have appeared in the Catholic press. A few are "Machine-Gunned Priest on Anti-

Communist Hit List," *Our Sunday Visitor* (June 8, 1980), 3; Ronald Burke, "Cry from Guatemala: They Killed Stan," *Maryknoll* (January 1982), 51–53; James Grote, "The Death of a Missionary," *Our Sunday Visitor* magazine section (October 18, 1981), 4; Patty Edmonds, "Oklahoma Priest Murdered in Guatemala," *National Catholic Reporter* (August 14, 1981), 7; Patty Edmonds, "Father Stanley Rother: A Holy, Hard-working Man," *National Catholic Reporter* (August 14, 1981), 3, 7; "Brother Slain in Guatemala 'Gave His Life for His Students,'" *National Catholic Reporter* (February 26, 1982), 8, 19; Joan Turner Beifuss, "Miller Eulogized," *National Catholic Reporter* (February 26, 1982), 19; Edward Brett and Donna W. Brett, "A Teacher and a Martyr in Guatemala," *America* (October 30, 1982), 253–255; Mordecai Specktor, "Revolution and the Church in Guatemala," *America* (June 5, 1982), 440–441; Frank X. Holdenried, "Terror in Guatemala," *America* (July 7, 1982), 31–34 (Holdenried would himself be murdered in Guatemala in 1983; see Brett and Brett, *Murdered in Central America*, 159–185); Mark R. Day, "Missionary Slain, Details Unclear," *National Catholic Reporter* (April 22, 1983), 2; Kevin Fitzsimmons, "Priest's Brutal Murder in Guatemala Is Part of Anticlergy Campaign," *National Catholic Reporter* (May 25, 1984), 10; William J. Price, "A War against the Church in Guatemala," *Our Sunday Visitor* magazine section (July 12, 1981), 8–10; Robert Holton, "Guatemala Another Central American Tragedy," *Our Sunday Visitor* magazine section (February 14, 1982), 4–7; Robert Holton, "The Tragedy of Guatemala," *Our Sunday Visitor* magazine section (February 21, 1982), 18.

3. "Guatemala: Religious Only a Fraction of Thousands Slain There," *National Catholic Reporter* (March 5, 1982), 22–23; Jean Molesky, "I Speak for My People: Guatemala's Persecuted Mayans," *St. Anthony Messenger* (May 1984), 12–17; "Report from Guatemala: Truth and Its Consequences, Who Will Listen?" *Commonweal* (September 23, 1988), 488–489; Warren Holleman, "The Human Rights Illusion," *America* (October 29, 1988), 318.

4. "Report from Guatemala: Truth and Its Consequences," 488; Carol Winkle, "Guatemala: A Refugee's Story," *Catholic Worker* (August 1987), 1; Ana Arana, "Bishop Helps Fugitive Indians Return to Guatemalan Homes," *National Catholic Register* (January 31, 1988), 1, 9; Louis Dubose, "Guatemala's Border Refugees," *America* (November 17, 1984), 317–320; Olivia L. Carrescia and Robert Dinardo, "The Yaxan Story," *Commonweal* (August 13, 1983), 429–431; Mark R. Day, "Guatemalan Refugee: Why Don't They Believe?" *National Catholic Reporter* (November 12, 1982), 6; Patrick McCaffrey, "Observers Say Refugees Still Flee Guatemala," *Our Sunday Visitor* (February 20, 1983), 4–5; Chris Hedges, "Guatemalans Flee Holy War," *National Catholic Reporter* (January 14, 1983), 2; Paul D. Newpower, "Guatemala: Fighting Subversion with Bullets and Beans," *St. Anthony Messenger* (June 1983), 32–34.

5. June Carolyn Erlick, "Exiled from Guatemala, Bishop Continues Work," *National Catholic Reporter* (April 16, 1982), 5; "Guatemalan Bishops Say Nation on Brink of Bloodbath," *Our Sunday Visitor* (December 13, 1981), 7; Romano Rossi, "Can Such Bloodshed Be Justified in the Light of the Gospel: Appeal of the Bishops of Guatemala," *Origins* (August 31, 1981), 7–8; "The Anguish of Our People," *Origins* (August 26, 1982), 165–166.

6. Linda Drucker, "The Pope and Holy War: Confrontation with Rios Montt," *Commonweal* (April 22, 1983), 230–232; Beatriz Manz, "Pope Urges Return of Dignity, Unity to Race, Religious-Torn Guatemalans," *National Catholic Reporter* (March 18, 1983), 8–9.

7. Carrescia and Dinardo, "The Yaxan Story," 429–431.

8. Isabel Rogers, "Thorn in the Flesh," *Commonweal* (February 10, 1984), 81.

9. Holton, "The Tragedy of Guatemala," 4.

10. Robert Holton, "Stark Terror Is the Beast on the Prowl in Guatemala," *Our Sunday Visitor* magazine section (February 14, 1982), 3.

11. Ibid.

12. Ibid.

13. Bowen, "Guatemala's War against the Church: No Roadblocks to Death," 361–364.

14. Ibid., 362.

15. Ibid.

16. Bowen, "How Things Are Getting Better in Guatemala," *Commonweal* (October 18, 1985), 555–558.

17. Ibid., 556.

18. Warren Holleman, "The Human Rights Illusion," *America* (October 29, 1988), 318.

19. Ibid., 318–319.

20. Ibid., 325.

21. Pat Ryan Green, "A Visit to El Salvador," *America* (November 24, 1984), 343–344.

22. Vincent J. Giese, "The '*Desplazados*': El Salvador's Poorest of the Poor," *Our Sunday Visitor* (May 27, 1984), 4.

23. James R. Brockman, "Five Years after Romero," *America* (May 18, 1985), 403.

24. John J. Quinn, "Notes on My Visit to El Salvador," *America* (May 3, 1986), 360.

25. Ibid., 362.

26. William Bole, "U. S. Bishops on Salvador's List of 'Undesirables,'" *National Catholic Reporter* (September 15, 1989), 7.

27. "Department of Injustice," *America* (May 3, 1986), 354.

28. Edward T. Brett and Donna Whitson Brett, "Run-For-Your-Life Crises Mark Lives," *National Catholic Reporter* (March 23, 1984), 6–7; Graham Clarke, "Guatemalans Arrive at Vt. 'Sanctuary,'" *National Catholic Reporter* (April 6, 1984), 5.

29. Patricia Scharber Lefevere, "On Trial in Texas: Is It Legal or Not to Help Refugees?" *National Catholic Reporter* (May 18, 1984), 1, 21–22.

30. "'My Head Is Not Bowed': Guilty Sanctuary Worker," *National Catholic Reporter* (May 25, 1984), 21.

31. "Smuggling, Sanctuary and the 'Objective Facts,'" *America* (November 16, 1985), 309.

32. Robert F. Drinan, "Kissinger Commission Puts U. S. on Wrong Side," *National Catholic Reporter* (April 27, 1984), 16.

33. "Church in El Salvador Deals with Civil Strife," *Our Sunday Visitor* (November 10, 1985), 4.

34. Arturo Rivera y Damas, "Church and State in El Salvador," *Priest* (July/August 1984), 32–37.

35. "The Day after Elections," *America* (May 19, 1984), 369.

36. Ibid.

37. "A Victory for Moderation," *America* (April 20, 1985), 314.

38. Kathleen G. Connolly, "The Murder of the Churchwomen," *America* (August 24, 1985), 88–89.

39. Jim Chapin and Jack Clark, "Paralysis Is Still the Winner," *Commonweal* (May 4, 1984), 268–270.

40. Jim Chapin, "After the Salvadoran Elections: A Time to Be Realistic," *Commonweal* (May 3, 1985), 269–271.

41. Vincent J. Giese, "Recent Runoff Election in El Salvador Expected to Escalate War, Not Bring Much Wanted Peace," *Our Sunday Visitor* (May 20, 1984), 3.

42. Matt Scheiber, "Duarte: 'Today My Country Needs Peace,'" *Our Sunday Visitor* (May 19, 1985), 4.

43. Jim Chapin and Patrick Laiefield, "El Salvador: Land of No Compromise," *Commonweal* (May 6, 1988), 269.

44. Ibid., 267–271.

45. Joseph P. Fitzpatrick, "The Church's Great Initiative for Peace in El Salvador," *America* (October 8, 1988), 213. For more on the National Debate as well as on similar debates initiated by the church in other Latin American countries, see Klaiber, *The Church, Dictatorships, and Democracy in Latin America.*

46. "El Salvador: The 1988 National Debate," *LADOC* (March–April 1989), 10–12.

47. Larry Hufford, "Stop All Military Aid Now!" *America* (February 21, 1987), 147.

48. Gene Palumbo, "Salvador's UCA Bombed Again," *National Catholic Reporter* (May 12, 1989), 8.

49. Gene Palumbo, "Hooded Men Break into Salvadoran Church," *National Catholic Reporter* (October 13, 1989), 10.

50. Gene Palumbo, "New Violence Wave Hits San Salvador," *National Catholic Reporter* (October 27, 1989), 6.

51. Gene Palumbo, "Salvadoran Refugees Journey Home, Six Supporters Arrested," *National Catholic Reporter* (November 3, 1989), 6.

52. Gene Palumbo, "Death Squad Blamed for Salvadoran Blast," *National Catholic Reporter* (November 17, 1989), 9.

53. Arthur Jones and Joe Feuerherd, "Bishop Now Closest to Poor in Salvador Is a Lutheran," *National Catholic Reporter* (September 29, 1989), 4.

54. Arthur Jones and Joe Feuerherd, "Salvador May Be Groping towards Uneasy Peace," *National Catholic Reporter* (September 29, 1989), 3–4.

55. Tommy E. Lash, "Rivera Damas Sees Hope in El Salvador," *National Catholic Reporter* (September 29, 1989), 5.

56. Gene Palumbo, "Salvador Torture Tactics New, Their Causes Old," *National Catholic Reporter* (September 29, 1989), 6.

57. Elizabeth Groppe Sniegocki, "Heartbreak Odyssey of a Salvadoran Mother," *National Catholic Reporter* (September 29, 1989), 5.

58. "Opening for New Prophet," *National Catholic Reporter* (September 29, 1989), 24.

59. Joe Feuerherd, "Trained to Kill in El Salvador," *National Catholic Reporter* (November 10, 1989), 1, 6.

60. "Ditch the Thugs and Killers," *National Catholic Reporter* (November 10, 1989), 24.

61. Thomas H. Stahel, "Of Many Things," *America* (December 2, 1989), 390.

62. "Now You Be Quiet, Oscar," *America* (December 9, 1989), 415.

63. Joseph A. O'Hare, "In Solidarity with the Slain Jesuits of El Salvador," *America* (December 16, 1989), 443–446.

64. Leo J. O'Donovan, "Letter to President Alfredo Cristiani," *America* (December 16, 1989), 445.

65. James Torrens, "For Julia Elba Ramos," *America* (December 30, 1989), 465.

66. Thomas H. Stahel, "Of Many Things," *America* (January 20, 1990), 26.

67. Joseph E. Mulligan, "The Blood of Martyrs: The Seed of Hope and Commitment," *America* (February 2, 1990), 145–146.

68. "Save El Salvador," *Commonweal* (December 1, 1989), 660.

69. Ibid.

70. Ibid., 660–661.

71. Ibid., 661.

72. Jon Sobrino, "Death in El Salvador: Why the War Goes On," *Commonweal* (December 15, 1989), 693–695.

73. "Fear, Accusations and Multiple Arrests Follow Jesuit Murders in El Salvador," *National Catholic Reporter* (November 24, 1989), 1, 8; "U. S. Taxpayer Money Is Being Used to Kill Priests and It Must Stop Now," *National Catholic Reporter* (November 24, 1989), 20. See also Mary Jo McConahay, "Salvador Military Escalates Church War," *National Catholic Reporter* (December 1, 1989), 1, 4; Mary Jo McConahay, "Church in Salvador Is under Heavy Fire," *National Catholic Reporter* (December 8, 1989), 1, 8.

74. "U. S. Taxpayer Money Is Being Used to Kill Priests and It Must Stop Now," 20.

75. "Americas Watch Hits U. S. on El Salvador, Says Policy 'Dismal,'" *National Catholic Reporter* (December 8, 1989), 5.

76. Joe Feuerherd, "U. S. Nationwide Reactions Protest Involvement in, Aid to Salvador," *National Catholic Reporter* (December 1, 1989), 6.

77. Joe Feuerherd, "U. S. Has 12-Year-Old Info on Slain Jesuits," *National Catholic Reporter* (December 1, 1989), 9.

78. "North Americans among 14 Arrested at Lutheran Church," *National Catholic Reporter* (November 24, 1989), 8; see also "Fear, Accusations and Multiple Arrests Follow Jesuit Murders in El Salvador," *National Catholic Reporter* (November 24, 1989), 1, 8.

79. "Bishop in Hiding Eulogizes Jesuits," *National Catholic Reporter* (December 1, 1989), 5; Mary Jo McConahay, "Church in Salvador Is Under Heavy Fire," *National Catholic Reporter* (December 8, 1989), 1, 8; Tim McCarthy, "Persecution Is an Orchestrated Bid to Cripple Church Analysts Charge," *National Catholic Reporter* (December 8, 1989), 1, 8.

80. "El Salvador Is Still Harassing Churchworkers," *National Catholic Reporter* (January 19, 1990), 7.

81. McCarthy, "Persecution Is an Orchestrated Bid to Cripple Church Analysts Charge," 1, 8; see also Joe Feuerherd, "'Going Home Hotline' Shares Salvadoran Information," *National Catholic Reporter* (December 8, 1989), 3.

82. Robert Boczkiewicz, "U.S. Catholic Lay Worker Expelled from El Salvador," *National Catholic Reporter* (December 22, 1989), 6.

83. "Casolo Release Gets Cool U.S. Reception," *National Catholic Reporter* (December 22, 1989), 7.

84. Mary Jo McConahay, "State of Fear Replaces Rattle of Gunfire for Church Workers and Others in El Salvador," *National Catholic Reporter* (February 16, 1990), 14.

85. "Outrage Reverberates across U.S. after Salvador Slayings," *National Catholic Reporter* (November 24, 1989), 9; Tim Unsworth, "U.S. Parishes Share Grief, Frustration, Pain of Salvadoran Sister Parishes," *National Catholic Reporter* (December 1, 1989), 1, 4; Joe Feuerherd, "U.S. Nationwide Reactions Protest Involvement in, Aid to Salvador," *National Catholic Reporter* (December 1, 1989), 6; Bill Kenkelen, "Jesuits Mobilize to Change Salvador Policy," *National Catholic Reporter* (December 1, 1989), 7; Tom Sheehan, "Weep Not for Ellacuría, but for Ourselves," *National Catholic Reporter* (December 1, 1989), 7; James K. Healy, "Getting into Trouble in the Name of Jesus Christ," *National Catholic Reporter* (December 1, 1989), 20; Joe Feuerherd, "Battle to Suspend U.S. Aid to El Salvador Intensifies," *National Catholic Reporter* (February 2, 1990), 6.

86. Joe Feuerherd, "Officials Disagree on Coercion of Salvador Witness," *National Catholic Reporter* (December 22, 1989), 6.

87. Chris Norton, "U.S. Groups Meet Salvador Officials," *National Catholic Reporter* (February 23, 1990), 6.

88. Tim McCarthy, "Cozy and Corrupt, Army in Salvador Mafia-Like Family," *National Catholic Reporter* (January 19, 1990), 7.

89. Tim McCarthy, "Brave Lives That Denied Death's Dominion," *National Catholic Reporter* (December 29, 1989), 1, 6–10.

90. Ibid., 9.

91. Ibid., 2.

92. Berryman, *Stubborn Hope*, 46.

93. Ibid., 54; Crahan, "Religion and Politics in Revolutionary Nicaragua," in Mainwaring and Wilde, *The Progressive Church*, 50.

94. Frank M. Oppenheim, "A Report on Nicaragua," *America* (March 8, 1986), 183–185.

95. Paul Jeffrey, "Touching the Heart of God: Peace Pilgrimage Crosses Nicaragua," *America* (April 26, 1986), 341.

96. "Winning and Losing," *America* (July 12, 1986), 2.

97. "U.S. Policy in Nicaragua," *America* (March 16, 1985), 205–206.

98. "A War of Analogies," *America* (May 11, 1985), 382.

99. "Sandinista Crackdown: Their Lies and Ours," *America* (November 2, 1985), 269.

100. Ibid.

101. "Idle Comparisons, Real Folly," *America* (March 22, 1986), 218.

102. "How to Lose Friends," *America* (July 30, 1988), 51.

103. "Nicaraguan Bishops' Advice," *America* (April 26, 1986), 334.

104. Thomas J. Maloney, "Church and State in Nicaragua," *America* (November 29, 1986), 340–341.

105. "Mr. Ortega and Bishop Vega," *America* (August 23, 1986), 61–62.

106. "Hasenfus Case: Who's on Trial?" *America* (November 8, 1986), 273.

107. "The Iranian Lessons," *America* (December 13, 1986), 373–374.

108. "Peace of Mind," *America* (March 7, 1987), 185–186.

109. "'Sleazy' Is the Word for It," *America* (April 4, 1987), 266.

110. "'No' to More Contra Aid," *America* (January 30, 1988), 83.

111. "And What of the Contras Now?" *America* (August 22, 1987), 75.

112. "Should We Go to War with Nicaragua?" *Commonweal* (June 21, 1985), 355.

113. "Facing Contraquences," *Commonweal* (May 17, 1985), 294–295.

114. Philip McManus, "The Dogs Never Lie: Costs of the 'Contras,'" *Commonweal* (June 20, 1986), 360.

115. Ibid., 361.

116. Edward R. Sheehan, "The Battle for Nicaragua: Church, Cardinal, and Comandantes," *Commonweal* (May 9, 1986), 264.

117. Ibid., 268.

118. Ibid., 267.

119. "Uncivil Targets," *Commonweal* (April 10, 1987), 195.

120. Ibid., 196.

121. Ibid., 196–197.

122. Ibid., 198.

123. Desmond O'Grady, "Exiled Bishop Defends Role as 'Voice of the Voiceless,'" *Our Sunday Visitor* (August 10, 1986), 3.

124. David Kelly, "An Examination of Liberation Theology, 'Spiritual Animator' of Latin America Church," *National Catholic Reporter* (August 17, 1984), 11–12.

125. Mary Beth Moore, "The Light Came! Living Liberation Theology," *National Catholic Reporter* (August 17, 1984), 13.

126. "Liberation Theology, under Attack, Must Be Judged on Its Own Merits," *National Catholic Reporter* (April 6, 1984), 14.

127. "Conflicting Attitudes Mark Nicaraguan Church," *National Catholic Reporter* (April 13, 1984), 12.

128. "Nicaragua: Oh, How Can It Please?" *National Catholic Reporter* (October 12, 1984), 12.

129. Patty Edmonds, "Obando Talk with U.S. Executive Told in Memo," *National Catholic Reporter* (July 20, 1984), 8; Chris Hedges, "Sandinistas Say Church Gets CIA Aid," *National Catholic Reporter* (August 31, 1984), 1, 33.

130. "Nicaragua Strife," *National Catholic Reporter* (July 20, 1984), 14.

131. Michael Garvey, "Under the Gun, and under the Cross," *National Catholic Reporter* (July 20, 1984), 19.

132. Chris Hedges, "Strife within Church 'Really War of Western Socialist Mores,'" *National Catholic Reporter* (September 7, 1984), 1, 25.

133. "Letters to the Editor," *National Catholic Reporter* (October 5, 1984), 17–18.

134. Joan Desmond Frawley, "Adios, Danny: Violeta Wins, and Penance May Be in Order for Some U.S. Christians," *National Catholic Register* (March 11, 1990), 1.

135. "Time for U.S. to Put Aside Hysteria and Yield to Idea of Nicaraguan Sovereignty," *National Catholic Reporter* (March 9, 1990), 24.

136. Holly Sklar, "Nicaraguans Voted Their Stomachs over Hearts," *National Catholic Reporter* (March 30, 1990), 20.

137. Bill McSweeney, "A Clear Victory for UNO, but Nicaragua's Future Is Hazy," *National Catholic Reporter* (March 9, 1990), 16.

138. Paul Berman, "A Thirst for Peace That U.S. Visitors Often Missed," *National Catholic Reporter* (March 9, 1990), 24, 16.

139. Ibid.

140. "Nicaragua Cries Uncle," *America* (March 29, 1990), 284.

141. Ibid.

142. Jeff Gillenkirk, "Reflections on Nicaragua's Holy War," *America* (April 14, 1990), 374–376.

143. "The Heat Is On," *Commonweal* (March 23, 1990), 173.

144. J. Bryan Hehir, "New World, New Roles," *Commonweal* (March 23, 1990), 174–175.

CONCLUSION

1. Leonard Dinnerstein, *Antisemitism in America* (New York: Oxford University Press, 1994), x.

2. Ibid., 4.

3. James Hennesey, *American Catholics: A History of the Roman Catholic Community in the United States* (New York: Oxford University Press, 1983), 63–100.

4. Ibid., 126.

5. Kenneth Scott Latourette, *A History of Christianity* (New York: Harper and Row, 1975), 1099–1101.

6. Charles Morris, *American Catholic: The Saints and Sinners Who Built America's Most Powerful Church* (New York: Times Books, 1997), ix.

7. Mark S. Massa, *Catholics and American Culture: Fulton Sheen, Dorothy Day, and the Notre Dame Football Team* (New York: Crossroad Books, 1999), 39.

8. Ibid., 1.

9. Ibid., 60.

10. Ibid., 78.

11. Cited in Morris, *American Catholic,* ix.

12. For more on Bishop Sheen, see Massa, *Catholics and American Culture,* 82–101.

13. Donald Crosby, *God, Church and Flag: Senator Joseph McCarthy and the Catholic Church* (Chapel Hill: University of North Carolina Press, 1978), 15.

14. James Terence Fisher, "Thomas A. Dooley," in Michael Glazer and Thomas J. Shelley, eds., *The Encyclopedia of American Catholic History* (Collegeville, Minn.: Liturgical Press, 1997), 450–451.

15. Ibid., 451; for a fuller account of Dooley, see James Terence Fisher, *Dr. America: The Lives of Thomas A. Dooley, 1927–1961* (Amherst: University of Massachusetts Press, 1997).

16. Massa, *Catholics and American Culture,* 129.

17. Dorothy Dohen, *Nationalism and American Catholicism* (New York: Oxford University Press, 1968), 52–53. Also see David O'Brien, *American Catholicism and Social Reform: The New Deal Years* (New York: Oxford University Press, 1968), 225; Mary T. Hanna, *Catholics and American Politics* (Cambridge, Mass.: Harvard University Press, 1979), 13–19.

18. Mary McGlone, *Sharing Faith Across the Hemisphere* (Washington, D. C.: U. S. Catholic Conference, 1997), 73–80; for more on this topic, see John B. Sheerin, *Never Look Back: The Career and Concerns of John J. Burke* (Mahweh, N. J.: Paulist Press, 1975); Robert E. Quirk, *The Mexican Revolution and the Catholic Church, 1910–1929* (Bloomington: Indiana University Press, 1973); Douglas J. Slawson, "The National Catholic Welfare Conference and the Mexican Church State Conflict of the Mid-1930s: A Case of Deja Vu," *Catholic Historical Review* (1994), 58–96.

19. Charles A. Meconis, *With Clumsy Grace: The American Catholic Left, 1961–1975* (New York: Seabury Press, 1979).

20. John Tracy Ellis, foreword to Hennesey, *American Catholics,* xi.

21. "And What of the Contras Now?," *America* (August 22, 1987), 75.

22. "Sandinista Crack Down: Their Lies and Ours," *America* (November 2, 1985), 269.

Index

About the Author

EDWARD T. BRETT is professor of history at La Roche College in Pittsburgh, Pennsylvania.